DEDICATION

To my wife Robin,
Who gets fed up with Church because she knows we fall short of what the world really needs...
Who despite ministry, moving, and my occasional forgetfulness, still loves me more than any other person on the planet....
You have shown me what love and loyalty really mean and I am humbled and blessed to have you in my life.
Because Jesus should make life better than it has, this book is intended to help the cause.

ACKNOWLEDGMENTS

5x5 began as a way to solve a problem at First United Methodist Church of Hanover, Pennsylvania. With a shortage of trained class leaders and teachers, we needed a reliable way to equip and disciple leaders. We developed the "5x5 Discipleship Group" as our own version of the early Methodist Class Meetings. I would like to thank the following people for their invaluable contributions to this project:

Rev. Joshua Rhone
Karen Bureau
Graham Campbell
Rita Clough
Jackie Spadt
Christopher Evans
Tommy Fitchett
Bill Ingram
Ann Jones
Donna Leese
Mary Ann Nickey
Judy Porowski
Claire Rankin
Elaine Strevig
Janis Wagner
Chad Wynn
Carol Yates
Alex Rapp
Keith Giles
Christopher Hitz
Dr. Mike McGough
Michael Steininger
Denny Kuhn
Jim Wymer

CONTENTS

PREFACE

Nobody follows Jesus anymore. Just look around, and you'll see what I mean. How often do you ever see someone show love to a person who is in their face? Have you ever once heard of anyone chasing a thief down the street screaming, "Hey, you forgot my DVD player!" or witnessed a person who has just been slapped in the face turn their head to offer the other cheek?

I doubt it.

That's my point. Jesus had some pretty radical teachings. Love your enemies. Pray for those who abuse you. Give to those who steal from you. Lend without expecting anything in return. Bless those who curse your name. Even the most casual glance at the words and teachings of Jesus will tell you this guy had unreasonable expectations of those who would dare to follow Him. It was almost as if He was trying to thin the crowd by raising the bar so high. He doesn't stop there. No sir. Jesus even goes so far as to say that those who follow Him must deny themselves and take up their own cross (an instrument of brutal torture and death). In fact, He says if you don't do this, you "cannot be my disciple" (Luke 14:27).

No wonder no one follows Jesus anymore.

Now, I'm not suggesting people don't believe in Jesus anymore. There are millions and millions of people out there who really do believe a guy named Jesus actually lived 2,000 years ago. They believe that He was the Son of God, and God the Son, and that He led a sinless life, died on the cross for their sins and rose bodily from the grave three days later. Yep. They all believe that. But, those people don't really <u>follow</u> Jesus, not the way He expected them to. Maybe that's why Jesus wondered out loud, "When the Son of Man returns, will he find faith on the earth?" (Luke 18:8). Maybe He knew after 2,000 years of Christianity, we'd just have given up on following

1

His specific example of how to live.

G.K. Chesterton once said, "It's not that Christianity has been tried and found wanting; it's that it has been found difficult and left untried."

I think Jesus really did expect His followers to live extravagant lives of love as He commands in Luke 6:27. He wasn't kidding around. He's pretty clear that the kind of love the world has is nothing special at all. "If you love those who love you, what credit is that to you? Even 'sinners' love those who love them. And if you do good to those who are good to you, what credit is that to you? Even 'sinners' do that" (Luke 6:32). Jesus was trying to get His potential followers to understand they were expected to model a standard of love that went far, far beyond what anyone living on this planet had ever encountered or dreamed of before. A kind of love that could change someone's life for eternity.

Once you understand this, it starts to make more sense. Jesus calls His followers to this kind of life for a reason—so we can show those who aren't aware of the kindness of God what it means to be loved, forgiven and shown mercy. Yes, Jesus expects us to actually do these things. Yes, it will hurt. Can you think of a better way to show those who are far from God that He really loves them, Christianity is the "real thing," and forgiveness is for them? Imagine a world where we all actually did this stuff on a daily basis. Would it change the world? Would it change the world's idea of Christianity? Of Christ? Would it set the teachings of Jesus apart from every single other religious figure who had ever lived?

Isn't it ironic to think the most radical thing a modern Christian could do today would be to simply do exactly what Jesus says? Yeah, it's really a shame that no one really follows Jesus anymore. But, can you imagine what would happen to the world you live in if even a few people actually did? Not only that, Jesus promises those who actually do put His words into practice will be blessed and have life abundantly. Maybe it's time to start following Jesus? Maybe it's time to take Him seriously? What do you think?

"Therefore everyone who hears these words of mine and puts them into practice is like a wise man who built his house on the rock" (Matthew 7:24).

-Keith Giles

1
FOLLOWING JESUS

If you are reading this, I assume a few things about you. First, I assume you are interested in a radically different way of life than the one you are currently living. Perhaps you have spent your whole life in a church but feel there must be more to Jesus than just attending a worship service. Perhaps you are brand new to Jesus and wonder what comes next. Maybe you are wrestling with the idea of God and faith and are searching to understand more about Jesus before you give your life to Him. Perhaps you are a committed disciple of Jesus but you are looking for help teaching others how to follow Him. Regardless of why you are holding this book, know that it will help you take your next step closer to God. But before we can talk about your next step, we must be clear about the first step we all take: choosing Jesus. Discipleship is about following Jesus every day with every part of our lives, but in order to do that we must at some point choose Jesus as the focal point and purpose of our lives.

Why should we choose Jesus? For centuries, the primary answer to this question has been "to escape the fires of Hell." In an effort to encourage more people to choose Jesus, well-meaning preachers have cranked up the flames and horror in order to literally scare the Hell out of us. The reason this strategy is so common is because it has worked for many centuries. But running away from Hell is not the same thing as pursuing Jesus. It's not that Heaven and Hell don't matter. They do. But God would much rather help you choose Jesus and build a life with Him than simply run away from something bad. Besides, Heaven and Hell are not the issues keeping most people awake in the middle of the night. Too many people are living their own version of Hell right here and now and desperately need to know that God can make a positive difference in their lives today as well as for all eternity. Running away from Hell is not enough. Escaping to spiritual

Heaven is not enough. By choosing Jesus, we are not escaping earth in order to reach Heaven, but helping God smuggle Heaven into this present world, which won't be easy, but it will give our lives a dignity and purpose that many have never had before. Jesus is beating back the darkness with light. He is repairing what is broken, uniting what is divided, rebuilding what has been destroyed and bringing back to life what has died. Eternal life begins for us in the here and now the very moment we choose Jesus who then molds us into His image, recruits us to join His redeeming work, and equips us to get the job done. Jesus is changing our lives for the better so we can help God make the world better, too. That is not a cosmic miracle that will happen in the distant future. It is happening right now, every day, all around us.

Before we celebrate the coming Kingdom of God, we need to acknowledge something important: God has a few problems with us. We are notoriously unreliable. We make mistakes. We are weak. We hold grudges. We are selfish. We lash out in frustration. We shoot for the target God sets before us, but time and again, we miss the mark. We call this tendency to fail "sin." Before we can be truly useful to God in transforming this broken world, we are going to undergo some repairs and renovations. To serve Christ, we need a heart like Christ and a mind like Christ. The Holy Spirit is poured into us to clean things up inside and to rewire our desires and thoughts to be more compatible with the way Jesus approaches things. As Christ cleans us up to fit into His plans, we get to enjoy the benefit of living a healthier, more sane life. Our character is strengthened. We experience more love, joy, peace, patience, kindness, gentleness, generosity and self-control. Many of us come to Jesus because life is a mess, a combination of the choices we've made and the brutality of the world around us. Sometimes it is just bad luck and we can't catch a break. We struggle and need help. Another gift Jesus gives is the support and unconditional love of others who have surrendered their lives to Jesus, too. We are no longer alone in the struggle. Maybe our biological family gave us nothing but heartache, abuse and neglect, but we can become part of a new spiritual family that we choose and who chooses us rather than the random luck of the draw that is birth. Together with this family, we can choose to be a part of the solution for what is wrong with this world rather than continuing to be part of the problem. We can choose to serve through God's power rather than suffer as helpless victims.

In short, that is why we choose Jesus: for life, for a fresh start, for the friendship of a truly supportive family, and for a purpose worth living and dying for.

Anything else, inside the Church or out, is part of the problem that Christ came to solve and will pass away leaving only what is truly loving, truly kind, truly just, and truly holy. We come to Jesus because we believe He is the greatest hope we have for a better life, a better world, and a better future that stretches into eternity.

To the Church of Jesus Christ, I ask you this: Search your lives and have the courage to let the Spirit sift your hearts all the way to the bottom. Allow the Spirit to judge whether you are fully surrendered to Christ or whether you are kidding yourself. After all, "not everyone who cries out 'Lord, Lord' will enter the Kingdom of God." Jesus said that. He also said a tree is known by its fruit. Your life is proof of where your heart really is. Don't look around the room and decide where those around you are. You are only responsible for yourself. You only answer to God for your own thoughts and actions, and only you will receive the rewards or consequences of those thoughts and actions. Unfortunately, love, joy, peace, patience, kindness, gentleness, generosity, and self-control are in very short supply in far too many congregations. As authentic disciples, our lives should reflect Christ. What passes for Christianity these days is too often cold, shallow, judgmental, cautious, fearful, begrudging, stingy, suspicious, easily offended, and concerned with self. Christ is not the sole property of certain political parties, nor should certain political parties be confused for the generous grace of Jesus. Our faith has been hijacked by those seeking to divide us for the sake of votes. For the Church to be the Church we must value our citizenship in Heaven far above any earthly flag or nation. We offer Christ to every nation, every culture, every person of every conceivable way of life. There will be new faces here looking to you for love, acceptance and support. Never forget that "*not all the sinners are out in the streets and not all the saints are in the pews.*" Jesus received harsh criticism from the religious leaders who did not approve of the company He kept. If you are never uncomfortable, you probably aren't following Jesus. If you never rub others the wrong way, you probably aren't following Jesus. (Rubbing others the wrong way may also mean that you are acting like a jerk and not accurately reflecting Jesus. The existence of annoyed people is not proof of holy obedience, but is often a byproduct.) If you only seek the approval of other people, you definitely aren't following Jesus. Commit to being a generous part of the solution for this world rather than part of the problem.

To those new to Jesus, be patient with us. God chose to work through ordinary people like you and me, which means Christ's Church will always be less than perfect. You will be disappointed by the Church now and then. That is nothing new. It has been that way since the Church was born. The New Testament introduces us to churches like Corinth who just couldn't seem to get it together and were petty, mean, critical, and divided. You know what else they were? They were sinners in the process of salvation. That's us. We are all sinners being shaped in Christ's hands. We are all a mixed bag. Even the nastiest person you meet here has good in there somewhere and the kindest person you meet here has sins of their own. No one is perfect. If we expect each other to be perfect, we will be disappointed every single time. But we do expect better from ourselves and from each other. That's what it means to watch over each other with love and to encourage each other to take a step closer to God. We hold each other accountable for the inevitable sins and slip ups and speak the truth to each other about it in love, not to punish each other but to improve. The renovating work of the Holy Spirit is not automatic but requires our input, effort, and cooperation. That is what discipleship is all about. We cooperate with the Spirit every day to be what God created us to be. We are all a work in progress because Jesus isn't finished with any of us yet. But He who began this work in you will be faithful to complete it. God keeps God's promises, all of them: life, a fresh start, the friendship of a supportive family, and a purpose worth living and dying for.

So, are you ready to choose? Will you choose Jesus? Will you surrender your life to Him? Will you follow His lead and make every day count? Will you deepen your love relationship with God every day? Will you learn to follow Jesus with the support and accountability of other people? Will you generously share what you have with God and with others? Will you obediently assist God by meeting the needs of others? Will you encourage others to take their next step closer to God? Someday, Jesus will return to us. We don't know when, but He is coming back. It could be a thousand years from now or it could be tomorrow. We just don't know, which is why we must never waste a single moment of a single day. Choose Jesus above all else and make every day count.

IF YOU CHOOSE JESUS, KEEP READING...

Since you are still reading this, I assume you are interested in giving God a chance. In the end, you will give God your whole life, but let's not get ahead of ourselves. That is a huge commitment and a huge gamble, since we only have one life to give. We usually date for a while before we get married, so let's get to know God a little better before we make any promises we're not ready to keep.

The first and probably weirdest thing about God is the mind-bending paradox that God is Three Persons yet One God. That is why we will be calling God "God" rather than "He or She." Even though I'm avoiding gender pronouns, I will use the traditional language of God the Father, God the Son, and God the Holy Spirit simply because it is biblical language used by Jesus. There are people who have a problem calling God "Father" and it has nothing to do with political correctness. Too many people are coming to God to heal from the abuse inflicted by their earthly parents. To them a father is a drunk, violent, abusive monster, words that can never describe the Triune God who invented the nurturing love of parents for their children. "Father" is the role played by the First Person of the Trinity which goes far beyond a family relationship. It is also the role of the commanding officer who develops the plans for the redemption of the universe. Even though God the Father assumes command, all three are equal. God the Father is not somehow "More God" than the other Two. It is a matter of the role being filled and the functions being carried out. God the Father creates plans. God the Son carries out those plans. "Son" is a role played by the Second Person of the Trinity that, again, means much more than a family relationship. God the Son is one who is under the authority of another who leads but also loves, protects, and provides. God the Son is tasked with carrying out the plans and completing the mission. God the Holy Spirit, or Third Person of the Trinity, is the mystical power used by God the Father and God the Son to make things happen. It is the power behind every miracle in Jesus' life on earth from conception to resurrection and is the power by which God gives us faith and transforms us as we grow as followers of Jesus.

Our One God is a group, not simply one person. This idea of what we call the "Triune God" or "Trinity" is deep and complicated and makes the average human brain hurt. God is so different from us that our human minds can never fully understand. You can reconcile One God being Three Persons if you think of God as a family or a community. It is an imperfect analogy that fails to completely express the true nature of God, but it is at least a step in the right direction. Just like there are nine players on one baseball team, there are three persons in our one God bound by love and loyalty and working together for the common good. No player on these sports teams is better or more important than any other. They all work together in different positions to win the game. No one Person of the Trinity is better or more important than any other. They only differ in the parts they play in the eternal mission. That is also why we insist that no one person in Jesus' Church is better or more important than any other. We only differ in the parts we play in the eternal mission. Wouldn't you like to be part of a family like that, bound together by love and loyalty and working together for the common good?

You can be. God created the universe and every single one of us so that we can be a part of this family too. This perfect Divine Family of Three has opened up the circle and invites us to join. God is a small group that is completely supportive and cooperative in everything it does, working together to accomplish the eternal mission that unites its members with a purpose worth living and dying for. It is no accident that Jesus began His work on earth by gathering the first disciples into a similar small group that learned how to be completely supportive and cooperative in everything it did, working together to accomplish the eternal mission that united its members with a purpose worth living and dying for. Jesus was born for this and died on a cross for this. The original disciples were born again for this and most surrendered their lives to the cause as martyrs, who are those whose deaths bear witness to their faith in Jesus Christ. (As is repeated elsewhere in this book, the Way of Christ is the Way of the Cross. The ability to suffer, while unfortunate, is a crucial skill of effective disciples.) This is how life is meant to be lived, not alone but together. Jesus continues to gather us into similar small groups to learn how to be completely supportive and cooperative in everything we do, working together to accomplish the eternal mission that unites us with a purpose worth living and dying for. That is what you will find in these pages, the invitation to join not only a group of like-minded followers of Jesus, but to become an eternal part of the Family that is God the Father, God the Son, and God the Holy Spirit in service to the rest of the world around us. That is a concept that so fills me with awe, I have tears in my eyes as I write. While the Triune God is hard to understand, the "Eternal Mission of God" is not. God really only wants three things from us:

First, God desires an intimate love relationship with us that lasts forever.

The love part is nice, but the forever part is problematic. God is immortal, which means God lives forever, but we do not. We die. Compared to God, our lives are incredibly short. Thanks to the death of Jesus on the cross, we are forgiven for our personal part in screwing up the world, but it is His resurrection that opens up life beyond death for us. That's great, but please remember, there is more to life than just waiting to die and go to Heaven. Life is to be enjoyed with God right now. If you keep reading, we will teach you how to love God, talk with God and grow closer every day. We must become more like God the Father, Son, and Holy Spirit in order to become part of the Family. We must fall in love with God and be able to express that love forever.

Second, God wants to help us love and care for each other.

The Three Persons of the Trinity are united, loyal, and cooperative but we human beings don't seem to get along well. We grate on each other's nerves. We get angry. We fight wars and stop speaking to each other. We are what's wrong with the world. We are all God's children, and God loves us equally. If only we could see in each other what God sees in us, we might stop treating life as a competition and begin to really look out for each other. That is what God wants and what God expects. Thankfully, God is making that happen by rewiring our selfish human brains and teaching us how to care for others. It is essential that we learn to love, accept, and support each other or we will remain incompatible with the Divine Family we are invited to join.

Third, God invites us to help God change the world.

If we are what's wrong with the world, then we are also an indispensable part of the solution. The world is repaired by us and through us one life at a time. We will remind ourselves again and again that God is changing lives and making the world a better place. God is recruiting us to help influence the world for healthy change. We help every person in the world find their part in God's Eternal Mission by beginning an intimate love relationship with God that lasts forever, then learning to love and care for each other as humans as God the Father, Son, and Holy Spirit love and care for each other. This gives our new lives meaning, purpose and direction.

Discipleship Means Following Jesus

Being a disciple of Jesus is being a follower of Jesus. We know what it means to follow. As children we play "Simon Says" and "Follow the Leader" where we follow our leader as exactly as we can like little ducks following the big duck. In the farmyard, when Mama Duck invites her ducklings to join her for a walk, she is the first in line, deciding where to go, by what route and how fast. The ducklings keep an eye on Mama and do what Mama does. They learn their way around the farm by following Mama. They learn to swim by swimming with Mama. They learn how to find food by finding it with Mama. They don't follow Mama just because they love her. By following her around, day after day, little ducks learn how to be big ducks. As big ducks, many will teach little ducks of their own someday.

Jesus is "The Big Duck." He led his first disciples so that they would one day be able to lead disciples of their own who one day would be able to lead disciples of their own. Jesus is always the leader of our small groups, too. We follow His example. We follow His instructions. We will break that down later in great detail so we will both know what that means and live it out. For now, let's just be clear: Jesus is in charge. He is our teacher, mentor, and guide. He decides the way we should go and we obediently do our part. We surrender our right to decide for ourselves. We surrender our right to be in control. From this moment on, we live our lives for Him. His purpose is our purpose. His mission is our mission. His life is our life. His heart is our heart. His mind is our mind. Jesus is not just a large part of our lives; our lives only have meaning in His. If you are new to Jesus, or if God has been, up until now, something you've done once a week on Sunday, you are in for an adventure! You are about to surrender everything to Jesus and find a life more meaningful than anything you have ever known! But this does not mean, as too many assume, that we are mindless drones guided by remote control. Nothing could be further from the truth. It takes heroic amounts of self-control to choose to give our lives and obedience to the cause of God. Remember what the cause of God really is. It is those three things that God desires:

> God desires an intimate love relationship with us that lasts forever.
> God wants to help us love and care for each other.
> God invites us to help God change the world for the better.

We are taught how to do this in order to teach others who will in time teach others. At some point, after growing with Jesus in a small group, we will each gather others in a brand new small group of our own. Those new disciples who follow Jesus will eventually do the same. It is as natural as the changing of the seasons.

Regardless of how much experience you have with Jesus at this exact moment, know this: God has already supplied you with everything you need to give your whole life over to God and live obediently for God's glory rather than your own. Throughout the pages that follow, you will be introduced to an avalanche of teachings, practices, resources, and realities that God has placed at your fingertips to equip you to live as God's beloved child and to be a subversive revolutionary through which God undermines this present world and replaces it with a better one. But just because this mountain of resources is already at your fingertips, it does not mean that becoming a disciple is instant or easy. You will question many long held assumptions about God, the Church, the World, and yourself in the days ahead. Don't be frightened by that. We cannot rely forever on what "someone else told me" about God. It is time to experience God for yourself. It is time to question, to learn and to make up your own mind. Be convinced. Own your faith as yours. That's how lives are transformed. Different Christians may explain how to walk this path differently, which should be expected. We are not interested in quibbling over particulars or making mountains out of molehills. We care nothing about proving ourselves or these teachings to be superior to anyone else's. That is the way of the world that would rather compete than cooperate. What we share here is deeply indebted to countless others. We simply share in the historic passion and purpose of Christ's Church for making disciples by actively discipling each other. Discipling is something that is taught and passed down ever since Jesus invested His life and time in the first disciples. That brings us to one more gift God has already given you in this new life: help. Do not think that simply reading a book will change your life. It can have a great impact, but we cannot become disciples on our own. It is not a solitary pursuit, but a team sport. We need the Holy Spirit and we need other, more experienced disciples to teach us how to follow Jesus by living life together with us. That is what "5x5" is all about. It is intended to simply be a helpful way to share ancient "holy knowledge and holy know-how" by walking the Path of Jesus together.

What is "The Path of Jesus" and How Do We Start Walking It?

There are so many words to describe this new life that we are living with Jesus. The Bible calls it "salvation," "being born again," and the "new life in Christ." Whatever you call it, the common thread is an active relationship with God. Like any relationship, it is marked by changes in things inside of us as well as things going on around us. Historically, the Church has focused on the inside stuff first, what we think, believe and feel. We are taught that belief in Jesus is all that is required:

"For God so loved the world that He gave His only begotten Son that whoever believes in Him shall not perish but will have everlasting life." (John 3:16)

What does it mean to "believe in Him?" It means we agree that the claims and promises made about Jesus are indeed true. Jesus, who was born the step-son of a Jewish carpenter in Galilee is in fact the "Eternal Son of the Triune God" who was fully human as well as fully divine, taught us the ways of God, died to take the consequences of our sins and was raised in resurrection to offer us eternal life. Some people, thanks to the constant help of the Holy Spirit, are able to believe that almost immediately and are ready to begin living every day with Jesus from that moment on. They pray, confess their sins, ask Jesus to take them "under His wing," and the rest is history. That is a beautiful moment that changes everything for us. All that's left is to start living as a disciple who is learning how to follow Jesus every day. It can be as simple as praying what has come to be known as "The Sinner's Prayer" or "The Believer's Prayer." There are many versions of this prayer but they have the same things in common:

First, we acknowledge that we believe the truth of who Jesus is.

Second, we confess and apologize for our sins and ask for forgiveness.

Third, we trust Jesus and choose to follow Him with our whole life.

Here is an example:

Believer's Prayer (Anonymous)

Lord Jesus, I want to know you personally. Thank you for dying on the cross for my sins. I open the door of my life to you and ask you to come in as my Savior and Lord. Take control of my life. Thank you for forgiving my sins and giving me eternal life. Make me the kind of person you want me to be.

If you've never consciously taken the initiative to claim the truth of Jesus, give Him control of your life, confess your sins, and begin living a new life for Him, you can do that right now. You can use any version of the prayer above as a guide. But I must impress upon you this word of warning: There are no magic words in the Kingdom of God.

Some assume that, just because they took thirty seconds to pray this prayer, their salvation is assured, and they never have to give it another thought. The same applies to the act of baptism whether your church baptized you as an adult or an infant. If you are new to Christ's Church, I have to apologize about baptism. No single teaching of Jesus has divided us more as a Church than the institution of baptism. Rather than spark a fresh debate over why, when, and by what method, I will simply remind you of something important from Jesus's baptism. It was the beginning of the rest of His life. With that life, he served the incredible plan of God the Father by pointing us toward Heaven, then dying and being raised to get us there. Baptism will be the beginning of the rest of our lives, too, as we dedicate ourselves to serving the incredible plan of God for us and our world. Yes, you acknowledged the truth of who Jesus is. Yes, you have confessed your sinfulness and asked for forgiveness. Yes, you have expressed your intention to live for Jesus. But, now it is time to actually give your life to Jesus and follow His example, His teachings, and His call every day for the rest of eternity. I don't want to get into a theological battle about how salvation happens for us so I will lean upon the apostle Paul who teaches in Ephesians 2:8 that *"We are saved by grace, through faith, not by our own works, lest anyone boast."* That's good enough for me. We don't live as disciples in order to earn our salvation. We receive salvation in order to live as disciples and followers of Jesus who help God change the world. That last part is what this book is all about: living as followers of Jesus.

Some of you reading this may not have sorted all of that out yet. You may not be ready to pray these prayers or take such a big step. There are parts of this story we just don't understand. Maybe you are struggling with what you have been taught about Jesus. You have doubts. Don't worry about that. Everyone has doubts. Doubts are simply questions that need answers. This story is understandably hard for some people to grasp because the work of God is beyond normal everyday life. It is both miraculous and supernatural. How do we work through our doubts? "It takes faith," we say, meaning "a leap of faith." Faith is the combination of belief and trust. While it is one thing to believe in my mind that my rusty, dented rowboat can ferry me safely across the deep lake, it is quite another thing to trust that boat by getting in and shoving out into the deep water. What reason do I have to trust it? What reason do I have to trust God? In our salvation, praying one of these salvation prayers is like saying I trust the boat. I may mean it with all my heart, but it means very little if I don't trust my life to it. Choosing to live every day obediently for God is like shoving out into the deep water. It is taking a risk on God, much like we took a risk on that leaky rowboat. I trust Jesus with my life, my family, my hopes, my dreams, my finances, and my future. I put it all at God's disposal to use in ways that further God's Eternal Mission. That is a huge step. So, you may ask, where do we get the courage to trust that much and take that leap of faith? Again, it comes from God who is working infinitely harder to reach us than we are to reach God. God the Father is giving you, through God the Holy Spirit, the encouragement and love necessary to take the risk of following God the Son.

The following analogy will help us understand how God is doing that. Imagine a frightened toddler wearing a life vest and swim goggles standing nervously beside the swimming pool as Mommy is waist deep in the water. Mother is inviting her child to join her in the water, and the child understandably has doubts. He is afraid of the deep water, but mother, arms outstretched, has promised to catch him if he would simply jump. Why would he jump? Why would he ever take the risk of jumping in over his head? He knows his mother. That's why he believes her and trusts her. Mommy invites, comforts, and encourages him to jump, assuring him that she will never drop him. With enough encouragement, his love and trust grow far stronger than his fear and doubt. So it is with your relationship with God. If you are afraid to jump into God's arms with everything you are and everything you have, it just means you need to get to know each other better. You need to spend some time together. God, through the Holy Spirit, has been calling out to you with arms outstretched since your birth. We are saved by grace, which means God gives us what we need to help our love and trust grow stronger than our fear and doubt. So, if you are not yet ready to pray a Believer's Prayer you can simply walk with God on the Path.

You may be wondering why we call it "The Path." The earliest believers, before they were called Christians, were simply called "Followers of the Way." This comes from Jesus' own words in John 14:6 as Jesus declares: "*I am the Way, and the Truth, and the Life. No one comes to the Father except by me.*" This has been interpreted very narrowly in the past as if Jesus is the secret password we need to say aloud to be permitted to begin a life with God. Jesus may have had something else in mind. The Greek word that is translated "the way" is '*odos* and means a journey, a path, or a road and metaphorically represents a way of life. The simple truth of Jesus is this: the way to our Father in Heaven is found in a simple way of life that is enjoyed every day. Even if you are still struggling with some doubts about Jesus, you can still spend time with God by taking a walk together on the path. Some teach that you must be fully "saved" before living as a disciple, that you must first pray the Believer's Prayer or it doesn't count. It certainly helps, but you don't have to. Take Jesus for a test drive by trying out His way of life that encourages honesty, self-control, compassion, service, and humility. We do not care to argue whether it was the chicken or the egg that came first. In the end it doesn't matter whether you gave your life to Jesus and now are beginning a new way of life, or whether you begin a new way of life that builds the trust necessary to give your life to Jesus. Simply believing the right things means little. Even the demons believe Jesus is God the Son, but that doesn't improve their lives at all. There have been scores of people who have "prayed the right prayer" but then lived the same old life they lived without Jesus. It is the Way of Life that changes us and the world around us. As a matter of fact, consider this shocking statement:

> *Even if there were no such thing as God, and Jesus was just an ordinary man, the way of life that He advocates of humility, kindness, compassion, respect, and sacrifice will heal the world on its own if more people gave it a try.*

Now add to that the divine gift of the Holy Spirit to provide the wisdom, power and guidance that can only come from God and we begin to grasp how the Kingdom of God grows in around us. But it takes disciples who are willing to go beyond an intellectual agreement with a set of beliefs to adopt a radical and healing way of life that puts Jesus and God's Eternal Mission first. Discipleship is not without its tests and challenges, but it is meant to be enjoyed, not endured. So, let's take a walk.

How Do We Teach This Way of Life With Jesus?

Christian writer Bill Hull, in his book "The Complete Book of Discipleship," (NavPress 2006) gives one of the best explanations of how we become disciples by observing how Jesus taught the original twelve disciples:

1. A disciple submits to a teacher who teaches how to follow Jesus.
2. A disciple learns the words of Jesus.
3. A disciple learns Jesus' way of ministry.
4. A disciple imitates Jesus' life and character.
5. A disciple finds and teaches other disciples to follow Jesus.

This observation by Hull is so foundational to our work, it will be repeated several times throughout this book. We learn from Jesus and do what Jesus does. Jesus did a lot of things to make us better and to heal the world. Jesus prayed. Jesus taught. Jesus served. Jesus fed the hungry. Jesus encouraged and invited others to draw closer to God the Father. Everything Jesus did falls into five categories:

1. A life of worship in which Jesus deepened His love relationship with God the Father.
2. A life of learning and teaching in which He taught the disciples how to follow.
3. A life of giving in which Jesus generously shared what He had with God the Father and other people.
4. A life of serving in which He carried out the plans of God the Father by meeting the needs of other people with kindness, compassion, and sacrifice.
5. A life of encouraging all people to take their next step closer to God.

There are literally thousands of ways we can imitate Jesus. It could take us forever to learn everything there is to learn. How do we teach it all? We will need some helpful way to picture this in our mind to keep it all organized. Allow me a brief story to explain how we are going to do this. Several years ago, I fell in love with hiking and it wasn't long before I felt a deep desire to go further. I wanted to try backpacking where I live, eat, and sleep out on the trail for days, weeks, or even months at a time. Unfortunately, I didn't know the first thing about it. I didn't have any gear and I didn't know what to do with it even if I had it. I decided to purchase a field manual for backpacking. Originally written in 1968 and updated every decade, "The Complete Walker" by Colin Fletcher (Alfred A. Knopf, 2003) has become the "Bible of Backpacking," teaching me everything I needed to have, to know, and know how to do on the trail. I would later go on to lead backpacking groups and church camps, teaching others what I had learned from Colin Fletcher.

Fletcher describes the gear and know-how that is needed for life on the trail. An average backpack may contain 40-60 pounds of gear during a long distance hike. That's a lot of stuff to keep track of. To make it easier, Fletcher divides all that gear into five major categories according to the rooms of a house:

THE KITCHEN is all the gear and know-how needed to provide nutritious food and clean water.
THE BEDROOM is all the gear and know-how needed to provide shelter and sleep.
THE CLOSET is all the clothing and know-how needed for different weather conditions.
THE BATHROOM is all the gear and know-how needed to ensure good health and hygiene.
THE WORKSHOP is all the gear and know-how to make repairs along the way.

He then organizes all the hiking knowledge and know-how in his book according to these five rooms. It's a good thing he does, because it helps keep the thousands of pieces of hiking information organized in our minds. It is a brilliantly practical way to teach, which is why his book has become the gold standard for anyone wanting to learn how to hike. When it comes to discipleship, there is also an overwhelming amount of things to learn as a follower of Jesus. We need a practical way to keep it organized in our minds in order to live this new life to the fullest. Backpacking requires the right gear, good knowledge to live in harmony with nature, the right know-how to get things done, and wisdom to make good decisions in every situation. You don't need everything in that pack if you are only going out for a short walk in the woods. You may not need it all every day. But if you intend to live, survive, and thrive on the trail, you will need it all eventually, and you better know how it all works before you need it in the woods! Be prepared!

Being a Follower of Jesus doesn't require much gear, but knowledge, know-how and wisdom are essential. When you make a list of everything a Christian does or should know, it can also get pretty overwhelming. You won't need it all if you are content with one passive hour a week with God in a worship service. You won't need all of it every day, but we intend to walk with Jesus through the rest of our lives and eternity, so we will most definitely need everything in these pages eventually. Too often we forget why these things are important to us as gifts to help our life rather than a burden of obligations. The things of God are not intended to make us feel guilty for not getting around to them like eating broccoli or doing sit-ups every day. That is an attitude of shallow faith. These things of God help make the peace, courage, and freedom we crave possible. Remember, we are not just passing through this world with Jesus hoping to escape to perfect Heaven. We are being equipped to help God change the world. We are servants through which God is subversively undermining this crumbling world as the better world is smuggled in under our noses. These things of God equip us for every assignment and mission Jesus may give us, some of which may be risky or even dangerous. We'd best be prepared, too. To help keep track of this overwhelming amount of holy stuff, let's follow Colin Fletcher's lead and break it all down into five major categories according to function:

WORSHIP is everything needed to deepen our love relationship with God.
LEARNING how to follow Jesus as we live life together with other people.
GIVING is generously sharing whatever we have with God and with others.
SERVING is how we honor God by meeting the needs of others.
ENCOURAGING is helping each other to take our next step closer to God.

As we observe the life and character of Jesus we quickly discover that everything He did falls into one of these five categories. We follow His example, so everything in our lives will fall into one of these five areas as well. We will call these "The Five Disciplines of Jesus." We choose the word "disciplines" because they are the active methods and processes by which we become a disciple. They are skills that will take time and repetition to develop because "practice makes perfect."

I think "The Jesus Way of Life" looks a lot like a long distance backpacking trip with a group of friends. Since "the way" also means a path or a trail, backpacking is a good image to understand the disciple's life. We have some ground to cover and some friends to join us along the way. On the trail, some of us will be better at the basic skills than others. We will learn from each other and get better together as we walk along. We will inevitably get on each other's nerves too, and we'll work it out and love each other even more. We will take care of each other when sick and injured and of course share our supplies with each other and anyone else we might meet on the trail who needs help. Most importantly, we will not let each other quit when hiking is no longer fun. I dream of one day hiking the Appalachian Trail from beginning to end. It is over 2,000 miles and takes several months to accomplish. Only a quarter of the hikers who start the trail each year complete the entire journey. They drop out for many reasons. Some are injured. Some were unprepared. Some are homesick, wanting to go back to what they gave up in order to hike. Some simply get tired of hiking every day. Day after day of what seems like endless walking is more than some people can handle. These are the folks who started the trail simply to cross it off the list. They want the accomplishment, but really don't love the experience of living on the trail. I'd like to complete the entire trail, but I am looking forward to life *on* the trail, not just the photo op in front of the Mt. Katahdin sign at the end. I just like being out there, swimming in mountain streams, sleeping under the stars, taking in the forest and fresh air. There is plenty of exercise, time to think, time to read, time to pray, and time to make new friends. It becomes a way of life. That's the real payoff. Finishing a trail is a bonus.

Our relationship with God works a lot the same way. Some people just want to get to Heaven when they die. They're not interested in day after day of endless living in this broken world. Their bags are packed and they are waiting for the chariot to come. But we must live in the tension between the "already" and the "not yet." Jesus has already died and has risen. We are already forgiven and adopted as children of God. But eternity is still to come. How shall we spend that time? Every day in between is a gift to be lived and enjoyed, not simply endured until it is finally over. We are not just marking time until the good stuff happens. This is the only life we will ever have. Why waste it by wishing it away? This is the good stuff, too. This is where hiking and discipleship begin to really overlap.

Before we leave this introduction, there is one more important thing to cover. It does not matter how skilled you are at pitching tents and boiling water in your backyard. This journey will take us far from the comforts of home into the heart of the mountain wilderness. We must know something about what to expect outdoors in the wilderness. We need to know which plants and snakes are poisonous and which are harmless. We need to know how to read the sky during changing weather. We need to understand something about the movements of wildlife around us and how to protect our camp and supplies from hungry bears and raccoons. There are realities of nature that we must understand, accept, and adapt to in order to survive and thrive. It is not always clean, or comfortable, or safe and it's not going to magically change simply because we want it to change. It is the same with life on planet earth, whether we live for God or for ourselves.

"The Five Disciplines of Jesus" are not practiced in a vacuum. We are not pitching tents in the backyard. We are praying, serving, learning and trying to be encouraging amidst stress, suffering, anxiety, disappointment and hostility. Life is not always conducive to a loving heart. We follow Jesus even when it is anything but fun. Life often gets in the way of following Jesus and unexpected crises can knock us right off the path if we are not ready for them. I confess that, as a pastor, I spend as much time helping grieving people cope with the pain and struggle of everyday life as I do teaching them how to pray and serve. The pitfalls and accidents of life too often become an interruption and obstacle to the life we have chosen and too much suffering can even cause some to question their decision to trust God in the first place. We naively expect God to protect us from all harm and danger, but the world just doesn't work that way and neither does God. As disciples, we must learn to accept these hard realities of the world around us. It can be argued that the grace and tranquility with which we navigate these hard realities set the Christian apart from everyone else even more than our daily practices of holiness. The world around us may not be dying to learn how to pray, but many need to know how to accept disappointment, control anger, survive grief and handle pain without being crushed by it. In this respect, warm-hearted Followers of Jesus also need the cold steel steadiness of fighter pilots who (ideally) never panic, never lose control, and never give up. This steadiness is promised to us in scripture as a fruit of the Holy Spirit, but very little direction is given to assist us in the pursuit and development of courage, self-control, and peace. As a Church, we do not regularly teach Jesus Followers how to develop tranquility, fearlessness, and freedom in all situations. Without these things, it is difficult to love our enemies, offer grace to those who need it, and avoid bitterness. This has done a great disservice to both those walking The Path of Jesus and the world we are helping to liberate. We intend to correct that deficiency starting now:

We must accept that there are some things in life that we can control and some things we can't.

Here are five things in life that are completely beyond our control. We call them:

The Five Undeniable Truths

1. WE ARE EACH RESPONSIBLE FOR OURSELVES.
2. WE SHARE THE PLANET WITH OTHER PEOPLE.
3. EVERYTHING COSTS SOMETHING.
4. LIFE IS NOT FAIR.

5. NOTHING LASTS FOREVER.

We can't change these things. They apply to everyone on earth at all times. We waste so much time and energy wishing we could change what has happened in the past or demanding to know why these things have happened to us in the first place! Simply put: Life is hard. Deal with it. That might sound harsh, but it is true. Just because we are walking The Path of Jesus, it doesn't mean we now live in a magic fairy land of unicorns and rainbows. We follow Jesus who lived with us in this same broken world, suffered, struggled, was treated unfairly, grieved the deaths of friends, was falsely accused, tortured and died! The Path of Jesus does not steer clear of danger and pain but plunges right straight through it. We are on that path too. We are not immune to the hard realities of life. Jesus accepted the cross and that willingness to suffer offers life to us all. The Path of Jesus always leads to the Cross. Knowing that, accepting that, and working with that gives us more power for Jesus than you may realize.

This, incidentally, is how "5x5" found its name. Walking The Path of Jesus is a matter of accepting the things in life we cannot change ("The Five Undeniable Truths") while focusing our energy on the things we can change ("The Five Disciplines of Jesus") and letting God take care of the rest. This is a way of life that can heal us and can heal the world. That may not be evident now, but it soon will be. We keep our focus on the Path by regularly praying "The Serenity Prayer" by Reinhold Niebuhr (1892-1971).

The Serenity Prayer

God grant me the serenity
To accept the things I cannot change;
Courage to change the things I can;
And wisdom to know the difference.

Living one day at a time;
Enjoying one moment at a time;
Accepting hardships as the pathway to peace;
Taking, as He did, this sinful world
As it is, not as I would have it;
Trusting that He will make all things right
If I surrender to His Will;
So that I may be reasonably happy in this life
And supremely happy with Him
Forever and ever in the next. Amen.

We must accept the things we cannot change, change the things we can, and seek to know the difference between the two. That covers so much ground, we could get lost in all the things we need to know and know how to do. 5x5 is simply a way of keeping it all organized in our minds so we can remember it when we need it most. Here's a memory trick that we can use to remember the entire framework of becoming a disciple. Take a look at your hands. Most of us have two hands with five fingers on each hand. Look first at your left hand. On one hand, we have the things we cannot change. We call them the Five Undeniable Truths. On the other hand, we have the ways God equips us to change the world for the better. We call them the Five Disciplines of Jesus. Our life and our faith are literally in our own hands.

The material in this book is organized according to these two lists of five. As hikers on the spiritual trail, think of the Five Undeniable Truths as the wilderness around us. We learn to recognize, accept, and work with the perils and pitfalls that are common to us all. We've identified them by taking a hard look at the world and observing what appears to be true for all of us. Since they are common to all, we need not be surprised or shaken when we run into them. Think of the Five Disciplines of Jesus as the things we learn how to do, like purify water, build campfires, and avoid blisters. They are the skills we need to accomplish God's Eternal Mission. By them, Jesus is equipping us to assist in bringing the Kingdom of God into reality. We've identified the Five Disciplines of Jesus by taking a closer look at Jesus and observing him in action. Everything Jesus does falls into one of these broad categories and we will cover a tremendous amount of ground as we explore them one by one. This is not the only way to explain the Christian life, but it is how we will learn to follow Jesus together.

A few last thoughts before we dive in. First, because this is a field manual it can be read straight through, or as a reference book allowing you to look up what you need when you need it most. Therefore, you may find material that is repeated in different sections because it is relevant in different situations. Second, while this book is a resource for those participating in a 5x5 Discipleship Group, which is a specific method of discipling each other, it is also quite useful for anyone who wishes to have a wealth of discipleship resources at their fingertips. Third, I believe this material can be useful to any Christian disciple, but recognize that we may see things differently. I have tried to keep denominational and theological controversies out of this project but I'm not so naive as to believe that everyone will embrace everything found within these pages. I am a United Methodist pastor in the evangelical tradition of John Wesley. That word "evangelical" has become divisive of late thanks to its association with

American political movements. I embrace the word as Wesley did, claiming to be part of a growing movement to offer Jesus to the world. My views on how the Bible works may differ from yours, but we can still unite in our mission to change lives and make the world a better place through the eternal gifts that Jesus offers. I will invite you to join me on this journey, despite our differences, because we have Jesus in common. To quote John Wesley: *"If your heart is as my heart, take my hand."* Lastly, this is not a self-help book. As you will learn, discipleship is a team sport. While this book is a thorough overview of the disciple's life it is no substitute for sharing life together with other believers in the congregation of your choice.

Ready to go? Let's take a closer look at what this all means for us. We begin with the things we cannot change.

2
THE FIVE UNDENIABLE TRUTHS

"To achieve freedom and happiness, you need to grasp this basic truth: some things in life are under your control, and others are not..."If it is not within your control, it is nothing to you; there's nothing to worry about." -Epictetus

Epictetus was a very wise man. He was born a Greek slave twenty five years after the resurrection of Jesus. He wasn't a Follower of Jesus. He was a Stoic philosopher in Rome. I can already hear the question forming in your mind: "Why in the world are we starting a discussion of Christian discipleship by talking about a pagan philosopher?" That is an excellent question. In many ways, wisdom is universal. God has revealed some things to us about ourselves as human beings simply by giving us brains capable of paying attention. People have been paying attention to human life since the beginning of time and have made some helpful discoveries that are just as true now as they were in ancient times. That is why, from time to time in the pages to come, we will include several astute observations from people of other cultures and faith traditions. We are not interested in what these faiths and philosophers have to say about God or eternity since Jesus alone will be our guide in matters of salvation. But much of what the Bible teaches us about ourselves can be found echoed eloquently all the over the world and many writers have dedicated themselves to exploring our human faults and foibles. That is why we are meeting Epictetus.

Epictetus lived a hard life, beaten repeatedly and crippled by his owner, yet he refused to let the difficult people and difficult circumstances of life determine his outlook. All Stoic philosophy begins with this quote from Epictetus that there are some things in life that we can control and other things that we cannot, or to say it another way: Some things are up to us and some are not up to us. His secret to finding peace, courage, and freedom was accepting the things beyond our control and turning all our energy toward the things we can control. We can't control the weather, the stock market, cancer, or being born into a family led by an alcoholic father. We can complain. We can cry. We can throw a tantrum, drink heavily, or be depressed, but none of these actions can change our situation. Epictetus could not change his bondage to an abusive master. He could not change his crippled legs or physical disabilities that resulted from the unfair beatings he endured. Was it unfair? Yes. Was it wrong? Yes. Should it be different? Yes. Was there anything he could do about it? No. Here lies the crucial decision: How do we choose to respond to the things in life that are unpleasant, unfair, and wrong? In short, we can't control anything external. We can't control events, other people, or bad luck. We can however control what goes on inside of us, our thoughts, feelings, likes, dislikes, and our ability to choose and decide for ourselves. The only thing we can ever control in any situation is ourselves. Roman Emperor Marcus Aurelius said:

"You have power over your mind, not outside events. Realize this and you will find power."

As you will see in the discussion below, we can choose to be derailed and defeated by the unplanned and unpleasant obstacles of life or, as Marcus Aurelius also said "the obstacle becomes the way." He actually said *"the impediment to action advances action. What stands in the way becomes the way."* Why is that important for disciples of Jesus Christ? It is important because we will face resistance, hostility, interruptions, and bad luck while serving the purposes of God in this world. If we collapse in a tantrum every time the world is unfair to us, the Eternal Mission of God will go unfulfilled. Our ability to suffer and endure without losing focus on the purpose of our lives is key to God's plan. Not only that, just as Marcus Aurelius taught, these moments of suffering and disappointment often turn out to be the seasons through which God accomplishes the most fruitful work. Remember, God is healing what is injured, repairing what is broken, and recovering what is lost. Alleviating suffering is God's business, so finding ourselves in pain certainly does not derail God's work nor disqualifies us from being a part of it. On the contrary, finding ourselves diagnosed with a tumor, or needing dialysis may actually clarify our call by allowing God to use us among the people we meet at the hospital waiting room. We will borrow heavily from the Stoic philosophers to express something inherently Christian because these philosophers so eloquently and effectively expressed what we need to hear.

We will focus on five things we cannot change. They are five undeniable truths. Accept them. My friend Jim is an officer in the Air National Guard and one of the more stoic and Christ-like souls I know. His response to difficulty is often tough love. In the military, we are not encouraged to whine and complain about our difficulties. We are told to "suck it up" and why not? We all have problems, don't we? Deal with them and keep moving. In my neighborhood growing up, we had a word for anyone not tough enough to "suck it up." That word was "wuss" (which rhymes with "puss" as in "pussy cat") If you cried after being tackled in a game of football, you were called a "wuss." It was not about shaming and belittling each other as much as it was about offering perspective. If you aren't seriously injured, your crying is holding up the game. We all had our bumps and bruises, but if we stopped playing every time something hurt, we'd never finish a single game. How we think about our pain determines whether we will keep playing or quit. Magnify that statement a thousand fold when talking about the pain and disappointment we encounter as servants of Jesus. God has given us the power to decide for ourselves how we will think about our pain and disappointment which is a very powerful gift.

The Five Undeniable Truths are:

1. WE ARE EACH RESPONSIBLE FOR OURSELVES.
2. WE SHARE THE PLANET WITH OTHER PEOPLE.
3. EVERYTHING COSTS SOMETHING.
4. LIFE IS NOT FAIR.
5. NOTHING LASTS FOREVER.

Let's take a closer look at each one in turn.

I. WE ARE EACH RESPONSIBLE FOR OURSELVES.

This is the First Undeniable Truth of Life: We are each responsible for ourselves. That means several things to us all at once. As said above, God has given us the power to decide for ourselves how we will think about our pain and disappointment which is a very powerful gift. This powerful gift only works if we take the responsibility to think for ourselves and choose our response. I cannot emphasize this enough. Too many people feel that having a happy life is a matter of luck. Life is what happens to us and we hope good things happen. We resent people who seem "luckier" than we are, who have what we want. This is nonsense.

First, we are required to live our own lives and take care of our own daily needs and obligations because no one else is required to take care of us. As pastor, I spend a lot of time with people in need. Poverty is a complicated issue with many causes and is a foundational concern of Jesus. People struggle because of illness, accidents, lack of education, or lack of opportunity. Sometimes, though, people struggle to keep a roof over their head because they are unable or unwilling to do what is necessary to survive. I encourage them to understand what they are responsible for and encourage them to take that responsibility seriously.

Second, we are required to choose the kind of person we would like to be and the kind of life we would like to live. There is no guarantee that we will achieve all our hopes and dreams in life since so much of this world around us is beyond our control. We are free to choose and must choose for ourselves what kind of character we wish to develop and what brings meaning to our lives.

Third, we are each responsible for our own thoughts, feelings, and decisions. We are not victims helplessly swept along in life by the cold world around us. We are free to think for ourselves. How we feel emotionally is directly linked to the way we think and interpret things. Nothing can make me angry unless I choose to be. Nothing can frustrate me unless I choose to let myself be frustrated. We are not taught to think this way. If we were, we wouldn't blame our tantrums on other people who may legitimately be frustrating and irritating people. We decide how we will respond and we own the consequences of those choices.

Fourth, we are responsible for our own salvation. We each must stand before God one at a time in judgment and will be solely responsible for the consequences of our choices and actions. While others may pray for us, encourage us, and offer Christ to us, no one can accept our salvation for us. That we must do on our own. Parents may desperately wish for salvation for their children, but they cannot make it happen. That is what the old saying "God has no grandchildren" means. We each must relate to God on our own.

As said above, we must accept that there are some things in life that we can control and some things we can't. The truth is, the only thing we can ever completely control in any situation is ourselves. We were created to take full responsibility for ourselves. According to Genesis, we are created in the image of God. That means there is something about us as human beings that we share in common with God that no other creature in the Animal Kingdom shares. It is Moses who helps us understand what that common trait is. When Moses met God at the burning bush he asked God to reveal God's name. God said "I AM WHAT I AM." This Divine Name tells us a lot about who God is, in particular that God is sovereign over God's own affairs. God is *autonomous*. What does "autonomous" mean? It means to be in charge of and to exercise control over oneself. No one decides for God but God. No one controls God but God because no one else can run God's life BUT God. It is this same autonomy that God has wired into us. We are responsible to live our own lives. We alone decide for ourselves. God respects our autonomy so much so that God will not even save us from sin and death without our permission. Admiral James Stockdale explained it this way as he addressed the United States Naval Academy:

"...I am totally responsible for everything I do and say; and that it is I who decides on and controls my own destruction and own deliverance. Not even God will intercede if He sees me throwing my life away. He wants me to be autonomous. He put me in charge of me. "It matters not how straight the gate, how charged with punishment the scroll. I am the master of my fate, I am the captain of my soul." ("Stockdale on Stoicism I: The Stoic Warrior's Triad)

Dr. Henry Cloud and Dr. John Townsend, in their insightful book "Boundaries," (Zondervan 1995) shed some helpful biblical light on taking responsibility for ourselves:

"Problems arise when boundaries of responsibility are confused. We are to love one another, not be one another. I can't feel your feelings for you. I can't think for you. I can't behave for you. I can't work through the disappointment that limits bring for you. In short, I can't grow for you; only you can. Likewise, you can't grow for me. The biblical mandate for our own personal growth is "Continue to work out your salvation with fear and trembling, for it is God who works in you to will and to act according to his good purpose" (Phil. 2:12-13). You are responsible for yourself. I am responsible for myself."

We can alleviate a portion of anxiety and suffering in our lives by taking some important lessons about autonomy and responsibility to heart. Let's be very clear what we are responsible for and what we are not, Also, we take notice of what we can ultimately control and what we cannot. Once we claim this, we can take life to the next level of maturity.

BECAUSE WE CONTROL OURSELVES...

A. We refuse to be controlled by external events and circumstances.
B. We refuse to be controlled by our feelings and emotions.
C. We refuse to be controlled by other people.
D. We refuse to be controlled by our material possessions.
E. We embrace our freedom and power to decide for ourselves.

A. We refuse to be controlled by external events and circumstances.

We are too often motivated by fear, frustration, and grief because of the events unfolding around us. Long before Jesus, ancient Romans, like Epictetus, taught that *"Man is affected not by events but by the view he takes of them."* The world does not decide if we are angry or happy. We do. Anger is a choice. Worry is a choice. Frustration is a choice. Joy is a choice. Regardless of what events transpire around us, it is not these events that affect us. It is the way we choose to think about these events that bring us misery or contentment. Psychiatrist Victor Frankl survived the death camp at Auschwitz and despite the violence, cruelty and suffering of his surroundings, he still believed that we have the power to decide how we will feel about it. In his landmark book "Man's Search for Meaning" (Beacon Press 2006) he writes:

"Between the stimulus and the response, there is a space. In that space is our power to choose our response. In our response lies our growth and our freedom."... *"Everything can be taken from a man but one thing: the last of the human freedoms—to choose one's attitude in any given set of circumstances, to choose one's own way."*

Or, as Roman emperor Marcus Aurelius explained:

"If you are distressed by anything external, the pain is not due to the thing itself, but to your estimate of it; and this you have the power to revoke at any moment."

It is infinitely easier to change ourselves and our reactions to things than it is to change the world around us. You may be wondering how this can be. How can we just choose to NOT be angry when someone insults us? How could the apostles and prophets take joy in suffering for God? How could they laugh in the face of danger, stay strong in the face of rejection and grow more determined through great suffering? They were blessed by the Holy Spirit to be sure, but let's not overlook the decisions they made to choose joy, faith, and courage despite their circumstances. We are to love God with all of our mind, as well as our heart and soul, and that means using the mind and freedom God gave us to choose for ourselves how we will feel and act. We are created by God to do just that. It takes some practice, but it can be done. Later we will offer some techniques to practice this kind of self-control. It is also important to add that we do not blame our events and circumstances. We are not victims. Again, Marcus Aurelius:

"Choose not to be harmed, and you won't feel harmed. Don't feel harmed and you haven't been."

"Reject your sense of injury and the injury itself disappears."

"You have power over your mind - not outside events. Realize this and you will find strength."

Is this not what Peter and John did when they rejoiced after being beaten for preaching Christ in Acts chapter 5? Is this not what Paul did after being arrested, beaten, and shipwrecked yet chose joy at the privilege of sharing this discomfort with and for Jesus? Because he chose to see this struggle as part of the mission, he accepted it, the way we accepted our bumps and bruises as kids as part of the football game. The game was more important to us than the pain, so we chose to take pride in our wounds and kept playing. Paul valued the mission of Jesus far above the discomforts along the way. He took pride in them as being part of the game and kept serving. Even when pain had no greater meaning, Paul was free to choose to accept it as unimportant. In 2 Corinthians 12, Paul reports asking God to remove the pain of some malady. God refuses, saying *"My grace is enough for you, for my power is made perfect in your weakness."* Paul could let that daily annoyance become a distraction, or a source of bitterness. God reveals something the Stoics also believed: *suffering is so normal it can only ruin life if we choose to let it.* Being beaten, shipwrecked and seeing friends executed can destroy us BUT ONLY IF WE CHOOSE TO LET IT! Everyone suffers. We will see that in the Fourth Undeniable Truth that "Life is Not Fair."

Never, EVER say "I didn't have a choice" to justify your actions. We always have a choice. This autonomy and responsibility God gives us over ourselves is the ultimate freedom. As we said before, not even God controls us. Pharaoh treated the Israelites like slaves, giving them no choice whether they would serve or not. God treated them, and us, like family. We choose to follow God of our own free will. Our obedience is our willing gift to give. It cannot be taken from us or demanded. Nothing can happen to me that can take away that freedom and control over myself. I can break my arm, but I am still free to develop my character. I can lose my job, but I am still free to love. The external events of our lives cannot ruin our lives unless we choose to let them. The bad events and nasty people have no power over us other than the power we give them. This power and freedom to choose Jesus means more to us than any discomfort or loss. We waste so much time and energy complaining and protesting the unfairness of what has happened to us. We do not decide whether or not we are going to have a good day based on whether the sun is shining or it is raining. We are not controlled by the things going on around us. We are controlled by something deep within: the freedom to choose.

B. We refuse to be controlled by our feelings and emotions.

External events cannot control us, and neither can the way we feel about them. Because God loves us, God has created us with a host of instincts, defenses, and responses that protect us from dangers in the world we live in. In more primitive times, when faced with a hungry lion, we needed to protect ourselves from this threat. Thus, we have a tendency to either gear up for a vicious fight or run away as fast as we can. We don't even think about it. It is automatic. This "fight or flight" response explains why to this day our heart pounds, our breathing deepens and our brain pours adrenaline into our bloodstream when we are angry or frightened. It's very helpful when facing a lion, but it is often overkill when someone hurts our feelings or insults us. Our emotions are a natural warning sign that something in our world is out of balance. They are an alarm, an alert, a display on the dashboard that provide information. Nothing more. What we choose to do with that information is up to us.

Have you ever been so angry that you broke something or said something harsh that you wish you could take back? Who is in control in these emotional moments: us or our feelings? We are not victims of our feelings. Our feelings work for us. Our thoughts work for us. But few of us have ever been taught how to take responsibility for and control of our emotions and decisions. We are not talking about shallow mind games where we simply pretend that things are better than they are. This is something much deeper. It is a core decision about what matters and what doesn't. As said above, the world does not decide if we are angry or happy. We do. Anger is a choice. Worry is a choice. Frustration is a choice. Joy is a choice. This is a much simpler concept than it might appear. There are some things in life that we can control and some things we can't. If we can control it, then we take responsibility and get to work. We do something about it. It we can't, then we don't worry about it. But we do worry, don't we? We fret, agonize, and worry about the future and grieve, regret and suffer over our past. It is pointless to concern ourselves with things we cannot change. Jesus tells us plainly *"Can any one of you by worrying add a single hour to your life?"* (Matthew 6:27) Of course not, so why bother? It is a complete waste of time and energy.

As Followers of Jesus, we take these things that are beyond our control to God in prayer. But then, after giving our needs and wishes to God, we agonize about how long it is taking God to fulfill our wish and then feel slighted when God chooses not to. Shouldn't prayer lead to peace rather than more grief and worry? Yes, of course it should. Ole Hallesby, in his book "Prayer" (Augsburg Fortress 1994) offers us the example of Jesus and Mary at the wedding at Cana. The bride and groom have run out of wine, which is certainly not the end of the world, but an embarrassment for the family. Mary reports to Jesus "They have run out of wine" and walks away.

She does not ask Jesus to do anything, but having given Him the need, trusts Him completely to do whatever He feels is best. We don't control God or other people and we set ourselves up for heartache when we try. Hallesby writes:

"Our prayer life becomes restful when it really dawns upon us that we have done all we are supposed to do when we have spoken to [God] about it. From the moment we have left it with Him, it is God's responsibility." ("Prayer." Augsburg Fortress, 1994)

It is now God's problem to care for, not ours. Here is where the acceptance of things comes in. If God brings a miraculous change into our life as a result of prayer, that is wonderful. If God does not, then we are merely going to experience the same struggles that are common to the trillions of human beings who have come before us. It is not the end of the world. As we will explore in an upcoming section, it is not an indictment of God that we suffer. Suffering is a natural part of life for all of us. How we choose to accept and live with that reality is entirely up to us. Let. It. Go. It will be what it will be. It is not our concern. To help with letting go, take a good look at the following diagram designed by Ryan Holliday at www.DailyStoic.com:

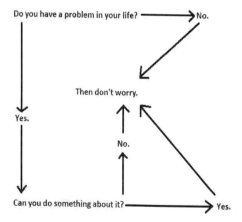

What does this diagram have to do with my feelings and emotions? Simple. If I have a problem, I do what I can to solve it. Fear and worry do not solve problems, but cause us to shrink from them. Anger only makes our problems worse. Our negative emotions accomplish nothing but destroying our peace. Remember, our emotions are simply the alarm bells warning us of a potential problem. Once we know we have a problem, we work the steps in the diagram above. I choose what I will do next. Just because I feel anger, it does not mean that I must choose to BE angry. We are not created to live in fear of or in bondage to anything, after all *"for freedom Christ has set us free"* (Galatians 5:1). I know this may sound strange, but it is weaved throughout the scriptures:

38 *For I am convinced that neither death nor life, neither angels nor demons,[a] neither the present nor the future, nor any powers, 39 neither height nor depth, nor anything else in all creation, will be able to separate us from the love of God that is in Christ Jesus our Lord. (Romans 8:38-39)*

"We are hard pressed on every side, but not crushed; perplexed, but not in despair; persecuted, but not abandoned; struck down, but not destroyed. (2 Corinthians 4:8-9)

Roman Emperor Marcus Aurelius said it best in one of my favorite quotes that demonstrates that our emotions have no power over us because we have power over ourselves:

"You don't have to turn this into something. It doesn't have to upset you. Things can't shape our decisions by themselves."

C. We refuse to be controlled by other people.

We care far too much what other people think. Most of our decisions in life are colored by a concern for what other people might think of us. We drive the car we drive, own the house we own, get a tattoo, or wear a particular hairstyle because deep down we care how people perceive us. Image matters to us. Fame matters to us. Pleasing people matters to us. Criticism matters to us. Have you ever stopped to ask yourself why that is? Emperor Marcus Aurelius did:

"I have often wondered how it is that every man loves himself more than all the rest of men, but yet sets less value on his own opinion of himself than on the opinion of others."

In his essay "Taming the Mammoth: Why You Should Stop Caring What Other People Think," Tim Urban argues that this is also part of our ancient evolutionary past:

"Evolution does everything for a reason, and to understand the origin of this particular insanity, let's back up for a minute to 50,000 BC in Ethiopia, where your Great [to the 2,000th power] Grandfather lived as part of a small tribe.

Back then, being part of a tribe was critical to survival. A tribe meant food and protection in a time when neither was easy to come by. So for your Great [to the 2,000th power]   Grandfather, almost nothing in the world was more important than being accepted by his fellow tribe members, especially those in positions of authority. Fitting in with those around him and pleasing those above him meant he could stay in the tribe, and about the worst nightmare he could imagine would be people in the tribe starting to whisper about how annoying or unproductive or weird he was—because if enough people disapproved of him, his ranking within the tribe would drop, and if it got really bad, he'd be kicked out altogether and left for dead. Being socially accepted was everything. Because of this, humans evolved an over-the-top obsession with what others thought of them—a craving for social approval and admiration, and a paralyzing fear of being disliked."

Approval from other people may feel good but it is hardly a matter of life and death. When we allow our personal choices to be affected by the approval or criticism of others, we surrender our power and freedom to others and become their slaves. *"Any person capable of angering you becomes your master; he can anger you only when you permit yourself to be disturbed by him."* Jesus taught that we cannot serve two masters. Why is this so important to us as disciples? It is important because taking a stand for Jesus will put us at odds with other people. Not everyone will embrace our loyalty to Jesus. Some will mock and reject it. If we are afraid of what other people think of us, our loyalty is to other people more than to Jesus. We are seeking to please them rather than pleasing God which gives other people tremendous power over us. Our witness is at stake. Our relationship with God is at stake. Jesus taught in Matthew 10:32-33: *"Whoever acknowledges me before others, I will also acknowledge before my Father in Heaven. But whoever disowns me before others, I will disown before my Father in Heaven."* Most importantly, the work God is doing in the world is at stake too.

A corollary to "I refuse to be controlled by other people" is the equally important "I refuse to take control of other people." The Golden Rule of Jesus is echoed in every major religion in earth: *"Do unto others as you would have them do unto you."* This is the value of "Reciprocity" which is freely extending to others what we expect to receive from them. We respect the fact that other people are responsible for themselves. They are responsible for their own thoughts, feelings, opinions, likes, dislikes and actions. I do not have a problem simply because another person has chosen to be angry. That is their rock to carry on their own. Their opinion is not reality. Praise does not make the horse beautiful neither does criticism make it ugly. People are allowed to think, feel and decide any way they want, but it does not concern us. There is simply nothing to be afraid of or worried about. And just as we do not blame events for anything, we do not blame other people either. We are not victims of other people's' words and actions unless we choose to be.

D. We refuse to be controlled by our material possessions.

Jesus was clear, we cannot serve two masters. We cannot serve God and wealth. We believe God blesses us with material things for three reasons:

1. To meet our needs
2. To meet the needs of others
3. To support God's work in the world

These are God's purposes for the things God gives us. We can get comfortable though and place a higher priority on the bank account, the house, or the car than on serving God. Sometimes God's assignments require us to give it away. Sometimes, God needs us to leave home and travel somewhere else to serve. We refuse to do what we know is right out of fear of losing what we own and enjoy. Also, we are too often devastated by losing our possessions and in our grief and resentment can blame God for that loss. Jesus always travelled light and taught His disciples to do the same. That way there is nothing holding us back from immediately responding with obedience. The prophets of Old and New Testaments also practiced a distrust of and detachment from physical wealth and possessions. Muslim prophet Ali ibn abi Talib writes that "*Detachment is not that you should own nothing but that nothing should own you.*" Wealth is a trap and can become a form of voluntary slavery. Do not surrender your God given freedom for human made things. That is what we call idolatry.

E. We embrace our freedom and power to decide for ourselves.

The refusal to take this responsibility is the cause of much of our unhappiness. We too often blame other people or bad luck for our misery and misfortune. If someone else is to blame for my unhappiness then I have little hope of ever feeling better because only someone else can fix it. I can't control other people so I can't force them to fix it. Also, other people are unable to control me so they cannot MAKE me be happy. It is a hopeless situation! When we blame others, or hold grudges, or fear, we give someone else power over us. Roman philosopher Epictetus once said: "*Any person capable of angering you becomes your master; he can anger you only when you permit yourself to be disturbed by him.*" You will find this recurring theme echoing through this "5x5 Manual." This is your life. Take the wheel and live it as you choose.

II. WE SHARE THE PLANET WITH OTHER PEOPLE

Now that we know we are all responsible for ourselves, it may be tempting to live as if our own life is the only one that matters. Philosopher

Ayn Rand taught that self-interest is the meaning of life and that altruism is actually harmful and destructive. Her ideas were developed into a philosophy called Objectivism and hold the self as the measure of all things. This idea has been picked up by certain practitioners of politics and many well-meaning Followers of Jesus have included it in their value system because of their political affiliation rather than their faith. It is at first glance understandable as it takes our first Undeniable Truth very seriously. But this assumption fails to hold all the Undeniable Truths in tension together, and Jesus clearly teaches something very different. We are responsible for ourselves, but God knows that life is not fair and because we share the planet with others and our wellbeing is tied to the wellbeing of others, we cooperate to ensure the greatest good for the greatest number of people. We protect our rights and freedoms best by protecting the rights and freedoms of all. Self-interest is not the evolutionary default for humanity. "Survival of the fittest" is taught to be a law of nature. That may work for animals in the wild, but human beings are created in the image and likeness of God and God is not a solitary Person but a small group. Because we are created in the image of God we are social creatures and possess a higher capacity for morality, compassion, and cooperation. Even animals in a herd will protect a weaker member from predators so surely we human beings can accept that helping each other is a natural thing to do. This kind of cooperation demands some revolutionary skills and disciplines. Giving and serving are the ways God has chosen to lift us above the cruel competition of animals and address the unfairness of a world that is free to unfold as it chooses.

Again, from Cloud and Townsend:

"We are responsible to others and for ourselves. "Carry each other's burdens," says Galatians 6:2, and in this way you will fulfill the law of Christ." This verse shows our responsibility to one another. Many times others have "burdens" that are too big to bear. They do not have enough strength, resources, or knowledge to carry the load, and they need help. Denying ourselves to do for others what they cannot do for themselves is showing the sacrificial love of Christ. This is what Christ did for us. He did what we could not do for ourselves; he saved us. This is being responsible "to." On the other hand, verse 5 says that "each one should carry his own load." Everyone has responsibilities that only he or she can carry. These things are our own particular "load" that we need to take daily responsibility for and work out. No one can do certain things for us. We have to take ownership of certain aspects of life that are our own "load."

The Greek words for burden and load give us insight into the meaning of these texts. The Greek word for burden means "excess burdens," or burdens that are so heavy that they weigh us down. These burdens are like boulders. They can crush us. We shouldn't be expected to carry a boulder by ourselves! It would break our backs. We need help with the boulders—those times of crisis and tragedy in our lives. In contrast, the Greek word for load means "cargo," or "the burden of daily toil." This word describes the everyday things we all need to do. These loads are like knapsacks. Knapsacks are possible to carry. We are expected to carry our own. We are expected to deal with our own feelings, attitudes, and behaviors, as well as the responsibilities God has given to each one of us, even though it takes effort. Problems arise when people act as if their "boulders" are daily loads, and refuse help, or as if their "daily loads" are boulders they shouldn't have to carry. The results of these two instances are either perpetual pain or irresponsibility. "

Therefore the Christ-like formula for giving and helping others generously and compassionately without weakening character and destroying personal responsibility is this:

"We bear one another's burdens so we each can carry our own load."

We help one another in the crises of our lives that threaten to harm us and destroy us in order to help people get back on their feet and take care of themselves. We distinguish between a burden and a backpack. Some politicians are correct that unless someone is truly disabled, receiving assistance is not intended to be a way of life or a career choice but must help people get back on their feet so they can once again take care of themselves and assist others. But we betray Christ by using Galatians 6 as a way to shame and belittle others. We use these verses as a guide to help responsibly, but must never forget that grace is treating people better than they deserve. Sometimes sacrificial kindness and generosity communicates the boundless love of God far better than a formula. For the followers of Jesus this goes beyond "tough love" to encouraging and equipping others to take one step closer to God and the purpose God has for our lives. We bear one another's burdens so that each can carry their own load and play their part in God's ultimate plan of a new and better world.

Sharing the planet with others means putting up with each other, too, which is sometimes easier said than done. We live and let live, meaning that, even if we don't enjoy each other's company, we can at least tolerate each other peacefully. Tolerance has become something of a dirty word recently. For many it has become the insistence that we are expected to bless everything and everyone despite our own firmly held convictions. Perhaps a healthier concept is one of "Reciprocity" that we mentioned earlier. It would be helpful to explore the idea more deeply. Rather than simply (or begrudgingly) allowing others to exist, reciprocity is offering to others what we expect from them. Jesus' "Golden Rule" is echoed in most world religions, calling us to take the initiative to "treat others as we would like to be treated." Perhaps the most groundbreaking words in the American founding documents are those that express that all are created equal and possess certain *"inalienable rights, among these are life, liberty, and the pursuit of happiness."* What is required then is an allowance of life, liberty, and the pursuit of happiness for all. While stated in the American founding documents, these ideas are universal and form the broadest statement of human rights that must be claimed and respected. We insist upon all three when claiming our individual responsibility but we cannot claim them in any way that denies them to others. This is the value of Reciprocity. It is in our own self-interest to provide them freely to others in order to protect them for ourselves. Even though ours is the only life that we have control over, it is hardly the only life that matters.

We are free to live as if we are the only person on the planet, but we are not. We share the planet with others and with more of us on the planet than ever before we must learn how to work together. As the poet John Donne wrote *"No man is an island."* I do not grow, roast or grind the coffee beans that I brew to make my cup of coffee in the morning. Someone else did that. I didn't milk the cow or mill the oats that went into my bowl of cereal. Someone else did that. No one is truly self-sufficient, but we are part of a cooperative network of humanity. Whether we like it or not, we are in this thing together. Our wellbeing is tied to the wellbeing of others. We must respect and protect the rights and responsibilities of others in order to ensure our own. We must cooperate to achieve the greatest good for the greatest number of people. We must, according to Jesus, love our neighbor as ourselves.

III. EVERYTHING COSTS SOMETHING.

Nothing in life is free. Everything costs something. You are free to make your choices in life, but every choice has a consequence. Every pro has a con. Every upside has a downside. You can choose to be rich and successful, but it might cost you time with your family or a relationship with your children. You can smoke two packs a day, but don't be shocked when you are diagnosed with lung cancer. You can eat all the cheesecake in New York, but don't get angry when your pants don't fit. You can choose to have a vital prayer life but it might cost you time otherwise spent watching television. You can choose to be fit but it will cost you sweat and effort. We can have most anything we want in life if we are willing to pay the price. Taking responsibility for ourselves means taking responsibility for the consequences of our choices. Cloud and Townsend call this "The Law of Sowing and Reaping":

"The law of cause and effect is a basic law of life. The Bible calls it the Law of Sowing and Reaping. "You reap whatever you sow. If you sow to your own flesh, you will reap corruption from the flesh; but if you sow to the Spirit, you will reap eternal life from the Spirit" (Gal. 6:7-8 NRSV). When God tells us that we will reap what we sow, he is not punishing us; he's telling us how things really are. If you smoke cigarettes, you most likely will develop a smoker's hack, and you may even get lung cancer. If you overspend, you most likely will get calls from creditors, and you may even go hungry because you have no money for food. On the other hand, if you eat right and exercise regularly, you may suffer from fewer colds and bouts with the flu. If you budget wisely, you will have money for the bill collectors and for the grocery store.

Sometimes, however, people don't reap what they sow, because someone else steps in and reaps the consequences for them. If every time you overspent, your mother sent you money to cover check overdrafts or high credit-card balances, you wouldn't reap the consequences of your spend-thrift ways. Your mother would be protecting you from the natural consequences: the hounding of creditors or going hungry. As the mother in the above example demonstrates, the Law of Sowing and Reaping can be interrupted. And it is often people who have no boundaries who do the interrupting. Just as we can interfere with the law of gravity by catching a glass tumbling off the table, people can interfere with the Law of Cause and Effect by stepping in and rescuing irresponsible people. Rescuing a person from the natural consequences of his behavior enables him to continue in irresponsible behavior. The Law of Sowing and Reaping has not been repealed. It is still operating. But the doer is not suffering the consequences; someone else is."

IV. LIFE ISN'T FAIR

We make ourselves miserable by having unrealistic expectations about the way things are SUPPOSED to be. But let's be brutally honest with ourselves: *We live in a world where anything can happen and usually does.* Accidents happen. Illnesses come. Disasters, both natural and human, occur. We are not immune to nor are we protected from random chance. We may be tempted to protest the injustice and demand to know "Why me?" Perhaps a more realistic question is "Why not me?" We are vulnerable in a dangerous universe where things happen. We shouldn't be shocked and shaken by misfortune. Expect it. We shouldn't live as though our loved ones will live forever. They won't and neither will we. We are also not protected from people who are free to hurt us. Bad things happen. Not everyone is nice. Not everyone treats us the way we deserve to be treated. Things don't always go our way. We are not all born with the same abilities or advantages which is why from time to time we all need help. Let's no longer deceive ourselves. Let's take off the rose-colored glasses and see the world as it really is. Remember these lines from the "Serenity Prayer":

"...Accepting hardships as the pathway to peace;
Taking, as He did, this sinful world
As it is, not as I would have it;"

There is a delusion running rampant through the Body of Christ that is weakening us and making us soft and ineffective as a Church. We somehow have come to believe that in our salvation the immediate solution to all our problems is simply a prayer away. God becomes Santa Claus who gives us whatever we wish for if we are good. As a result we have become completely unable to suffer, unwilling to endure, and resentful of God for not answering our prayers. We are like spoiled children with unrealistic expectations. We have misunderstood what it means to follow the Way of Jesus. It is the Way of Suffering, the Way of the Cross. Jesus did heal, but his mission was not to set up a global healthcare system to keep everyone healthy forever. Jesus did feed the hungry, but his mission wasn't to establish global food distribution networks to eliminate hunger forever. Jesus performed miracles to point our attention to the Father and to give us a glimpse of the coming Kingdom of God. This Kingdom must be smuggled in under the noses of the powerful as we undermine the current world. That is painful and unpopular work. Contrary to popular belief, the world will not cheer and embrace the global changes that Christ is bringing about. It will resist. It will fight back. The current order will defend itself. God has chosen the Way of Suffering to do the greatest work among us. Very rarely does God detour us around the hardships and pain of life. Rather, God takes us by the hand as we plunge right straight through it, developing faith and character through the ordeal. As Paul writes in Romans:

"3 We also have joy with our troubles, because we know that these troubles produce patience. 4 And patience produces character, and character produces hope. 5 And this hope will never disappoint us, because God has poured out his love to fill our hearts. He gave us his love through the Holy Spirit, whom God has given to us" (Romans 5:3-5).

Or consider the words of James:

"Consider it pure joy, my brothers and sisters, whenever you face trials of many kinds, because you know that the testing of your faith produces perseverance. Let perseverance finish its work so that you may be mature and complete, not lacking anything." (James 1:2-4)

This is just two of many verses from the Bible in which God's people seem to embrace seasons of difficulty, not as obstacles to faith and obedience but as the seasons in which the most progress is accomplished.

We change what we are able to change in life and give the rest to God. But if God doesn't give us the resolution we were hoping for, we accept it. We deal with it. We endure. We persevere. We don't throw a tantrum like a toddler in a grocery store who isn't allowed to get a piece of candy. We don't wish our lives away wishing that things were different than they are. Even though the life we planned takes a detour, we are not lost. Emperor Marcus Aurelius said: "*The impediment to action advances action. What stands in the way becomes the way.*" The misfortunes that seem to be obstacles to walking the Path of Jesus BECOME the path. It may not be the life we want, but it is the only life we have, so we simply live it as it is. If God allows it, it must not prevent God from achieving God's plan of bringing the Kingdom of God to its fullness. God doesn't create or send the misfortune. There's plenty of that occurring naturally in the world already. We learn to want what God wants, or as Jesus prayed "Not my will, but thine." That's life as it is. As the Rolling Stones sang: "You can't always get what you want." Life isn't fair. Deal with it.

The Challenge of Loving Life As It Is

Most American Christians are hedonists. Hedonism was a school of philosophy in ancient Greece and Rome that taught that the purpose of life is pursuing pleasure and avoiding pain. We want to be comfortable above all else. The vast majority of our prayers contain requests to take our pain and discomfort away. These are the exact things the devil tempted Jesus with in the desert: comfort, safety, power and popularity. The problem here is that the pursuit of pleasure and avoidance of pain makes things like sacrifice and endurance impossible. We will only follow Jesus while it is comfortable and convenient and that makes for a weak and ineffective Church. We love God only when life is good. Comfort gets in the way. Seneca, the Roman statesman and philosopher writes:

"If we coddle ourselves, if we allow ourselves to be corrupted by pleasure, nothing will seem bearable to us, and the reason things will seem unbearable is not because they are hard but because we are soft."

V. NOTHING LASTS FOREVER

The poet William Butler Yeats, in his poem "The Second Coming" wrote: "*Things fall apart. The center does not hold.*" We live in a universe where things break down. Things get old. Things wear out. I offer Lord Kelvin's Second Law of Thermodynamics which introduce the idea of "entropy". Simply put, it states that things wear out when left to their own devices. If you ignore it, it will slip away. Ignore the house and it will eventually fall down. The young grow old. The fit get flabby. Clean things get dirty. It takes real effort to keep things in top shape. We have to keep winding the clock. We have to keep cleaning away the cobwebs. We have to keep oiling the machine. We have to keep studying and using our minds. We have to keep doing push-ups and sit-ups. Otherwise, things will fall apart. Life takes work to keep it livable. That goes for our relationships with other people, too. A good marriage doesn't stay good all by itself. You have to pay attention to it. You have to keep putting some effort into it to keep it at its best. The same is true of our love relationship with God. You may have a powerful mountaintop experience with God, but it will fade over time. A good relationship with God doesn't stay good all by itself. You have to pay attention to it. Everything costs something.

It also means that we will not live forever either. Everyone dies. We only get one life. We only go around once, which means that life is unspeakably precious. It also means that life is too important not to enjoy. William Irvine, in his book "A Guide to the Good Life: The Ancient Art of Stoic Joy" (Oxford University Press, 2009) writes:

"More generally, we should keep in mind that any human activity that cannot be carried on indefinitely must have a final occurrence. There will be—or already has been!—a last time in your life that you brush your teeth, cut your hair, drive a car, mow the lawn, or play hopscotch. There will be a last time you hear the sound of snow falling, watch the moon rise, smell popcorn, feel the warmth of a child falling asleep in your arms, or make love. You will someday eat your last meal, and soon thereafter you will take your last breath."

Let this not be a morbid burden upon your mind but a cheerful reminder to enjoy every experience in life as if it were our last. We squander too much of our lives waiting for the next thing to happen. Life is too precious for that. Take nothing for granted.

More On Accepting Life As It Is

Life is hard for most people. It just feels like the universe is constantly working against us and it takes real effort just to get through the day. Like swimming upstream, it can wear you down and if you quit swimming you will go backwards. That's what the Five Undeniable Truths clearly express. Murphy's Law is real. Life is hard and nothing we can do will ever change that, but God is changing that. That is what the Kingdom of God is all about, a world that is not hostile to life, health, peace, and joy. Jesus teaches us to use these destructive forces to make life better instead of worse. We accept the things we cannot change, seeking grace to respond to the challenges of life with courage, freedom, and serenity. This is crucial because as disciples, we do some of our best work with Jesus among the rocks. How do we offer Christ to those broken and battered by life? We turn to that discussion now.

3
THE FIVE DISCIPLINES OF JESUS

What follows is what we are calling the Discipleship Path. It is the direction our lives take when we not only follow the footsteps of Jesus but also allow Jesus to guide our steps. Disciples of Jesus follow Jesus. We follow Jesus' example, teachings, and daily guidance through the Holy Spirit in every decision we make. We turn now to a collection of teachings and spiritual practices that change lives and makes the world a better place. Just as we fill our backpack with specialized gear and fill our heads with the practical knowledge and experience to respond well in any situation on the trail, we follow Jesus every day equipped with "holy knowledge" and "holy know-how." The word "holy" means to be set apart by God for a special purpose. Our purpose as disciples is helping Jesus turn our broken world toward the eternal Father's Kingdom. We learn to accomplish this purpose by listening to what Jesus says, watching what Jesus does, and practicing this holy knowledge and holy know-how with the help and guidance of other more experienced disciples and the Holy Spirit. Jesus did so much, but as already mentioned, everything Jesus did can be boiled down to just five distinct kinds of spiritual practices:

THE DISCIPLINES OF WORSHIP
THE DISCIPLINES OF LEARNING
THE DISCIPLINES OF GIVING
THE DISCIPLINES OF SERVING
THE DISCIPLINES OF ENCOURAGING

Let's take a close careful look the Five Disciplines of Jesus. Be prepared to learn, but also be prepared to practice what you are learning. Give your life to it. Remember, you are beginning to learn a way of life that allows God free reign to change the world. As we said before:

Even if there were no such thing as God, and Jesus was just an ordinary man, the way of life that He advocates of humility, kindness, compassion, respect, and sacrifice will heal the world on its own if more people gave it a try.

Ready to change the world? Let's begin, one careful step at a time..

4
THE DISCIPLINES OF WORSHIP

It has been repeatedly said that Christianity is not a religion, but a relationship. We are invited to have a dynamic friendship with the Creator of the Universe, which is a pretty shocking thing to say. It is also hard for many to believe because we serve a God we cannot see, hear, or touch. How do we deepen a friendship when there is nowhere to mail our letters to or no phone number to call? Like any human relationship, this one also takes time and effort to keep it at its best. Think about two people who get married. They meet. They spend time with each other. They get to know each other. They talk. They tell each other about their lives, their childhoods and their families. They give gifts to each other. They help each other through the tough times. As they grow closer and begin to depend on one another, there comes a time to claim that mutual trust and commitment to each other. That is what marriage vows are all about. We grow closer to God the same way. We spend time with God. We talk. We get to know each other. We learn about each other's past and life story. We give each other gifts and help each other through times of need. We share life together, and sooner or later, we make some more formal commitments to each other. And like a healthy marriage, we can't stop spending that quality time with one another and expect the relationship to always be at its best. But that can be challenging since God exists in the spiritual realm and we live in the material one. Forgive the analogy, but it is not unlike science fiction stories of parallel worlds that exist side by side but are completely unaware of each other. God has ways of crossing over and communicating with us but these ways are going to be different than the way we humans talk with each other. There are five ways we can experience God. (There are actually a lot more than that, but let's look at these first.) They are:

I. Bible
II. Prayer
III. Spiritual Disciplines
IV. Worship
V. Sabbath Keeping

I. THE BIBLE

The Bible is the primary way God has chosen to tell us God's story. There are lots of ways God communicates with us through these pages which means there are different ways to read the Bible. Five is the "magic number" in 5x5, so we will look at five different ways the Bible can be useful in strengthening our love relationship with God.

I. THE BIBLE:

A. Read to Know God
B. Read to Hear God
C. Read to Follow God
D. Read to Love God
E. Read to Remember God

A. Read to Know God

As just discussed, when two people meet and become friends, they want to get to know each other. We talk about who we are, where we live and what we do for a living. We tell each other our life stories about our past, our families, and our childhood. We share our likes and dislikes, our hopes, dreams and plans for the future. We also share our values and character and declare what we stand for in life and what will we not tolerate. God reveals all of this in the pages of scripture. We read these stories and writings to get to know and understand God better. God has been active throughout human history and we see God at work in the stories and history of the Hebrew Bible, the ministry and message of the prophets, the teachings and passion of Jesus, and the faithfulness of the apostles. This is the way most people read the Bible, like a novel, enjoying the story. Just remember that the Bible is actually a collection of sixty six different kinds of books, so not every part of it is a page turner. If we try to read it the way we read other books we might become frustrated.

1. How Does the Bible Work?

One of the most baffling things about the Bible is that while all Christians embrace the Bible as a divine source of inspiration and guide to life, nobody seems to agree on how to read it and what it means. From the very beginning of the Church in Peter and Paul's day, different gatherings of believers practiced and explained their faith a little differently. There has ALWAYS been variety and diversity among followers of Jesus. It is one of the reasons why the four gospel writers tell the story slightly differently from each other. Therefore, we should not be overly concerned by these differences now. Today, a major factor in explaining these differences of opinion among us is identifying a difference of perspectives about what the Bible is and where it came from. Let's break it down into three "schools of thought." As Tom Head writes in "The Absolute Beginner's Guide to the Bible" (Que Publishing, 2006): *"This may be the most controversial part of this entire book."* But regardless of how you approach the Bible, the 5x5 approach to discipleship will still be helpful to you. I am indebted to Tom Head for the following conversation.

a. "Secularist" School of Thought

If "sacred" refers to the divine things of Heaven, "secular" refers to the regular things of human beings. A secular worldview does not recognize the existence of God or anything supernatural. This school of thought views the Bible as 100% human invention. It embraces the Bible as an important piece of ancient literature containing poetry, mythology, and an insight into the values of ancient human culture. While this view treasures the Bible as an important piece of literature, it does not recognize any spiritual authority in it and does not employ the Bible as a practical rule of life. It, therefore, offers very little to promote a personal love relationship with God or a life of obedient discipleship.

b. "Fundamentalist" School of Thought

I put "Fundamentalist" in quotations because we are using the word here in a more general sense than it is commonly used. Fundamentalism is a conservative branch of Christian theology and practice that goes beyond simply explaining what the Bible is and how it works. We are here speaking of a wider group of believers who believe the Bible is 100% the work of God with no human input other than writing it all down through dictation. It is revealed by God rather than inspired by God. Because the Word is divinely spoken, it is considered literally true, error free, and is to be simply obeyed rather than interpreted. The Bible is of supreme importance for determining our values, priorities, morality, actions and purpose.

c. Pros and Cons of the Fundamentalist Approach.

The undeniable strength of this approach is a deep belief in God, deep respect for the Bible, and deep devotion to take it seriously and live it obediently. By taking every word of scripture as literal and factually true, we make all parts of scripture equally binding on our lives with no contradictions, but a simple reading does find a few. For example, Paul writes in Galatians 3:28 "*There is no longer Jew or Greek, there is no longer slave or free, there is no longer male and female; for all of you are one in Christ Jesus*" which suggests a radical equality among all those saved by Christ. However, he then goes on to say in other places that women are not permitted to speak in church, that they must obey their husbands in all matters, and that slaves must obey their masters rather than claim their freedom. But Paul also wrote in Galatians 5:1 "*For freedom, Christ has set us free.*" So which is it? Taking these passages literally and as binding on our lives, we may find ourselves treating women as second class citizens and making slavery legal. It also may require us to ignore the existence of different genres of writing and figures of speech, such as parables, metaphor and hyperbole. Jesus teaches in Matthew 5:30 "*If your right hand causes you to sin, cut it off and throw it away.*" He says the same things about what to do if your right eye causes you to sin. Taking this literally, we are being commanded to mutilate ourselves rather than simply appealing to God for forgiveness through confession and repentance. A literal approach assumes the Bible is factually correct in every matter and thus may require us to ignore the factual evidence of sciences such as geology that the earth is millions of years old and embrace that the earth is only ten thousand years old. This approach can seem hostile to reason, logic, and research. Quoting Proverbs 3:5, we trust in the Lord with all our heart and lean not on our own understanding. We distrust any human thought or wisdom as unreliable and tempted by sin in favor of the security of an absolute and unchanging scripture. It can also reduce our relationship with God to reward and punishment that encourages a legalistic view of humanity over a compassionate one.

d. "Modernist" School of Thought

Some believe that these words are the result of faithful believers who were inspired by God and who expressed and explained God the best they could. *The Bible is seen to be what discipleship is: a collaboration between God and humanity that bears the fingerprints of both.* For an everyday example of how this works, think about a preacher proclaiming God's Word from the pulpit. Have you ever been moved by something you heard a preacher teach in worship? Of course you have! Because the preacher is pointing to God at work in the world as accurately as possible, relying on the pages of the Bible and the Holy Spirit, we can accurately claim to have heard God speak through that human teacher. It is true that the divine communication came through an imperfect human being who is limited by their own experiences, culture and sin. Still, we see both divine and human fingerprints in the preaching of a godly sermon. The existence of one does not rule out the reliability of the other. The apostle Paul wrote in 2 Corinthians 4:7 that "*we have this treasure in jars of clay, to show that the surpassing power belongs to God and not to us.*" God stores eternal treasure in imperfect containers, which do not spoil what is divine, but makes common things holy.

I write as a Christian influenced by the Wesleyan tradition. As a United Methodist, we understand the revelations of God through four interconnected methods. The first is SCRIPTURE which is primary, but we come to understand that scripture through an ongoing conversation between TRADITION, EXPERIENCE. and REASON. Tradition is understood to be the ways the Church has understood and explained a passage in many different generations, places, and cultures. Experience is our everyday human experience. Do the teachings of Jesus prove reliable to the daily difficulties of life? How do ancient perspectives relate to contemporary discoveries of science, discovery, and history? If the humans writing scripture are informed and limited by the human understanding of their day, how do their reliable expressions of God take on fuller meaning with the discoveries of our day? God did command us to love the Lord with not just our heart, but also our mind. Critical thinking is a God given ability and need not be banned from our faith or reading of the Bible. That is where reason comes in.

Since we can experience this divine/human cooperation in our own lives and churches, why should we be surprised to find it in the scriptures? Some study and interpretation is required and that interpretation requires us to understand the time and place in which these words were written. Context is important because people always experience God in very real times and places. Few of us are experts in ancient languages, customs and history, so some tools are helpful to read the Bible to know God better.

e. Pros and Cons of Modernist School of Thought

The Modernist view encourages us to think things through using the reasoning power God has given us. We read the Bible not only for the clear instructions it offers, but as examples of discipleship. Every writer of scripture pointing to God at work is still limited by their time, culture, and personal experience and yet boldly chooses God. By accepting that some of the trouble spots we have in scripture, such as the treatment of women and slavery, are the result of human nature rather than God's divine nature we can find a way forward through some of the most difficult parts of the Bible. In Paul's day, there were specific expectations of Roman society concerning women and slaves. Choosing to rightly overturn these expectations would have been controversial to say the least and the infant Church may have spent all its time defending itself over these matters rather than spreading the Gospel. Remember, Paul was writing at a specific time and place in history. The Good News was so new, the highest priority was to spread it as far as possible rather than get mired in culture wars. It's not that slavery is embraced by God or the Church. It's not that the treatment of women is unimportant. But we can't accomplish everything at once. It would just have to wait until Jesus was embraced by enough people to start changing the culture. But by assuming Paul is speaking to every Christian in every time and place, the Church did embrace and support slavery and continued to hold women in lower regard than men. By studying the historical and cultural background, by paying attention to genre and figures of speech, by comparing and contrasting different texts we can get a better picture of how the writers of scripture were cooperating with God in a time and place very different from our own.

The weakness of this approach is the temptation to explain away anything in scripture that we do not like. Human ingenuity can rationalize anything. It is a weakness of our fallen nature that sticks with us even as we are being saved as disciples of Jesus. Whereas those of the Fundamentalist school of thought may sometimes embrace the letter of the law rather than the spirit, the Modernists, in their zeal to embrace the spirit of the law can dismiss the letter altogether. We must guard against the temptation to explain away everything divine and miraculous through logic and reason. The Modernist embrace of reason can lead it to become the Secularist View when we forget to emphasize the cooperation of both human beings and God in the same scriptures.

f. What Happens When We Read
We believe that Jesus the Living Word speaks through the Written Word. The Bible, regardless of how it came to be, is never an end in itself. We do not just read and glean facts from it the way we read a school textbook or a magazine article. As we pour over the written words, Jesus sits with us and we pour over it together. Jesus speaks by way of the Holy Spirit, raising questions, pointing out certain things, and opening our eyes. Every time we read the Bible, it is an interaction with God. Reading the Bible is always time with God and a form of prayer.

2. Bible Tools and Resources
Few of us are experts in biblical history, culture, translation, or interpretation, but these things do help us gain a clearer understanding of the scriptures. This Modernist approach may sound like it requires too much detective work on our part. The good news is, we have help. God has called many faithful people to the life work of studying and explaining the Bible to the rest of us and the fruits of their labor are readily available through a variety of resources.

a. Bible Translations

The Hebrew Bible was written in Hebrew. The New Testament writings were crafted in Greek and Aramaic. We need to have these ancient texts translated into the languages we speak and understand. There are several strategies employed by translators.

Some strive to provide the most accurate word by word translation. Others will take a phrase and translate the idea of the phrase, focusing on providing a better sense of the idea without trying to mimic the word for word structure of the original authors. Some, like the Living Bible, are translations that paraphrase, telling the story in its own words. It can be a bit overwhelming to decide which translation is right for you. I recommend you start with the translation used by your congregation in worship. You may want to ask your pastor for recommendations. The most important thing is choosing a translation you can understand. The King James Bible contains some of the most beautiful passages in the English language, but was written in the time of Shakespeare. Many find it as hard to understand as Shakespeare's plays because the English language has changed so much in the past 500 years. Make sure you can understand what you are reading. Some will tell you that *"if it ain't King James, it ain't Bible."* That is, to put it politely, nonsense. It also begins to smack of idolatry when we worship a particular set of words on the page as passionately as we worship the God revealed through them. We worship the Living Word (Jesus) who is revealed through the Written Word.

b. Study Bible

A good Study Bible is worth its weight in gold and can help us understand what we are reading. I credit the purchase of "The Life Application Study Bible" as the most important single thing I ever did to become a follower of Jesus. Study Bibles contain the translated text of the Bible but also contain extensive footnotes and articles to explain the history, background and culture that may not be familiar to us. It teaches how certain scriptures can help us to live our lives for Jesus. There is a dizzying variety of study Bibles to choose from. Take your time when choosing to determine the one that is best for you. An excellent study Bible may be all the reference materials you need, but there are more resources you may find helpful:

c. Bible Commentaries

A Bible Commentary gives the same kind of information as the study notes in a good Study Bible, but in much greater depth. It is a book or multi-volume set of books that explain the history, cultural background, text and translation questions as well as offering interpretations on the meaning of the text and ways in which these interpretations apply to everyday life. Remember though that every commentary is written with a specific goal and theological viewpoint in mind. Some are very academic, while others interpret the Bible from a particular point of view, such as a Women's Bible Commentary, Catholic Bible Commentary, John Wesley's Notes on the Bible, etc. Just pay attention to the purpose of the commentary to see if it is what you need.

d. Bible Concordance

Imagine having an index of every word in the Bible. That is what a concordance is and is helpful in doing word studies or when you are trying to remember a favorite verse but can't remember exactly where it is in the Bible. I find Google frankly to be a faster way to find what I need. I am not good at remembering the chapter and verse of a text, so I will search for it online. Many of these resources we are discussing are available for free if you have access to the internet.

e. Bible Atlas

This a collection of maps from different periods of history that help us to understand the geography of the stories of God's People throughout the Bible.

f. Bible Dictionary

A Bible dictionary is just like a regular dictionary but defines Bible terms, people and places.

B. Read to Hear God

The Bible is not limited to the words frozen on the page. While we are reading about God, God speaks to us by the Holy Spirit. The Living Word speaks through the Written Word. Imagine a room filled with radio waves. We cannot hear the sound of the countless broadcast signals in the air around us all the time without the help of a radio that allows us to tune the signals to a frequency we can hear and understand. God is speaking all around us all the time, too. We can learn to read the Bible in a way that helps us tune in that Voice of God so we can hear it and understand it. The Written Word is important to us but it serves the Living Word which speaks fresh messages to us every day.

We teach the practice of "Lectio Divina" or sacred reading. It is a method of praying the scriptures in order to hear God's Living Word speak through the Written Word. The practice is rather simple. First, select a brief portion of scripture. Read it several times silently, paying attention to the details that are presented. Look for what claims your attention, like a troubling thought, a positive insight, a deep question, or a peculiar detail. Then meditate over the passage allowing the Spirit to guide your thoughts. Meditation is "holy thinking": just think about it. After this reflection talk to God about it in prayer. Talk as long as you like. When you are finished rest in silence. You will find more complete instructions on how to pray the scriptures through "lectio divina" in our upcoming discussion of prayer.

C. Read to Follow God

To say that God is Lord is to say that God is in charge. That means that we need to know what God expects of us. Throughout the scriptures we receive instructions from God on how to live our lives. We are given specific instructions on how we live with God, how we live with each other and how to make the world a better place through our actions. From the Ten Commandments, to the wisdom of Proverbs, to the teachings of Jesus, God gives plenty of instructions for us to follow. It's not about being bad or good or simply about following rules. There is a powerful quote that has been attributed to Dietrich Bonhoeffer that:

"Being a Christian is less about cautiously avoiding sin than about courageously and actively doing God's will."

Bonhoeffer did not actually write those exact words (regardless of what the internet claims) but they sure express the heart of his message and view of discipleship. We live lives that are useful to God by being compatible with the new and better world that God is preparing for us. Only God can teach us how to do that and it is found in the scriptures. We read the Bible paying close attention to any commands, instructions, or expectations given by God in the text then strive to live our lives accordingly. We will speak later about "being called by God." There are special assignments God gives directly to us individually, like Moses at the burning bush. Not everyone receives a call like that, but we are all called to live according to God's plans. The Bible is full of teachings and instructions that guide us along the kingdom-building Path of Jesus. Read them. Learn them. Practice them. Live them.

D. Read to Love God

The heart of the Bible is the reminder that God loves us. We sometimes read the Bible to remember just how much God loves us the way we re-read old love letters. We read the Psalms, the New Testament letters and the words of Jesus to claim once again God's promises to us. We remember how God has accepted us just as we are and has moved galaxies to be close to us. We are reminded of the tenderness it took for God to join us in human flesh, sharing our death, and being raised again to give us life that never ends. Why would God go to such lengths? God loves us and wants to spend forever with us. Sometimes we only read the Bible to remember that so that we might never take it for granted.

E. Read to Remember God

Ben Franklin had a way of expressing a great deal of truth in a very few words. His proverbs and words of wisdom, like "*A penny saved is a penny earned*," have become part of our everyday conversation and help to guide us in our everyday decisions. The Word of God is equally helpful to guide us in our everyday decisions but like these helpful proverbs we have to have them handy at a moment's notice. Thus, we memorize scripture. By doing so, we are carrying around a collection of verses everywhere we go.

Andy Rau, who writes for biblegateway.com offers ten tips to help memorize scripture:

1. Choose a verse to memorize that speaks to something in your life right now.

A Bible verse that's relevant to what you're going through is easier to memorize than one that speaks to a topic that's abstract to you.

2. Start small.

Choose a short verse to start with… and make it even shorter by breaking it down into pieces. Memorize the first five words in the verse first, and when you've got them down, add the next five. As you become more confident, you can add more words, sentences, and even entire verses—but don't add anything new until you've got the previous words down pat.

3. Write it down.

A vast majority of [disciples] suggested this simple strategy: *write the verse you're memorizing down on paper.* But don't just write it once; write it many times—five or ten times is a good start (and some people write out their memory verses up to 50 times!). Physically writing the words out is an extremely useful tactile memory aid.

4. Say it out loud.

Just as writing a verse out can help in memorizing it, so speaking the words aloud is an excellent way to burn them into your memory. One person suggested turning the radio off during your commute to work or school each day and reciting your memory verse out loud instead!

5. Incorporate the verse into your prayers.

When you pray, include elements of the verse in your words to God. Pray that God will help you understand and apply the verse to your life. Pray for God's help in fixing the verse in your heart and mind.

6. Put it everywhere.

Many people suggested writing your memory verse out on multiple index cards or sticky notes (combine this with tip #3 above!) and putting them all over the place, so that you'll see the verse many times throughout your day. Tape the verse to your bathroom mirror or computer monitor. Tuck it into your purse, lunch sack, car glove compartment, school textbook, pockets... anywhere you'll see it. One person suggested making the verse your computer desktop background, and another goes so far as to laminate the verse and hang it in the shower!

7. Use music to help.

Do you find it much easier to remember lyrics than spoken words? Try setting the Bible verse to a simple tune (perhaps repurposing a song you already know well) that you can sing to yourself. (If this sounds like a strange suggestion, consider that many famous hymns and worship songs use Bible verses as their lyrics, and were written specifically as aids for Bible verse memorization.)

8. Make it a game.

Turn the act of memorizing into a personal challenge! You might write the verse out on flashcards, leaving key words blank, and quiz yourself. Get some friends or family members to help quiz you, or even to memorize the verse along with you and encourage/challenge you.

9. Translate the verse into a different language.

This tip isn't for everyone, obviously, but several Bible Gateway fans suggested that if you're comfortable in more than one language, try translating your verse into a different language. Translation requires an intense focus on the meaning and language of a verse—an obvious help for memorization.

10. Repeat, repeat, repeat!

Whatever strategy you follow in memorizing a Bible verse, *do it repeatedly*. Write it down, speak it out loud, sing it out, pray it—but whatever you do, do it over and over until it's a natural, reflexive action. The goal isn't to reduce it to a mindless, repeated activity, but to slowly press the verse into your memory through repetition. Repeat your memorization activity over the course of several hours, days, or even weeks to pace yourself—there's no prize for memorizing a Bible verse fastest; the point is to internalize it over time. And that means you shouldn't be discouraged if it takes a while for the verse to "stick"—keep at it, and it *will* take root!

II. PRAYER

Before we go any further, I have to come clean: I'm terrible at prayer. Because I am a pastor and the writer of a discipleship blog, I have to explain that. After all, why should you keep reading what I have to say about prayer if I'm not very good at it? We all have our heroes of the faith. We all have people we look up to and wish we could be more like. I wish I could save souls like Billy Graham. I wish I could serve the needy like Mother Theresa. I wish I could build a massive congregation like Adam Hamilton, Rick Warren, or Andy Stanley. I wish I could pray like John Wesley and George Muller. Wesley rose every day at four in the morning so he had enough time to pray for several hours. Muller ran an orphanage in England with no funding other than what God provided in answer to prayer. There is a famous story of a morning when there was no food in the house and fifty children to feed at breakfast. They set the table then sat down to pray, thanking God for providing the meal. While they were praying there came a knock at the door. It was a local baker who felt a leading by God to bring bread. Shortly after, a man from the local dairy came to the door. His milk wagon had broken down nearby and the milk would spoil before the wagon was repaired and the milk taken to market, so he thought it best to allow the children to drink the several large milk cans full for breakfast.

Compared to that, I'm terrible at prayer. I would be too chicken to lead hungry children in thanks for breakfast when the table was empty! Yet, God showed up. That takes a lot of faith. I have faith, but I would shrink away from doing what George Muller did because it feels like I am putting God to the test, demanding a miracle, and setting the kids up for disappointment. Here are some other reasons I'm terrible at prayer:

I'm not as regimented as John Wesley. I pray, but I try to fit prayer into my life rather than living my life around prayer. Wesley's early morning prayer hours were non-negotiable. They came first. Instead of being too busy to pray, he knew he was too busy NOT to pray.

My mind wanders. I often start out well, but as I sit in silence, my mind starts to wander. I feel guilty about that sometimes because I'm talking to God. Have you ever felt your mind drifting away somewhere else when talking to your grandmother at the nursing home? How about when talking to your spouse or your boss? It is not only inconsiderate, it can get you into trouble. I pray because I want to draw closer to God, not offend God because I'm daydreaming in the middle of our conversation.

I sometimes fall asleep while praying. That's embarrassing. Remember watching that kid trying unsuccessfully to stay awake in class? Remember how embarrassed he looked when he woke up to see the whole class looking at him? Ever been that kid? (That's why I never EVER give anyone a hard time for falling asleep when I preach. God gives us what we need most in worship, and for some people that is evidently a few more minutes of shut eye!)

I don't hear God talking back. There are those people who begin sentences with "the Lord has revealed to me..." I know that we all receive different spiritual gifts. I almost never "hear a word from God" when I pray, but some people do. Some people in church will say that in order to manipulate the situation. They know that many people who struggle with prayer will defer to them if "God told them so."

I've never prayed a miracle into existence. Again, let's keep theology in mind. Miracles are also gifts of the Spirit given to some and not others, so I shouldn't expect to rival the apostles by healing the sick and raising the dead. Maybe it's because I've never trusted enough to ask for something really bold like breakfast at the Muller orphanage.

I am not the only person to feel unworthy when comparing myself to the "Olympic Champions of Faith." But remember, just because I can't outrun Jesse Owens or Usain Bolt, that doesn't mean I should never run. Just because I can't serve like Mother Theresa, it doesn't mean I don't serve. Just because I can't pastor like Andy Stanley, it doesn't mean I don't pastor my flock. And just because I can't pray like George Muller, it doesn't mean I don't pray. Whoever said that discipleship is a competition anyway? God doesn't hold up scoring cards to rate our performance when we serve or pray. Which brings us to the real point.

What if the people who score a zero, one, or two in prayer are actually more easily able to enjoy the gift of prayer than those who know they score a perfect ten? How is that possible?

Why Being Terrible at Prayer is Actually a Good Thing

My single favorite book on prayer is "Prayer" by Norwegian Theologian Ole Hallesby which we've referred to previously. In it, he says one of the most amazing things I've ever heard:

"What is that attitude of heart which God recognizes as prayer? I would mention two things. In the first place, helplessness. This is unquestionably the first and the surest indication of a praying heart. As far as I can see prayer has been ordained only for the helpless. It is the last resort of the helpless. Indeed the very last way out. We try everything before we finally resort to prayer. This is not only true before our conversion. Prayer is our last resort also throughout our whole Christian life. Prayer and helplessness are inseparable. Only those who are helpless can truly pray. Listen to this, you who are often so helpless that you do not know what to do."

"To pray is nothing more involved than to let Jesus into our needs. To pray is to give Jesus permission to employ His powers in the alleviation of our distress. To pray is to let Jesus glorify his name in the midst of our needs. The results of prayer are, therefore, not dependent upon the powers of the one who prays. Our intense Will, our fervent emotions, or our clear comprehension of what we are praying for are not the reasons why our prayers will be heard and answered. To pray is nothing more involved than to open the door, giving Jesus access to our needs and permitting him to exercise his own power in dealing with them. He who gave us the privilege of prayer knows us very well. He knows our frame, he knows that we are dust. That is why he designed prayer in such a way that the most impotent can make use of it. For to pray is to open the door onto Jesus. And that requires no strength. It is only a question of our will. Will we give Jesus access to our needs? That is the one great and fundamental question in connection with prayer."

So, if I am reading this correctly, there is no such thing as bad prayer. I am not disqualified because I'm timid, unfocused, undisciplined, and sleepy. I am qualified simply because I come. I welcome Jesus in, despite my distractions, weariness, caution, and guilt. After all, the only rule in prayer is that we must be completely honest with God about who we are and what is going on inside and around us. Prayer is not necessarily more effective because I'm more skilled at it than other people. Prayer is effective simply because we come to God, stay for a while, and are completely open while there. When I am terrible at prayer, I know I can't make anything happen through prayer. I am powerless. This realization is what is needed most. God has the power, not us. We will not arrogantly get in God's way. We will not dare to think we have a better solution for our problems than God. We will not give God orders. We will give God our problems and our helplessness to do much about them and let God do the rest. THAT is faith. THAT is prayer. That is what George Muller was doing all along.

So, are you terrible at prayer? No problem. Effective prayer doesn't depend on us being good at it. Instead, we depend on God to be good in all things. So just be terrible at it with God. Does your mind wander? No problem. Just daydream with God. Are you falling asleep during prayer? No problem. Rest in God, then thank God for watching over you while you slept once you wake up. Spend time together with God and see what happens. Now that we have that out of the way, let's take a closer look at the different ways we can connect with God in prayer.

There are five categories of prayer that we will explore with Jesus:

A. Silence
B. Talking to God
C. Listening to God
D. Written Prayer
E. Group Prayer

A. Silence

Have you ever wanted God to speak up? We want God to shout. We want God to shake the ground and light up the sky with divine flashing neon messages so there is no way we will NOT hear and understand. But God is evidently under no obligation to drown out our noise. The world is too loud. Period. I offer that observation as our next step in trying to hear what God has to say. I've made the claim that God speaks. I was driving downtown the other day and passed the local United Church of Christ congregation sporting a banner out front that boldly proclaimed "*God is Still Speaking.*' Indeed!...So why don't we hear it? One reason is that the world is too loud. God is still speaking, but God is not shouting. God is evidently under no obligation to shout over our noise and busyness in order to be heard. We had two kinds of teachers growing up. There was the kind that would raise their voice loud enough to shout us into obedience and silence. Then there was Mr. Caskey my history teacher. He would simply speak in a normal, calm tone, going on with the business at hand like what material would be on the upcoming test. If we wanted to hear, we had to shut up and listen. That's how God works. We have to quiet down. I used to think that God had more to say in ancient times. But that's not it. In the ancient days of campfires, starlit nights and silent temples, silence was a much easier commodity to come by. There was no traffic, no planes overhead, no radios blaring. It was a slower, quieter reality. We are so unfamiliar with silence because we insist on drowning it out with news, noise, music, or TV. We create artificial background noise that is around us all day long. Then we naively think that ten minutes of prayer at bedtime will be enough to tap into the Creator of the cosmos. We will need to turn off the noise.

How to Get Quiet

First of all, we can't do much to change how many planes fly overhead or how much traffic drives by our house, so we may need to get away to a more quiet spot. I love the forest, but I don't have the time to drive out into the woods every day. I can choose to turn off the noise. I can drive without the radio or iPod playing. I can turn off the television. I can stay off the computer. I can slow down and take it easy. If the traffic is still too loud, I can always buy a box of ear plugs at the drug store and have all the silence I want anywhere I want it. These things are completely within our control. But just sitting in a quiet room may not be enough. We are often shocked to learn how loudly our own thoughts are blaring inside our heads.

The noise inside our own minds is uncharted territory for most of us and it takes time in silence to get there. To truly hear God the following formula is all we need: "*When we are as quiet on the inside as the world outside, we are ready to hear God.*" How can we be "loud on the inside?" Our thoughts. I once spent five days straight in a tree stand in the forest during hunting season from sunrise to sunset in complete silence. I was as still and silent as the forest was still and silent. With nothing moving, no noise, no outside stimulus to respond to, all I had were the thoughts in my head. By day three my thoughts were so loud I wanted to plug my ears! This is why prisoners placed in solitary confinement for long periods of time suffer psychological and emotional damage. I can't make my brain stop thinking because that is what brains do. Trying not to think is like trying to keep your heart from beating. There is a remedy to find peace and silence within. There is a form of prayer called "contemplative prayer" that is not about talking or listening, but about rest and silence. Father Thomas Keating of "Contemplative Outreach" has spent years teaching others how to find this peace and rest in God. He offers some steps we can take to enter silence and listen for the Presence of God within.

Practicing Contemplative Prayer

STEP ONE. First of all, get away and slow down. We must first make the effort to take a break and find some quiet, out of the way place. Psalm 46:10 states "*Be still and know that I am God.*" Be still means slow down, settle down, stop, relax. Settle down and relax in a quiet silent place. I find this to be not only relaxing, but a great way to practice humility as I trust God to take care of things while I allow the world to turn on its own for a while.

STEP TWO. Stay there until you are as quiet on the inside as it is on the outside around us. The biggest obstacle to the quiet on the inside is the constant barrage of distracting thoughts in our head. As I said a moment ago, it is impossible to stop thinking. It's what our brain does, all the time. It even thinks when we are asleep, which is why we have dreams. Expecting our brain to not think thoughts is like expecting our heart to stop beating or our lungs to stop taking in air. We can't do that. The trick is not to stop thinking, but to stop paying attention to those thoughts. Father Thomas Keating, in his book "Foundations for Centering Prayer and the Christian Contemplative Life" (Continuum 2002) explains it in a way that really makes sense.

As we look within ourselves, we are becoming aware of our soul, which is the spiritual part of us. That's also where the Holy Spirit lives within us. Father Keating encourages us to imagine looking down from above on a river filled with boats. Our ordinary thoughts are like boats sitting on a river that are so closely packed together that we cannot see the water that is holding them up. We can't keep them from coming, but the less time we spend examining and inspecting every boat, the sooner they can continue on their way downstream. Likewise, the less time we spend examining and inspecting every thought, the sooner it can continue on its way. The more we send the boats downstream, the farther apart they get, and suddenly we can see the water below them. The more we send our random thoughts downstream, the more we become aware of our own soul below them. Letting our thoughts just pass by isn't all that easy. We humans have a hard time not doing things. There is a solution. When a baby is suddenly interested in playing with the electric socket in the wall, how do we usually get them away from it? We give them something else to occupy their attention: a toy, a rattle, a stuffed bunny. We give them something safe to take their mind off of something dangerous. What about my random distracting thoughts? How do I keep my mind off that? I give myself something else that points me back toward God rather than away.

STEP THREE. Choose a sacred word or phrase. It might be as easy as silently whispering the word "Jesus" to ourselves whenever we are aware that we are thinking about something else. Turn each distracting thought away by silently whispering your sacred word: "Jesus. Jesus. Jesus." Let it go. We give ourselves a break. We do not have to be so attached to every little thought that wanders into our awareness. The less attached we are to our random thoughts, the more space there is between them. The more space there is between them, the quieter we become. Then we are aware of the deep silence and stillness within. This stillness within is the "peace that surpasses all understanding". This does take some time and some practice. For some of us, just sitting still for a half hour doing nothing will take some discipline. It could take a week or two until you begin to feel more comfortable with it. For others, just getting comfortable sitting in complete silence will take time but it is worth the time. Maybe you live in a part of town that never gets quiet. No problem. Simply pick up a fifty cent pair of earplugs at the drugstore and it can be as quiet as Elijah's mountaintop. We will feel funny doing nothing. But remember, it's not nothing.

STEP FOUR. Sit long and quiet enough to really hear your own thoughts. Then keep sitting quiet and still as you learn to let your thoughts and worries go, turning them away with your sacred word and tuning in to God within. Contemplative Prayer is about resting in God's Presence revealed through silence. It takes practice, but is a crucial skill to center our lives in God.

B. Talking to God

In the earliest Harry Potter books, Hermione Granger knows all the right words and how to say them with the proper inflection in order to cast spells that actually change things like making objects levitate or catch on fire. Ron Weasley could never quite remember the right order of things and his spells usually backfired or had no effect at all. Prayer is not at all like learning to cast spells at Hogwarts, but we talk about it the same way. We treat prayer as magic words to be memorized and recited when we rattle off the Lord's Prayer without a thought of what it actually means. We believe our prayers are not answered because somehow we are doing it wrong. We've shared repeatedly that there is only one rule to prayer and that is to be completely honest with God about what is going on inside and around us. How can we mess that up? We can't, unless we are holding something back from God. So, what exactly are we doing when we pray and how does it actually change things in the world?

In the beginning of creation we learn something important. God makes it clear that God intends creation to be something God and human beings do together. God created all the animals but relies on Adam to name them. God made it rain for forty days and nights, but Noah and his family built the ark. God gave instructions to the people, but Moses wrote them down. God sent messages, but it was the prophets who delivered them. During the Exile of ancient Israel, God needed to punish the people for their endless disobedience, but it was Babylon that actually pulled the walls of Jerusalem down. Jesus offered hope, a healing way of life, and eternity but it was up to the apostles and the Church to spread it around. *God can do anything but chooses to work in this world through the assistance of human beings.* It might be hard to accept, but God chooses to be limited by us. How is God limited? God can do anything, but needs a human agent to work with and through, which brings us to prayer.

Prayer is not just the way God communicates with us to recruit volunteers for the mission like Moses at the burning bush. The act of prayer creates an opening for God to work in our world in real and powerful ways.

Remember, we learned earlier that prayer does not depend on our skill or abilities to make things happen. I shared a quote by O. Hallesby that redefined prayer for a lot of us:

"Our intense Will, our fervent emotions, or our clear comprehension of what we are praying for are not the reasons why our prayers will be heard and answered. To pray is nothing more involved than to open the door, giving Jesus access to our needs and permitting him to exercise his own power in dealing with them."

In other words, I don't have to be "good" at prayer. I don't have to know what to say or even how to say it. Prayer is simply opening a door for God into our world through our willingness to help. God's grace does the rest. It's a poor analogy, but it is as if I tune God in, then boost the signal to the rest of the world like a broadcast antenna. Mary, after she conceived by the Holy Spirit, said *"my soul MAGNIFIES the Lord!"* What does that mean? A magnifying glass makes things bigger and clearer. It also brings things into focus. Like Mary, in prayer, we help bring God into focus for the rest of the world. You know what else a magnifying glass can do? It can gather and intensify the rays of sunlight until they burn whatever they touch! In prayer, without saying a word, but willingly allowing God to pour through us, God's grace is amplified, intensified, and directed toward the people and situations most in need of healing. In intercessory prayer, we focus on a need, such as peace in North Korea or restoration after hurricanes, and God's grace is amplified there to make a difference the way sunlight through the lens can burn paper.

That's why it doesn't really matter if I daydream or lose focus while praying. Our most important task is to keep the door open. As I write this, a department store in town is going out of business. They have hired people to stand by the side of the road holding signs announcing the final clearance sales. It looks like a boring job to me. All they have to do is stand there all day long and keep the sign visible. They can sit down and fall asleep as long as the sign is visible to passing cars. Can prayer really be that easy? We simply keep the door open for God while God does the rest? Besides, what could I possibly ask God to do that would be a better solution to the problem than what God already has in mind? *"Thy kingdom come, thy will be done on earth as it is in Heaven."* If we slow down and think about the Lord's Prayer while we are reciting it, we see that we have been asking God all along to do whatever God thinks best. But God needs a willing accomplice in this world to do it. In prayer, we hold the door open, invite God in, and say "I'm with you God! Do what you need to do!"

But all that being said, sometimes we really need to talk to God to figure things out and get some things off our chest. Talking to God is not difficult. It takes no special skills or techniques to talk to God. The only rule needed for prayer is this:

"Always be completely open and honest with God about everything going on inside of you and around you."

We have to let God in to be a part of it, and only when God is allowed to be a part of our problems is God free to do something about it.

Peter Grieg teaches in "The Prayer Course" (www.payercourse.org) that talking with God is like climbing up on our Father's lap and spending time together because we love each other. Rules aren't required to sit on God's lap. That's why I don't feel guilty about daydreaming or falling asleep during prayer and neither should you. It is evidence of how comfortable we are on our Father's lap. Rehearsed patterns of prayer aren't necessary either, but Jesus did provide a basic etiquette of prayer in the form of The Lord's Prayer. This is not a prayer to be memorized and regurgitated like magic words. It is a suggestion of loving ways to communicate with God that improve the relationship. At its heart, that is what etiquette and manners are all about, treating others with the kind of respect and kindness that makes others comfortable and glad to be with us. Jesus teaches in this prayer the ways that we love and respect God and deepen our relationship through:

Adoration: Tell God how much you love Him and why.
Surrender: Give God full authority to choose our direction.
Confession: Admit our imperfections and need for forgiveness.
Petition: Ask God to meet the personal needs of the group.
Intercession: Ask God to meet the needs of others.

So, in short, talking to God has no rules other than being completely open and honest with God about everything going on inside of you and around you. We can strengthen the bonds of our relationship through the simple etiquette of prayer, such as expressing our affection for God, accepting God's guidance and leadership, admitting and apologizing for our mistakes, giving thanks and appreciation for the gifts God gives, and discussing the needs of other people with God.

C. Listening to God

Now while talking to God may be pretty easy, listening to God takes a bit more work. There are many ways to listen to God. Here are three:

1. Meditation

Meditation in our society has a lot of different connotations. Often, when we hear the word, we think of someone in India doing yoga and chanting with incense. Christian meditation, however, is not about chanting or burning incense. It is simply about thinking. The Christian theologian Richard Foster, in his book "The Celebration of Discipline' (HarperCollins 1998) suggests that anyone who can worry can also meditate, because they both involve thinking. When we worry, we dwell on our problems. We rehearse them in our minds, turning them over and examining them and fretting about how big they are. The longer we think about the problems the worse they get. By contrast, when we meditate, Foster suggests, we think about the good things of God, turning them over and over again in our minds and taking comfort from how they help us get to know God better. It is as simple as that. It is listening to what God has to say, then thinking about what God has said, mulling it over, examining and exploring, in order to obey it.

2. Prayer of Examen

A second way to listen to God is to look back over our day and reflect on where God has been with us. It is called the Prayer of Examen, and has been practiced by Christian believers since the days of St. Ignatius in the 1500's. Ignatius believed that by reflecting on our days in this way, we increase our sensitivity to the workings of God in our lives. He believed that God often speaks to us through our deepest feelings and longings, through what he called "consolation" and "desolation." We would say that God speaks through the good things as well as the bad things in our lives. Consolation can be defined as whatever draws you close to God, fills you with life, and makes you feel that all is right in the world. Desolations are those things that pull you away from God, alienate you from others, and drain your energy and vitality. We prefer to use some different words that make more sense to us. We look back over the "highs" and "lows" of the day. This would allow us to be attentive to the indwelling presence of the Holy Spirit and create space for God to shape our souls and direct our lives.

To begin a practice of The Examen, follow these guidelines:

1. Sit quietly and relax.
2. Think back over the last 24 hours and look for your "Highs of the Day."
For example, you might ask:
- For what moment today am I most grateful?
- What experience of the day felt most life-giving to me?
- When today did I feel most contented, most like myself?

- When did I sense God's presence most fully today?

3. Think again through the last day and look for your "Lows of the Day." You can use one of these questions as a guide:

- For what moment today am I least grateful?
- What experience of the day drained life from me?
- When today did I feel the most discontented, uncomfortable, and the least like myself?
- When did God seem absent in my life today?

4. Spend a moment in prayer, thanking God for your consolation, and asking for help with the low points.

This can be a great way to spend time with God at the end of the day, to unwind together before going to bed. Regardless of how today went, God can show us how to make tomorrow a little better. A third way to listen to God is by prayerfully feasting on the scriptures.

3. Lectio Divina

All around us, all the time, God is constantly communicating His thoughts and desires for us. A lot of people don't believe that because they've never heard God out loud. We just need a little help tuning God in. Roman Catholic author M. Basil Pennington in his book "Lectio Divina: Renewing the Ancient Practice of Praying the Scriptures" (The Crossroad Publishing Company 1998) explains it beautifully. He observes that at this exact second, the air around us is filled with all kinds of voices and music. They are radio waves that, because they can't be heard by human ears, require a radio to tune them in to a frequency we can hear and understand. It is the same with the Voice of God. God can miraculously speak in a tangible voice that all can hear, but day to day God is speaking in a different frequency...a spiritual frequency. There is no radio on earth that can tune in the voice of God. But it can be done by allowing the Living Word to speak through the Written Word of God. Every time we open the scriptures we are having an encounter with God. We practice a prayerful way of reading the Bible that allows us to experience what God is doing right now, live and in person. It is an ancient practice known as Lectio Divina which is Latin for "sacred reading." It is not difficult and employs only four simple steps.

The first step is called "*lectio*" or simply reading. After you choose a passage of scripture, one story or one section of teaching you just read it. Read the passage slowly and reflectively. Think about what you are reading. Imagine it. Hear the sounds, see the sights, smell the scents, feel the warmth or the cold. You may want to read it two or three times, reading more slowly each time.

The second stage is *meditatio*, or reflection. During this stage you identify an image, word or phrase and think deeply upon it. Ponder it and turn it over again and again in your mind.

Refer to our discussion above about "meditation," or thinking about the things of God. You allow that image, word or phrase to interact with your thoughts, dreams, or desires. Focus on whatever captures your attention, a word, a question, a character in the story. Whatever grabs you, stay with it and mull it over.

The third stage is *oratio* or response. During this stage you allow your heart to speak to God.

Whatever you are thinking or feeling about this scripture, tell it to God. Ask your questions. Share your insights. Talk it over and enjoy it together with God.

When you've finally talked yourself out in prayer it is time for the fourth step: *contemplatio* or rest. During this stage, you allow yourself to let go of thoughts, ideas, and words. It's a time where you can just sit and rest in God's presence.

READ: Read the selection through several times.
THINK: Meditate upon whatever caught your mind and imagination.
PRAY: Talk to God about your thoughts and questions.
REST: Rest in God's silence.

That's it: READ, THINK, PRAY, REST. Doing this, we tune in the voice of God allowing God to guide us and shape us.

D. Written Prayer

1. Written Prayers

Sometimes, we need some help to pray. Paul teaches that even when we are unable to pray, the Spirit intercedes for us with sighs too deep for words. We pray for each other, too. Sometimes it is the saints of the Church that have come before us that help us find the words to pray through written prayers that have been passed down through the generations. We have already shared "The Serenity Prayer" of Reinhold Niebuhr that has helped countless people in their encounters with God. There are many written prayers that so poignantly express deep truths of God that they are prayed over and over. There is a misconception among some that prayers must be extemporaneous to be valid. There is nothing wrong with praying a written prayer. Here are some ways to help pray through the words and witness of others.

Consider the "Prayer of St. Francis

Lord, make me an instrument of your peace.
Where there is hatred, let me sow love,
Where there is injury, pardon
Where there is doubt, faith,
Where there is despair, hope,
Where there is darkness, light,
Where there is sadness, joy.
O Divine Master, grant that I may not so much
seek to be consoled as to console,
not so much to be understood as to understand,
not so much to be loved, as to love;
for it is in giving that we receive,
it is in pardoning that we are pardoned,
it is in dying that we awake to eternal life.

--- St. Francis of Assisi

a. Pray It As Your Own Words

Just as an actor speaks the words of a script as if they are her own, we can simply pray these words as if they are our own. Simply read them with an attitude of prayer. This is familiar enough to anyone who has prayed "The Lord's Prayer." These are words given to us by Jesus, written down by Matthew and passed down through the generations. Remember, Jesus gave us this prayer in order to teach us to pray. Praying written prayers can teach us how to pray as well. After all, as children we learn to speak by imitating those around us. Praying the written prayers of generations of saints that have come before us can help teach us to pray and widen our prayer language.

b. Pray Like Jazz

Jazz music is about enjoying the freedom to make it up as you go. We pray that way too. But jazz starts with some chords and snippets of melody that give the musicians a place to start. We start with what is written by the composer but then follow the inspiration to add music that is all our own, improvised in the moment. We might pray just a line of St. Francis' prayer, then spend some time talking to God about what it means to us. Here's a brief example of what that might sound like:

Selection from Written Prayer:

"Lord, make me an instrument of your peace..."

Improvised Personal Prayer:
"Use me Lord. I know you change lives and make the world a better place. You bring peace. You calm our anxieties and settle our petty conflicts. I want to help you do that, Lord. Work through me to bring the peace that surpasses all understanding."

Selection from Written Prayer:
"Where there is hatred, let me sow love..."

Improvised Personal Prayer:
"I can't believe Lord that the KKK still has a foothold in our county. I can't believe how angry people get with each other over the slightest things. I grow weary of campaign ads that spend more time tearing down opponents than building up our citizens. It seems we are so ready to believe the worst about each other and our tempers are short. Help me Lord to know how to offer grace, and patience, and kindness and love. Help me to throw water to extinguish the fire rather than gasoline to feed the flames."

This is also a freeing way to pray the scriptures in addition to Lectio Divina.

c. Pray Using "Lectio Divina" Method

We learned above that we can pray the scripture through the method of Lectio Divina or sacred reading. We can apply the same method to the text of written prayers.

READ: Read the prayer through several times.
THINK: Meditate upon whatever caught your mind and imagination.
PRAY: Talk to God about your thoughts and questions.
REST: Rest in God's silence.

2. Journaling

It can be helpful to write our prayers to God as if writing a letter. Keeping a journal has been a helpful spiritual discipline for millions of people. Just as there is only one rule in prayer, there is only one salient rule to prayerful journaling: be completely honest and open with God about what is going on in us and around us. Just write it out. Studies have proven that students who write notes out by hand learn and remember the material better than those who typed or used an audio recorder. There is something about the physical act of writing that engages the mind at a deeper level.

Don't worry about style or spelling. Don't worry about anyone else reading it. Those concerns will only distract you and cause you to look upon your writing with a critical eye. Concentrate on what you feel and what you are trying to say and just let it flow. You will be surprised how the floodgates can open and your hand will sometimes struggle to keep up.

The act of writing is prayer. Even if you never read these words again, you are praying in a very deep way. However, since you have written these words down, they are written prayers in their own right and can be prayed again the same ways we prayed the "Prayer of St. Francis."

You can:

a. Pray It As Your Own Words
b. Pray Like Jazz
c. Pray Using "Lectio Divina" Method

3. Liturgies

Sometimes, even with the best of intentions, we need a plan in order to pray. Several years ago, I was overweight and out of shape and decided I needed to do something about it. I purchased a workout video from BeachBody.com called "Power 90." It helped me to get back in shape because it provided all the structure I would need to exercise every day. I didn't have to wonder what I would do each day. Instead, it claimed that if I "Just Push Play" every day, over time I would improve my physical health. It worked. I didn't have to waste any time deciding how I would exercise each day and I had a lot of options. I could walk, run, ride a bike, lift weights, or go for a hike.

Sometimes I couldn't decide and sometimes I didn't really feel like it, so my indecision became an excuse for procrastination. Our prayer life can also become mired in indecision and procrastination because we aren't sure which of these methods we want to choose. If you find this to be a problem, perhaps a daily prayer liturgy will get you back into the routine. "Just push play."

In the Roman Catholic tradition, great care has gone into producing a book of daily prayer liturgies to guide and equip the Church and its leaders in prayer. Like "5x5" it is a method, a discipline that provides enough stability to keep our lives focused on God long enough for God to change us. "The Liturgy of the Hours" (or "The Divine Office") provides "prayer services" to be read and prayed at various times throughout the day. These prayer services include scripture selections from a three year lectionary of daily readings, prayers for special occasions, liturgical seasons, and litanies that guide us through a series of categories of needs that we can pray for each day. "The Liturgy of the Hours" is a massive gift to the Church and praying through the whole thing would require purchasing it in a four volume set. It is available online for free. You simply pray the liturgy scheduled for the day.

"The Book of Common Prayer" is a similar resource originally developed by the Church of England. In the United States, the Episcopal Church uses its own version. There are many other prayer books that offer daily liturgies from a variety of sources and traditions and many are available online in both text and audio form..

A gentle reminder about using liturgies: Variety is the spice of life and also nourishes our prayer lives. If these liturgies begin to feel mechanical you may want to take a break from them for a season and focus on another method of prayer. That goes for all methods of prayer actually. The moment you begin to feel like you are just going through the motions, change things up. Keep it fresh. This is after all an encounter with God intended to deepen the relationship. Imagine you are dating someone but you go to see the same movie and eat at the same restaurant every time you go out together. That relationship is in a rut. Try something different. Pray in a different place. Have a different kind of conversation with God now and then.

D. Group Prayer

Prayer is not just something we do alone with God. It is a huge part of what we do together as followers of Jesus. We pray during worship. We pray at the beginning and endings of our church meetings, studies and events. We gather in special prayer meetings to seek God's guidance for the direction of the Church and to offer intercessory prayer for the wider world. Too many disciples would prefer to be hung by their thumbs than to be asked to pray out loud in front of others. Some people are extroverts who enjoy being in groups of people and don't mind speaking up in public. Others are introverts who are more comfortable with silence and solitude and speaking in front of a group is stressful. Whatever the legitimate reason for our hesitancy, not knowing how to pray need not be one of them.

1. Praying Out Loud

Some people feel out of their element when asked to pray out loud. If we are praying every day in our quiet time with God, then we are always in our element. Here are some things to keep in mind.

"We and Us" not "I and Me"

You are leading others into an encounter with God. It is our privilege to speak for the group, so remember that you are not praying just for yourself. Include everyone in the group. "Lord WE ask you to forgive US" rather than "Lord, I ask you to forgive ME."

Pray to the Occasion

If you are opening a church council meeting in prayer, feel free to pray for the council, the decisions to be made and the wisdom needed to make them. If you are opening a Bible Study, pray for the Holy Spirit to teach us. If it is Christmas Season, Lent, Easter, Summer, or back to school, feel free to pray to the occasion.

Patterns of Prayer

If you are not sure what to say when called upon to pray, just do as Jesus taught us and use the pattern contained in the Lord's Prayer:

Adoration: Tell God how much you love Him and why.
Surrender: Give God full authority to choose our direction.
Confession: Admit our imperfections and need for forgiveness.
Petition: Ask God to meet the personal needs of the group.
Intercession: Ask God to meet the needs of others.

Pray to God, not to Other People

Don't worry about being eloquent, poetic, or well spoken. You are not performing. You are praying. Remember the only rule in prayer that matters: Be honest with God about what is going on inside and around us. Beautiful words and witty turns of phrase are not needed and can actually be a distraction. Just talk to God.

2. Prayer Liturgies

Prayer liturgies, like the "Liturgy of the Hours" or "The Book of Common Prayer" are meant to be prayed as a group as well as during times of private prayer. Group members can take turns leading the prepared parts of the service and can just "follow the script."

3. Prayer Meetings

There are no right ways or wrong ways to hold a prayer meeting as long as we spend more time praying than talking about praying. That might sound like an odd thing to say, but take it to heart. We spend time in the beginning of the gathering agreeing on the plan. If it is to be a prayer for discernment, then we will review the decisions that are being made. If it is to be a prayer time for intercession, we may raise some prayer needs for the group to take to God. We will also decide how we will pray together. Will we, like a Quaker Meeting, pray in silence until someone is moved to pray aloud? Will we divide the group into smaller prayer teams to each focus on a specific assigned need? Will we take time to share testimonies of answered prayers? Will we fill a hat with prayer needs written on slips of paper that are pulled out and prayed over during the meeting then taken home to be prayed over during the week to come? The only limit to the variety of prayer methods is our own creativity.

4. Prayer Partners

In my first appointment as pastor I had a friend named Denny. Denny showed up unannounced at the door of the parsonage one day and asked if this was where Pastor Greg lived. He then informed us that he would begin worshipping at our church. Out of curiosity, my wife Robin asked him how he had heard of our church. With a strange uncomfortable look on his face, Denny said that God had told him to come and that he was to pray for me. It seemed very spooky and supernatural at first, but over time I would see God speaking to Denny in more dramatic ways than this. We became friends and prayer partners, meeting every Sunday morning before worship to pray together for each other, the services that were about to begin and for the parish as a whole.

It became clear why God had sent Denny to pray for me. I would never have survived my first appointment without it. I was a full time seminary student, serving three small congregations, with a daughter in kindergarten and one that had just been born. The stress of holding it all together began to take a toll on our marriage. It was a Wednesday morning and after we got our oldest off to school, we began to argue about how difficult things had gotten. I was given an ultimatum. I had to choose between ministry and marriage because the two could not peacefully coexist. I called my District Superintendent who came and counseled with us all morning. Our problems weren't solved but we were working things through. By late afternoon we just wanted to enjoy each other and our kids. We parked the car where no one from the parish could see it, took the phone off the hook, and closed the curtains. We would get a pizza, watch a movie, and hide from the world.

Then the doorbell rang. When Robin opened it, we saw Denny. He was standing, not on the door mat, but back from the door off the steps on the sidewalk. He had a bouquet of flowers in his hand. We invited him in but he declined and simply said: "I don't know what has been going on here today, but since 9 am this morning God has been beating me up because of you. It lasted all morning until mid-afternoon. I don't know why, but I know I'm not supposed to come in. I just need to give you these flowers and tell you everything is going to be OK." He did and he left. That remains to this day the most powerful experience of prayer I have ever been a part of.

There is only one Denny, but everyone should have a prayer partner like him. Having someone praying for you every day is a powerful thing. Praying for them in return is equally powerful. That much concentrated prayer tends to open lives up to experience God like never before. Choose your prayer partner wisely. You want someone committed to prayer, who is dependable, and will hold you accountable when you need it. It helps to pray with someone who shares your belief that God changes lives and makes the world better. Pray with someone who expects God to come through in a big way. If God doesn't deliver that person to your doorstep, then find someone willing to grow in this experience with you. You will not regret it.

5. Praying Over Others

"Is anyone among you sick? Let them call the elders of the church to pray over them and anoint them with oil in the name of the Lord." (James 5:14 NIV). What does it mean to "pray over" someone? It is basically praying for someone and with someone at the same time. When we are struggling physically, emotionally, or spiritually we need help praying. We pray for others every day using intercessory prayer. Praying over someone is intercessory prayer that is up close and personal. It is customary to lay on hands, which is a way of sharing the grace and Spirit of God with others. It is as if we are saying "whatever portion of God's grace and Spirit I have, I share it with you." Being prayed for is an act of great comfort and great power. As I write these words, I am suffering from a herniated disc. When I met with our Monday Prayer Group, the group began by forming a circle around me, laying on hands, and prayed for my upcoming surgery. It is unfortunate that many churches accept this work from pastors only, which biblically speaking, is nonsense. It is the baptized spiritual leaders of the church who are mature in the faith and sharing in the Holy Spirit who are called and commanded to share this gift with those in need. There is nothing magical or special about a pastor. (I should know. I am one.) The blessings aren't better or healing more likely because a pastor prays over us rather than a lay person. Too many churches plateau and their pastors burn out because they are like Moses in the desert trying to judge every dispute among the people of Israel. We run ourselves ragged trying to be all things for all people and to be present to pray over every crisis. We are called as pastors to *"equip the saints for every work of righteousness"* (Ephesians 4). It is empowering to recognize and accept the gift of prayer from one another within the

Church. It is a holy privilege to say "The Spirit in me recognizes the Spirit in you, and I welcome the opportunity to meet God together."

Here's how we pray over each other:

a. Get Personal

Whether you are in a hospital room, living room, or in the back of an ambulance, prayer is personal. Know the name of the person with whom you are praying. If they are able to hold a conversation, spend a little time getting to know this person as more than the illness or crisis but as a whole person.

b. Work Together

Ask the person "What would you like us to pray for today?" or "What would you like to tell God?" or "What should we ask God today?" Allow the person to be as active a part of the process as possible. Also, James says to call the elders (plural). Take someone else with you. Illness and crisis can make us feel very alone and a small group praying with us is a tangible reminder that as members of the Body of Christ, we are not alone. This is also a great way to model prayer ministry for those just learning.

c. Leave it to God

O. Hallesby writes that it is pointless to tell God what we would like God to do. God has infinitely better solutions than we do, so it is best to share our needs with God and leave the solutions to God. Tell God the need. Trust God with the solution.

d. Get "Hands On"

There is something healing and reassuring about a simple touch. Don't be afraid to hold hands while you pray together. Don't be afraid to lay on hands, often on the top of the head, on the arm or shoulder. (Not everyone likes to be touched, so I always ask permission.) Anointing with oil is a powerful sign of blessing and grace. The combination of conversation, prayer, and touch helps make the presence of God very real and tangible.

e. A Process for Praying With Someone in Need

If you keep these ideas in mind, you will never be at a loss for words. Prayers aren't powerful because of their eloquence. They are beautiful because of their sensitivity to the reality of the moment and bring awareness of God joining us in that moment. That being said, I've been called on to pray for the worst tragedies with no notice at all. I've worn my clergy ID badge to the emergency room to visit a friend and been grabbed by a nurse to pray for family in the next bay whose father just died seconds before. I will take a few seconds to talk with the family, to get to know their names, what has happened, and how they are feeling. Then I use this simple "script" to keep things relevant and focused:

Why we are here.
"Gracious God, this is a difficult moment for us. After a long and difficult battle with cancer, Dad has finally finished his fight."

What is going well?
"We are grateful to be here with him as he passed. We are also grateful for the skill and tenderness of Dad's doctors and nurses here."

What could be better?
"We knew this moment would come, but we always thought there'd be more time. We aren't sure what to do next or how we will go on without him."

What do we know about God that makes us think God can help?
We know that you love every one of us and you love Dad. You gave us life in order to spend time with us and you extend that time in resurrection and eternal life. And even now, in the pain of our grief, you provide comfort by sharing your Holy Spirit with us."

Ask for help.
"Comfort us and strengthen us for what we will face in the coming hours and days. Please accept Dad into your kingdom and bring yourself glory through even this. Amen."

f. A Word on Suffering:
Suffering is real. Bad things do happen. It is one of our Five Undeniable Truths: Life is not fair. We live in a world where anything can happen and usually does. This creates a problem for us because it can cause us to question what we know about God. Here are the three most important qualities of our Triune God that make suffering harder to understand or accept:

- God is All Powerful
- God is All Knowing
- God is All Loving

God is omnipotent. God can do anything because nothing is impossible for God. We are told in James that *"the prayer of faith shall heal the sick."* O.

Hallesby writes that prayer requires faith because if we don't believe God can do something about our problems, there is no reason to pray in the first place. But when the prayers aren't answered to our satisfaction, when the tumor continues to grow, it seems that God is either powerless to do something or God just doesn't care. We are taught that God is love and we cannot understand why an all-powerful Friend wouldn't use that power to help us if we are indeed friends. Friends help each other. So we assume the worst, either God is angry with us, God wants us to die of cancer, or God doesn't care. Or maybe God doesn't know, so we pray desperately to fill God in. But God is supposedly all knowing, so that must mean that God either can't do anything about it or doesn't care what happens to us. Either way, it throws a mighty big monkey wrench into our love relationship with God.

Or maybe we are the problem. The apostle James writes that that "*the prayer of faith shall heal the sick.*" He is Jesus' half-brother, so if anyone knows how this stuff works, it should be him. Perhaps we don't have enough faith, or we don't know how to pray properly. Despite what it seems to say in James, faith is not an automatic "get out of suffering free card." We don't need guilt for being a bad Christian on top of our suffering. How do we understand God in the midst of this suffering? These questions will come up when we pray over those in need.

Peter Grieg teaches in "The Prayer Course" that suffering is the result of three possible sources:

- God's World
- God's Will
- God's War

God's World
God has designed a world that is free to turn according to natural laws and systems. Weather patterns, the movement of the earth beneath our feet, even our own illness and death are natural parts of how the world works. Also because of our freedom and these natural laws and systems, there are consequences to our choices and actions. Newton identified it in his natural laws that for every action there is an equal and opposite reaction. Life has consequences. Everything costs something. If I eat fast food every day I really shouldn't shake my fist at God for giving me heart disease. Everything costs something. Life is not fair. We live in a world where anything can and usually does happen. We strive with God's help to accept the things we cannot change and change the things we can.

God's Will

Many assume that God has determined everything that will ever happen long before any of us were born and we are just playing our part in the role God has written for us. Everything in life is predetermined so when bad things happen, we can simply shrug our shoulders and assume "God has a reason." While it is true that God works in mysterious ways, this assumption blames God for everything. God does intervene in the freely turning world. Miracles are when God, for whatever reason, breaks in and interrupts the natural laws and systems by changing something. Tumors do sometimes disappear. The mystery that we cannot understand is why God chooses to intervene at certain times but doesn't at others. It is not God's will that we live in these mortal bodies forever. Postponing death by extending mortal life is not God's plan. Resurrection, eternal life and a new creation are God's ultimate plan so God will not heal every disease or fix every problem. God has something better in mind. Because this mortal life is all we know, it means everything to us. It is hard to accept losing it or the ones we love. We gather together to comfort one another in our grief, which is the painful process of accepting what we cannot change, and keep ourselves focused to the larger purposes of God that are playing out around us.

God's War

We are caught in the crossfire of an ongoing war between our creating God and Satan who is trying destroy everything God creates. In addition to the natural suffering and loss of life, we occasionally suffer as collateral damage in this epic struggle between good and evil. Satan is powerless to destroy God outright, so sows discontent and discord through sabotage, like the senseless terror attacks and bombings in the Middle East and around the world. It is usually innocents who are targeted, the suffering of whom puts pressure on the real powers they are trying to combat. "*For we do not wrestle against flesh and blood, but against the rulers, against the authorities, against the cosmic powers over this present darkness, against the spiritual forces of evil in the Heavenly places*" (Ephesians 6:12 ESV). This is why we love and care for our enemies. The evil people do to each other is not just the result of our free choices but also through the influence of spiritual terrorists who know that "hurt people hurt people." We tend to pass on the frustration, anger and pain we feel to others. Our "enemies" who hurt us are pawns in a much larger game. They too need to be rescued from the broken life. God is actively working against the sabotage of the Enemy. Jesus' work on the cross and in resurrection assures the victory and his recruitment of disciples who will join Him in the mission of waging peace continues the operation of helping God finish the job.

III. SPIRITUAL DISCIPLINES

In the springtime, when it is finally warmer, we always open up the windows to let the fresh air in. After being closed up all winter, the house is stuffy and stale, so the fresh air is such a welcome change. Sometimes we don't even realize how stuffy things have gotten until the fresh air comes. The breeze is so refreshing, we want it to fill the whole house. If you want the breeze to move completely through the house, you have to open more windows. It is the same with our souls. Everyday life can become a dull grind. Our hearts and minds can become a stale mix of worry, frustration, boredom, and fear. We know that God has promised that perfect love casts out all fear (1 John 4:18), which gives us a vague hope that our love relationship with God should make us feel better. We don't like to feel this way and we wish we could flush out these feelings with the fresh air of a loving God. The Greek New Testament word for the Holy Spirit is *"pneuma"* which literally means breath or wind. God breathed life into the newly created humans in Genesis and they became alive. Jesus "breathed" the Holy Spirit upon his disciples after his resurrection, the same Spirit that raised him from the dead. We sense that this life-giving Spirit could make our life somehow better but we are not sure how to go about making that happen. We remember that the Holy Spirit came upon the disciples at Pentecost as a mighty rushing wind (Acts 2) and wish we had windows we could open to let more of the fresh air of the Holy Spirit in. The good news is we do.

For thousands of years, God's people have drawn closer to God through a variety of spiritual practices that we call spiritual disciplines. We also call them the "means of grace." Grace is a big word that comes from the Greek word *"charis"* that means "gift." Grace, simply defined, is all the things God gives us, like life, salvation, and simple encouragement by the Holy Spirit. The means of grace are simply the ways this grace finds its way into our lives. These practices are everyday stuff we've always been encouraged to do, like prayer, Bible reading, fasting, and worship. We have treated these disciplines as things that are good for us that we know we should do but somehow don't, like doing sit-ups. Think of these practices instead as windows to your soul that, when opened, allow the fresh wind of the Holy Spirit in. Want the Holy Spirit? Open a window. Try making Bible reading a regular part of your day. Want more Holy Spirit? Open another window. Accompany your reading with prayer. The more time we spend with God, the more windows we open, giving God more access to our lives. Yes, there are times when God just overwhelms us out of the blue, but more often than not, God is looking for our signal that we are ready for God. James 4:8 reads that we are to *"draw near to God and God will draw near to you."* God respects our freedom and privacy and does not wish to be an unwelcome guest. We put out the welcome mat, or open a window through the means of grace. Do not succumb to the temptation that just because you didn't "get a lot" out of your reading or your prayer time wasn't "great" that somehow it didn't work. We read the Written Word through which the Living Word speaks. The Written Word may leave us cold or uninspired, but the Living Word is still whispering into our souls in ways we may not immediately perceive. Is life leaving you feeling stressed, frustrated, angry, or bored? Is your faith getting stuffy and stale? Open a window. Let the breath of God refresh your life! We've already discussed the spiritual disciplines of Bible reading and prayer. Let's explore a few more.

A. Self-Denial

It is natural for us to do what feels good. We don't even think about it. If it feels good...If it tastes good...If it's easy...If it's comfortable...we just naturally go there. But Jesus' work of saving and changing the world will not always be easy, for Jesus or for us. There will be tough choices. There will be struggles. Being a Christ Follower doesn't always feel good. Our assignments don't always taste good. It is not always easy. It's not always comfortable. Remember the wisdom "*What is right is not always easy, and what is easy is not always right.*" For Jesus, doing what's right included surrendering himself to death on cross. It wasn't good for Jesus personally, but it was very good for us who are saved by it. That's what sacrifice is all about, being willing to lose, suffer, or struggle so someone else doesn't have to and that doesn't come naturally to us. We naturally seek out comfort, security and popularity instead.

Discipleship doesn't have to be a life or death struggle, like Jesus, but it is always a choice. Discipleship is all about choices, and whether those choices are big or little, they will either move us closer toward God or farther away. Obedience is impossible without self-denial. As a matter of fact, Jesus states that it is the first thing necessary to be a disciple: "*If any wish to become my followers, let them deny themselves, take up their cross daily, and follow me.*" *(Luke 9:23)* This is a basic skill of being a disciple: We recognize the natural temptation to do what is easy or comfortable, and choose instead to follow our convictions and our call. This is a skill that we can learn and practice through the spiritual exercise of fasting and self-denial. Self-denial is simply giving something up for a period of time for spiritual reasons. Jesus fasted in the desert and the devil tempted Him with comfort, security, and popularity rather than the cross. It was a pretty shrewd move because these are things that naturally feel good to us. These things were also the greatest obstacle to our salvation and the salvation of the entire world. If Jesus was not able or willing to choose the cross over what is easy or comfortable or what feels good, then we are all lost. God the Father's plan fails. Likewise, if we in smaller daily ways are not able to choose obedience over what is easy or comfortable or what feels good, then the Father's plan fails in our lives and God will have to turn to someone else to work through.

Now maybe you are saying to yourself "I'm in trouble then because I have no willpower. If there's a cupcake in the break room at work it's going in my mouth. How exactly am I going make these kinds of decisions for God every day?" We practice. Soldiers train and practice so that when they are in the heat of battle they are ready for it. Sports teams run drills, practice skills, run their plays over and over so that when they are facing a real opponent the struggle feels familiar. We've been here before. We know what to do because we've practiced it. The more we practice, the more naturally it comes to us. The spiritual disciplines of fasting, self-denial and self-control are ways to practice these daily choices with God in safety BEFORE we are facing the same crafty opponent that tempted Jesus in the desert. Through these spiritual exercises our willpower, our faith, our self-discipline, our self-control get stronger and we can endure the temptations better. And most importantly, we get better at relying on God's power that is made perfect in our weakness.

So the last question would have to be "How do I fast? What do I do?" Well, it's quite simple really. If you are abstaining from food, start small. Replace one meal with prayer and see how you do. Then maybe two meals. As was the practice in Jesus' day, begin the day with prayer, instead of breakfast, then pause in the middle of the day for more prayer instead of lunch, then finish the day with prayer and dinner. Some people choose to do this one day a week, others two days a week. There are no rules about when or how often to do this, just don't do it every day. Never EVER even consider something like forty days. This is a supernatural fast. We would suffer starvation if we ever tried it. Fasting is not about damaging ourselves, it is about focus. We give up something normal in order to focus more on God, which is why it doesn't have to be food. It can be any normal thing in our lives that would cause us to squirm or struggle without it. That's good because fasting from food is not for everyone. Some medications or medical conditions make it dangerous to fast, so check in with your doctor. Also remember why we fast. It's not about cutting calories or losing weight. It's not about vanity or looking good. It's not about proving how fantastic we are by not giving in to temptations. It is for spiritual reasons to focus on God and what God wants, rather than on what we want. We practice making uncomfortable choices by choosing to refrain from something that is perfectly acceptable. We learn how to depend on God.

B. Self-Examination

The Ancient Greek philosopher Socrates once said "*The unexamined life is not worth living.*" It is barreling through life with no idea where we are going and without ever stopping to see where we've been. It is never learning from our mistakes, never changing direction, and never setting a purposeful course for our life. For Socrates, the purpose of life was personal and spiritual growth. This requires a life lived on purpose guided by reflection and self-examination. We move forward while making constant course corrections. The alternative is either the chaotic crash and burn of trial and error or the brain dead fog of living on autopilot. The unexamined life is not worth living. As followers of Jesus, we couldn't agree more. Let's take a closer look at "Self-Examination."

When you are trying to lose weight, it is important to step on a scale now and then to know how you are doing. People with diabetes check their blood sugar several times a day and adjust their food intake accordingly. Likewise, we must examine our own lives and check in on our progress as disciples. We have spoken earlier about the Prayer of Examen where at bedtime we look back over our day and review where God was active in our lives. We can use other yardsticks to test our progress then adjust our lives accordingly. Here are several helpful ways to look in the mirror:

1. The Ten Commandments

It can be as simple as reading through the Ten Commandments and taking note of which you have kept faithfully and which you have broken. Think about why you have let these things happen. What kinds of things are going on in your life that seem to encourage you to let your guard down? Do you notice any patterns? What can you change to do better in the future? Confess your sins and seek forgiveness. Ask the Holy Spirit to warn you when you are going astray.

2. The Beatitudes

Read through the Beatitudes (Matthew 5:2-12) and ask yourself if any of these qualities are a reflection of who you are. These things are considered blessings because they are so compatible with the coming Kingdom of God. We all want to go to Heaven, but will we fit in when we get there? Ask yourself: Am I peace maker? Do I hunger and thirst for righteousness? Be honest with yourself. Ask God to reveal this to you. How might you choose to live in the future to reflect the Beatitudes. This is a work of the Holy Spirit to wear away our rough edges and develop these God-pleasing kingdom qualities in us.

3. The Sermon on the Mount

In Matthew, chapters 5-7, Jesus describes in vivid detail what life looks like for those who choose to follow Him into the coming Kingdom of God. He holds nothing back and tells it like it is. This sermon both inspires and challenges us. How faithful are we to these teachings? How well do we reflect the character and example of Jesus in everything we do, say, and think? Take time to read this sermon verse by verse and reflect upon your life. Ask God to open your eyes. Ask for forgiveness. Commit to change. Ask for grace.

4. The Fruits of the Spirit

In Galatians 5:22-23, Paul listed evidence of the Holy Spirit's work in our lives. Just like a healthy fruit tree bears good fruit, a growing life begins to make the world better by adding more love, joy, peace, patience, kindness, goodness, faithfulness, gentleness, and self-control. From week to week, ask yourself "Am I more loving? More patient? More kind? More self-controlled?" Welcome the Holy Spirit to accomplish this in you.

5. The 5x5 Daily Questions

Another discipline we can employ is by asking ourselves a Daily Question based on our 5x5 Framework of Undeniable Truths and Disciplines of Jesus::

1. How did I deepen my love relationship with God this week?
2. How am I learning to follow Jesus? With whom?
3. How am I generously sharing what I have with God and with others?
4. How am I serving God by serving others?
5. Who am I encouraging to take their next step closer to God? What is my next step closer to God?
6. Am I taking full responsibility for my life? My choices? My mistakes?
7. Am I sharing the planet with others in a way that pleases God and helps others?
8. Am I accepting the consequences of my choices and accepting the cost of my decisions?
9. Am I struggling against the unfairness of life in a way that is keeping me from following Jesus?
10. Am I paying the proper attention to my life, relationships and faith to keep them healthy?
11. Because life is short, am I living as one who is prepared to die?

3. The Servant's Heart: G.H.O.S.T.S.

As we will read in a later section, to have a servant's heart, like Jesus, we will grow in six qualities. They are:

GRACE: Treating others better than they deserve.
HUMILITY: Considering others as more important than ourselves.
OBEDIENCE: Acting according to the orders and instructions of those in
authority over us.
SACRIFICE: Attending to the needs of others instead of our own.
TRUST: The risks we take when we decide the authority over us is reliable
SUBMISSION: Recognizing and yielding to authority of another over us.

We can examine our levels of grace, humility, obedience, sacrifice, trust, and submission in our daily dealings with God and other people.

C. Self-Study

Have you ever seen the TV game show "The Newlywed Game"? Newlyweds predict how their spouses will answer a variety of questions to reveal how well they know each other. Hilarity ensues when their answers do not match. It is no laughing matter though when we are not on the same page with God. Do we know enough about God to predict how God would react to something unexpected? Maybe you remember the "WWJD" bracelets that ask the question "What would Jesus do?" Like the "Newlywed Game," we have to know Jesus to predict what he would do. This is why we study. In 5x5, we seek to gain holy knowledge and holy know-how. This is "loving God with all of our mind" as well as our heart, soul, and strength.

1. We Study the Bible.

We have already spoken above about the Bible. I won't repeat it here other than to remind you that our personal efforts to study and understand the Bible are encounters with God. We strengthen the relationship by getting know more about who God is and what God has been doing.

2. We Study Theology.

Just as biology is the study of life, theology is the study of God. It takes the scripture stories, commandments, warnings and promises of God and puts them under the microscope to explain who God is. When we say that God is forgiving or God is just, we are making a statement about the character and personality of God. Some theology is dense, abstract and difficult to read, written by scholars and deep thinkers. There is benefit in their work of studying and explaining God, but theology need not be scholarly and hard to understand. We all study theology as we begin to learn how to understand and explain God to others.

3. We Study Christian Living.

Because you are reading these words right now, you are studying the Christian life. As we become more familiar with God, we become more familiar with living a life that pleases God. We want to live in such a way that we can help change lives and make the world better. Following Jesus is a way of life that is taught and we have a lot to learn from our brothers and sisters in Christ who have come before us.

D. Reading as a Means of Grace

There are plenty of other things to read that draw us closer to God than just the Bible. Anything that inspires us and keeps our thoughts on God can be a means of grace. Christian fiction is a growing genre, but any good literature that brings the mind back to God and the meaning of life can deepen our love for God. Spiritual biographies can also shine a lot of light on the way God works in our lives. When I was younger, I stumbled upon a book about George Muller who ran an orphanage in England on prayer and not much else. As a Methodist I enjoy reading about the ministry of John and Charles Wesley and am encouraged in my ministry of helping to change lives and make the world a better place. I've grown much deeper in my sense of call by reading the stories of great heroes of the faith like Dietrich Bonhoeffer, Archbishop Oscar Romero, and Rev. Dr. Martin Luther King, Jr. I read devotional books like "My Utmost for His Highest" by Oswald Chambers, the writings of Henri Nouwen and Richard Foster, collections of sermons, and even poetry. I enjoy C.S. Lewis and am blessed by "The Chronicles of Narnia" as much as "The Screwtape Letters" and "Mere Christianity." There is no shortage of good books to read to keep us connected to God.

E. Media as a Means of Grace

We live in a digital age which means there are endless sources of inspiration to build our faith. There is no way to catalogue here every kind of media that you can turn to other than books and the Bible. I spend a lot of time on the internet feeding my faith. I find helpful blogs and websites, listen to some excellent teachers, join in some dynamic worship services, and watch all kinds of videos. I am as moved by watching a video of the International Justice Mission combating human trafficking as I am cheered by watching "Veggie Tales". If it feeds your faith it is a means of grace. If it is a means of grace, it is an encounter with God.

F. Music as a Means of Grace

I can't imagine worship without music. I love to sing and I'm getting better on guitar. Music is a gift from God that stirs us deep inside. Even in my quiet time I like to listen to music, sing some favorite hymns and songs, and make music on my guitar. Again, if it feeds your faith it is a means of grace. If it is a means of grace, it is an encounter with God.

IV. WORSHIP SERVICES

Sometimes I think I worship too much. The church I serve as pastor offers four worship services at two different campuses. I worship on Saturday evening. I worship twice, sometimes three times on Sunday morning. I lead services at local nursing homes and speak regularly at seasonal luncheons and prayer breakfasts. Recently, I only had one service to lead at 10:45 am. One! I was up at the regular time. I had breakfast, was on my second cup of coffee, and still had time to look over the sermon one more time. I slipped easily into prayer while swinging gently on the patio swing in my back yard. I enjoyed the leisure of just dwelling quietly with God. That's when it hit me: I actually don't worship enough. I may attend too many worship services throughout the course of a month, but that has become work, not worship. Jesus modeled for us the disciplines of worship which is everything we do to deepen our love relationship with God. Jesus spent time alone before the sun came up far from the pressing crowds. He spent time on the mountain top. He did whatever He needed to do to connect with his Father before the crowds gathered. When worship becomes work…When we put more attention on gathering up all the details and putting on a smooth show than on deepening our love relationship with God, we are missing out on something beautiful. Leave it to human beings to turn something beautiful into something complicated. How about you? Do you feel closer to God when leave a worship service? By all means worship as much as you can! Deepen your love relationship with God, no matter what it takes!

When I compare the way Jesus connected to His Heavenly Father to the average worship service, worship feels too much like a show. It really doesn't matter whether it is a contemporary worship service or traditional. We are either putting on a classical music concert or a rock show. The room is set up as an auditorium with rows of seats facing a stage. Worshippers feel like an audience that comes to watch and be moved, excited, taught, or inspired. Because it is passive, our experience of God depends largely on how well the performers perform. Musicians must be professional quality. Preachers must be exceptional. The event must be flawless or it fails to impress and falls flat. This appealed to me early in my ministry and seemed to be a large part of my initial sense of call. I studied theater in college and worked professionally as an actor and stage manager. I thought my professional skills of showmanship were a perfect match to this calling. But worship was never meant to be a show. Worship is not a performance that turns us all into Siskel and Ebert giving the choir and the pastor thumbs up or thumbs down for this week's attempt. We were never invited by God to join together in worship to become critics or passive members of the audience waiting to be "fed," entertained, or inspired. Let's picture our worship in a very different way to understand why we are there and how it draws us closer to God. Imagine a child's birthday party. We give gifts to the guest of honor. We tells stories about the guest of honor. We sing songs to the guest of honor. We enjoy spending time together with the guest of honor. We light and put out candles and eat together. We may not know everyone at the party, but everyone at the party knows the guest of honor.

Worship should be more like that child's party. God is the Guest of Honor when we gather for worship. It is poor form to attend someone's birthday party asking "what's in it for me?" Nothing, really. The party isn't for us. We are throwing this party for someone else: the Guest of Honor. We give gifts to the Guest of Honor. We tell stories about the Guest of Honor. We sing songs to our Guest of Honor. We laugh and enjoy spending time together with the Guest of Honor. We light and put out candles and eat together. We may not know everyone at the party, but everyone at the party knows the Guest of Honor. How would it change the way you worship next weekend if you came prepared to use every part of the service as a way to say "I love you, Lord?" What if every song were sung to God rather than about God? What if every sermon and scripture were stories about how fantastic God really is? What if every offering were given with love, anxious to see the smile on God's face when the gifts are opened? What if we were eager to meet God's other friends and enjoy their company, too? Too often our worship feels more like a funeral than a party. We do not gather to ask "who died?" but to celebrate that Jesus is alive! That doesn't mean that we have to wear a lampshade on our heads, but it does mean that the message can be more than a dry academic lecture and that laughter is not forbidden. It is OK to feel something real in worship, because God is not fake.

Unless you are a pastor, choir director, or worship leader in your local church, there is very little you may be able to do to change what actually happens in a worship service. But remember, we are responsible for ourselves and we can always change the way we approach the experience. Seek God. Spend time in the service becoming aware of God's presence around you. Be aware of God in everything you say, sing, pray, or give. Ask God to speak through the music you are listening to. Ask God to speak through the person reading the scriptures, the person preaching, and the person praying out loud. Ask God to move throughout the room and inspire all in attendance. If you seek God in all things, you will be blessed in even the most poorly led time of worship.

How to Listen to a Sermon

As a pastor who preaches, I can tell when people are following with me or not. I've had people sitting attentively on the edge of their seat, hanging eagerly on every word. I've had people fall asleep and snore louder than I was speaking. I remind myself that the experience of listening to the sermon will have less to do with me than the Holy Spirit. Before preaching, I often pray: "Lord, speak this day either through me or in spite of me. Move me out of the way if you need to. We want to hear your Voice and know your will for us, so we can live it out with your grace." I trust that, as long as the listener has intentionally placed themselves in God's care during the sermon, God will provide whatever gift they need most. For some people, I guess they needed twenty more minutes of sleep! I know that daydreams during sermons are often conversations with Holy Spirit. Many times, something will be said in a sermon that catches our attention and we start thinking about that idea while the preacher moves on to the next thought. That daydream may be the most important gift of the day. I know this happens because I regularly greet people after worship who thank me profusely for teaching on something I never mentioned out loud. I used to be confused by that, checking my notes to see if I forgot something. I never said anything about it, but evidently the Holy Spirit said plenty about it when the two went on a daydream together during the sermon. Preaching, like discipleship, is a team effort. It is a partnership of the preacher, the people, and God. We all bring something to the experience and make it a greater blessing than we are capable of on our own. There are times when a preacher is so eloquent, charming, and even funny that our attention can be drawn to what a good speaker he or she is rather than toward the presence of God. Likewise, even a poorly skilled preacher can offer an idea worth daydreaming about with the Holy Spirit. Seek God above all else. Remember Jesus told us to seek and we shall find. Seek God, the Guest of Honor, and no weak preacher, misspelled bulletin, leaking ceiling, or out of tune choir can ever get in the way of the spiritual gift God wants to give.

V. SABBATH KEEPING

In Egypt there was no "down time," no breaks, and no days off for the people of Israel. Why? Because they were slaves to pharaoh who owned them like cattle. Pharaoh decided that their only purpose in life should be to work, make bricks, build pyramids, and die. Pharaoh thought there were far too many Israelites in Egypt and his whole plan was to kill them off through grinding, unending, back-breaking labor. The plan was not about constructing a better empire. It was about destroying the Children of Abraham. That's the hardest part of being a slave. Your destiny is in the hands of the one who owns you, and if the one who owns you is bent on your destruction, your life will be stressful, tiring, painful, and short.

I write as an American Christian in the twenty-first century and find it ironic that I live in one of the freest nations on earth, where slavery has been outlawed for over 130 years and yet we insist on treating ourselves like slaves. As a nation we are stressed, worn out, sleep deprived, stretched thin, and ready to break. It is not a coincidence that a recent study concluded that a high number of Americans fall asleep at work (or school) every day because they aren't getting enough sleep at night. Another study concludes that a lack of sleep makes it harder to keep emotions under control. Maybe that's why the roads are filled with too many people, with too much to do and not enough time to do it who end up shooting at each other over a parking space. Maybe that's also why families and marriages are fraying and falling apart because we are too tired and too busy to deal with each other before there is a major problem. Another study concludes that too little sleep throws our metabolism out of whack and contributes to obesity.

Sooner or later we wake up in the middle of the madness and ask ourselves "Why am I doing this?" We resent the endless tiring grind that is our life. We begin to blame our boss for the extra work and deadlines. We blame our kids for having one more soccer practice we have to run them to. We blame our church for constantly asking for more money and time that we don't have to give. We feel guilty when we are invited to serve in ministry, to read the Bible and to pray because we have no idea where to find the time for it. Our life has no meaning anymore and we just want to stop the ride and get off, but there is no one to blame, is there? We are not slaves. No one owns us. We are free to be the masters of our own destiny which means we have chosen to do this to ourselves. Evidently, we have no clue who our real Master is.

After God freed Israel from slavery God taught the people something very important:

"I am your God and you will be my People. You are MY people. Your destiny is now in My hands, so you should know a few things about Me. I know a thing or two about hard work, too. I created all that you see. I did all of this in six days, but on the seventh day, I rested. I did not rest because I was tired. I did not rest because I was exhausted. I did not rest because I was worn out. I am not limited in my strength or limited in my power. I rested because I chose to rest. I decided that my labors were enough and I chose to STOP. My Children Israel, I am your Master now, not pharaoh. I am not bent on your destruction. I wish to preserve your life. You are not unlimited in strength and power. You will grow tired. You will fall exhausted. You will wear out and break. Your ambition will drive you on, working harder without a rest. As your Master, I say that your labors are enough. I choose to stop. You shall work for six days, but on the seventh day you will rest. Your family will rest. Your animals will rest. Even your servants and employees will rest, for they are not your slaves either. You shall observe the Sabbath Day and keep it holy."

The traditional Jewish Sabbath, or day of rest, was from sundown Friday to sundown Saturday. It is to be an entire day off with nowhere to go and nothing to do. It was a bold move by God, stating in the clearest terms possible that we are not slaves. We are not slaves to pharaoh, our bosses, our work, our activities or even our ministries for God. Our schedule has no power over us. We have power over our schedules. This power has been granted to us by God who is our true Master. The word "Sabbath" conjures up images of the Ten Commandments and reserving a special day of rest. While that will be part of our discussion, we are considering Sabbath-keeping as the larger discipline of carving out time from our daily life for time alone with God. The vast majority of disciples beginning 5x5 zero in on their failure to consistently make time for God as the first and most pressing thing they want to address as followers of Jesus. *The world does not give us Sabbath. We must take it.* You might want to highlight that because it is crucial. Too many of us take time with God only when it is convenient AND when we feel like it. Sometimes we feel like it, but it isn't convenient. Sometimes it is convenient but we just don't feel like it. Imagine trying to keep a marriage healthy when we never spend any time together. We are nourishing a love relationship with God that is vital and personal...and that takes time. It also takes self-discipline and self-control. Remember, you are responsible for yourself. You alone are responsible for your schedule. Make the time. Take the time. Protect the time. Here are several ways to carve out and protect our time with God:

A. Daily Quiet Time
B. Weekly Day of Rest
C. Retreat
D. Strategies
E. Practicing the Presence of God

A. Daily Quiet Time
Carving out some quiet time every day is not easy for everyone but it can be done. It helps to develop some habits and routines that work for you. Morning people are fresh early in the day and might be sleepy in the

afternoon. Night owls may have a hard time praying early in the day, but may find vital time with God late at night. It is important to choose a time that meshes with the rest of your schedule and that allows you to be at your best with God. The amount of time and what you do with that time are entirely up to you and God. Just remember that this daily time is an encounter with God and regular contact makes us more sensitive to God's voice and leading.

B. Weekly Day of Rest

While prayer and devotion are a part of every day, the Sabbath day of rest is not a day of enforced devotion. In Exodus God explains that the day of rest is an answer to pharaoh's slavery. Slaves work around the clock. Slaves never get a day off or vacation. As children of God, we are not slaves to anyone or anything. We are not slaves to our jobs or our bosses. In the ancient world, it was radical and counter-cultural to take a day off. God rested on the seventh day of Creation and we follow God's lead. Sabbath is about rest, taking a break, kicking back, enjoying some time and catching our breath. We are restored, refreshed and rejuvenated by this time and are able to go back to work even harder the next day. This rest comes in many forms.

1. Physical Rest

This one is easy. Stretch out on the hammock and take a nap. Have a day with no deadlines, no to-do lists, and no plans. Be lazy. Sleep in. Relax. Our body recovers when we rest. Give your body a chance to catch up.

2. Active Rest

Snoozing is not the only way rest up. There is nothing wrong with having some fun. Go for a hike. Take a bike ride. Go to a ball game or a movie. Challenge your kids to a game of Monopoly. Play in the dirt and plant some flowers. The ancient Israelites took the Sabbath command to refrain from work very seriously and wrote elaborate rules as to what kind of physical activity was permitted on the Sabbath and what was not. No disrespect is intended to our observant Jewish brothers and sisters but this Sabbath looks more like a prison sentence than a vacation. The idea of this day is to be refreshed and renewed. Recreation is a way many of us shake off the cares of the week. Recreation is a good word. It doesn't just mean a hobby or past time. But one well-placed hyphen and we find "re-creation" or being made new.

There is a lot of debate about whether Sunday (The Lord's Day) is THE Sabbath day. The Jewish Sabbath (capital "S") is always sundown Friday to sundown Saturday. Sunday in the ancient world was like Monday is to us today. It was the first day of the week and it was a work day. The old blue laws which closed businesses on Sunday were a well-intentioned attempt to make it more convenient to take the day off. I will never forget an interesting encounter I had on my way to worship as pastor. My car was running on fumes so I stopped on my way to church to fill up. A gentleman from my congregation was filling up his tank at the next pump, so I nodded and said good morning. After worship he came up to me embarrassed and apologized for pumping gas on Sunday. I smiled and reminded him what I had been doing when we saw each other! He was truly worried that he had done something wrong by "working" on the Lord's Day. It was sad. In the first century, everyone went to work on the Lord's Day and worship was in the evening. Jesus said "*We were not made for the Sabbath. The Sabbath was made for us.*"

3. Spiritual Rest

And yes, sometimes having a lighter day with no schedule is just what we need to linger in prayer with God longer. I can leisurely read more scripture. I can sit in meditative silence longer. I can curl up on God's lap and fall asleep in God's arms. Relax and enjoy!

C. Retreat

A retreat is an extended time away from our everyday life to draw closer to God. It can be as simple as going camping in the woods for a weekend to spending time at a specialized retreat center. What you do with that time away depends on you and what you feel you need. It can help to have a plan in mind before you slip away. Here are some common ways of using retreat time:

1. Silent Retreat

It's as simple as it sounds. Stop talking and spend time listening to God. You may want to practice Contemplative Prayer, seeking the Holy Spirit in the silence within. The idea is to listen and seek peace.

2. Prayer Retreat

Most of our prayers are too short. Either we share the same handful of concerns or we don't listen for God's reply. Either way, we can use some real conversation with God. When our lives feel dry and our faith is weak, soaking in prayer can rejuvenate us and our love relationship with God.

3. Study Retreat

Perhaps there is a book we've been wanting to read or we want to feast on God's Word rather than snack. It is a great gift we can give to ourselves to immerse ourselves in scripture or read deeply to understand some facet of our life with God.

4. Discernment Retreat

When we have something we need to figure out or an important decision we need to make, time away to focus and think can help us hear God guiding us toward the right decision. Discernment can be found throughout all of these other methods combined.

5. Group Retreat

Sometimes we want to get away with some fellow disciples and grow together. The group can decide to engage in a variety of things from prayer, to study, to worship, to holy conversation. A group retreat may do more than draw us closer to God. It can strengthen our friendships with each other as well.

D. Sabbath Strategies

As we said before, we sometimes have a hard time making our quiet times a priority. The world will not give us this time with God. We must take it. Here are some strategies you can try if willpower isn't your strong suit.

1. The Unquestionable Calendar

Sometimes people won't leave us alone. We can tell them "I'm sorry, I can't right now. I need my quiet time with God." Folks don't really respect that. Do you know what they do respect? Your calendar. For someone reason, if I say "I'm sorry I have an appointment at that time. I'm not able to help you then," people accept that without question. The calendar seems to be the one unquestionable way to set your priorities. Place your daily quiet times, weekly days of rest, and retreats on your calendar as unbreakable appointments. The calendar works as a placeholder for these encounters with God and a handy reminder to you. Then when someone asks you to help them move a refrigerator at nine o'clock (and who can really turn that sweet temptation down?) you can simply reply, "I'm sorry, my schedule won't permit that." You don't need to tell anyone what you will be doing at nine o'clock. It is none of their business. You are responsible for yourself and owe no one excuses or explanations for how you choose to spend the time you have, especially when you choose to spend that time with God.

2. The "Do Nothing" Principle

Even with our "prayer appointments" on our daily calendar, it is no guarantee that we will actually pray. It can be hard to force ourselves and the whole thing falls apart. That's where The "Do Nothing" Principle comes in. It is quite simple, yet very powerful. If I have committed to twenty minutes in prayer, then I sit down for twenty minutes. I don't have to pray if I don't want to, but I can't do anything else until the twenty minutes is up. I have to sit there and do nothing. I will either have good peaceful rest doing nothing, or I will get restless and start to pray in order to have something to do. There is an Aesop's Fable about a contest between the wind and the sun to determine who was strongest. It was agreed that whoever could make the man down below take off his coat was the strongest. The wind blew and tried to strip the coat right off the man's back. But the harder it blew, the tighter the man wrapped the coat around himself. The sun smiled warmly at the man and as the temperature rose the now sweating man took off his coat. The wind tried to make him take off the coat. The sun made him want to. That is the genius of this principle. The harder we try to force ourselves to do something, the harder we resist. But through the boredom of sitting with nothing to do, we want something to do. Prayer now looks pretty interesting compared to being stuck with nothing. Give it a try.

3. The Prayer Room

Jesus taught us to find a private place to hide from the world and pray. *"But you, when you pray, enter into your closet and lock your door, and pray to your father who is in secret, and your Father who sees in secret will reward you in public."* (Matthew 6:6). You may not need to literally go sit in your closet, but many find it helpful to have a specific place to pray and study. Perhaps it is a specific room, a chair, a table. Maybe it is in a corner of your garage or laundry room. But it is a designated place where prayer happens. Perhaps you have stocked your place with the things you need to get closer to God, like a Bible, a notebook to write things down, or your journal. Don't think of it as a place of comfort or rest. This is not just a place to sit on God's lap and rest. This is also your prayer workshop where you and God get things done.

4. Accountability

Sometimes we need someone to answer to in order to make sure we are following through. If we won't take our quiet times faithfully on our own then we need the accountability of someone else who will not give us permission to fail.

E. Practicing the Presence of God

Brother Lawrence served as a monk in the Carmelite Monastery in Paris in the latter part of the seventeenth century. Lawrence was not educated and so was unable to work as a cleric reading and copying scripture. He was employed in the kitchen and his meal preparation schedule made it impossible for him to take part in the prayer and worship services. If you've ever had to work on Sundays, you know how cut off from God we can feel when we are not able to worship with others. Lawrence decided that since God is everywhere, he could experience God just as easily in the kitchen as he could in the sanctuary. He decided to focus on God's Presence with him at all times. He decided to talk with God in an ongoing conversation throughout the day. He would honor God through his daily work. If he was peeling potatoes, he would peel them as a service to God. If he was stirring the stew, he would stir it to bring honor and glory to God. He would treat everyone with the love and patience shown to him by God.

Brother Lawrence's simple spirituality was practical, elevating the menial and mundane obligations of life to holiness. Our daily work becomes our ministry. Our workplace becomes our sanctuary. Lawrence did not struggle to set aside quiet time with God. God was a welcome participant in every moment of his life. We can "practice the presence of God" too. Just make God a part of everything you do. We can imagine God standing next to us, sitting in an empty chair across the table, or standing somewhere in the room. I used to imagine God sitting in the comfy chair in my office or perched on top of my bookshelf. I sometimes ask God things out loud as if there were someone else in the room. It sounds a bit odd at first, but God is in the room. God is with us. God is listening, guiding, helping all the time. Whatever work I'm doing I do for God. When I was little, my grandfather would invite me into his workshop when he was fixing the tractor or sharpening mower blades. He would ask me to help him. I really didn't offer much help, but he included me in what he was doing so we could spend time together. When we practice the presence of God we are welcoming God into our workshop so we can spend time together.

5
THE DISCIPLINES OF LEARNING

The Savior's Apprentice

God the Father poured grace into the lives of a group of fishermen and tax collectors. There was so much they didn't know. Jesus was their Leader, their Teacher, their Rabbi. He was the one who would explain to them the mysteries of God. He would open their eyes to the big picture of how the world really was and what the world was destined to become. He would explain it through the scriptures, the Law and the prophets. He would explain it through clever stories we call parables. He also taught them that they had a part to play in God's Plan for the world. They listened carefully to everything Jesus said. They watched carefully everything Jesus did. They shadowed Jesus as He travelled from town to town, teaching and healing those who were sick. They helped Him feed the hungry by passing out the loaves and fish. But the day finally came when the only way they could keep learning was to go out and serve on their own. That's how an apprenticeship works:

I teach, You listen.
I do, You watch.
We do together.
You do, I watch and applaud.

The disciples carefully watched everything Jesus did. They shadowed Jesus as He travelled from town to town, teaching and healing those who were sick. Then, they helped Him feed the hungry by passing out the loaves and fish. They served together with Jesus, side by side. But the day finally came when the only way they could keep learning was to go out and serve on their own, but Jesus kept an eye on them, offering guidance, answering questions, and celebrating their victories. He was preparing them for the day they truly would serve without Him, continuing His work of sharing the Kingdom after Jesus returned to His Father in Heaven. We, as disciples, learn to follow Jesus and take our place in God's Plan the same way.

A disciple is an apprentice – someone who is learning from Jesus how to live the life He wants us to live. Unless we are apprenticed to Jesus we cannot live out the mission and calling that Jesus gave us. We have to be disciples if we want to make disciples. We can't bring others to a place of being apprenticed to Jesus if we ourselves aren't apprenticed to Jesus. But if we are disciples of Jesus, progressively becoming like Him in thought, word, and actions, we will live out our calling. The question we haven't answered is, "So what do we actually do if we want to be disciples of Jesus?" After all, being a disciple of Jesus has got to be more than a vague spiritual feeling. Being a disciple has to be more than just trying harder. As shared earlier, Bill Hull describes how Jesus transformed these raw recruits into mature disciples. According to Hull, these are the five hallmarks of a disciple in training:

1. A disciple submits to a teacher who teaches how to follow Jesus.
2. A disciple learns the words of Jesus.
3. A disciple learns Jesus' way of ministry.
4. A disciple imitates Jesus' life and character.
5. A disciple finds and teaches other disciples to follow Jesus.

Being apprenticed to Jesus is a regular pattern of everyday life. We take His direction, doing things Jesus' way. We obey His commands and instructions, and follow His example. We do what Jesus did...and Jesus did a lot of things:

Jesus fed hungry people.
Jesus comforted hurting people.
Jesus welcomed children.
Jesus never allowed violence.
Jesus confronted religious hypocrisy.
Jesus put kindness and compassion above all else.
Jesus stayed in constant contact with the Father through prayer.
Jesus taught others to pray.
Jesus talked with an outcast, foreign woman.
Jesus spent time talking with enemies as well as with friends.
Jesus forgave those who harmed Him.
Jesus obeyed the Father's will even when it hurt.
Jesus is patient with the ignorant.

Jesus met people where they were.
Jesus spoke truth to those in power to defend those who had no power.
Jesus trusted the Father despite His fear.
Jesus treats us better than we deserve.
Jesus got His hands dirty touching the poor and the ill.
Jesus accepted suffering and struggle as part of God's work.
Jesus challenges us to change.
Jesus taught others to follow God.
Jesus healed the sick.
Jesus comforted the broken hearted.
Jesus resisted temptation.
Jesus invited others to join Him in His ministry.
Jesus shared the good news with as many people as possible.
Jesus kept moving around.
Jesus gave to the poor and needy.
Jesus fasted.
Jesus was baptized.
Jesus knew the Father's purpose for his life.
Jesus recognized and complimented people for their faith.
Jesus confronted and commanded demons.
Jesus forgave sins.
Jesus accepted even the most unacceptable people.
Jesus forgave the unforgivable.

This goes much deeper than just doing what we see Jesus doing. A parrot can mimic speech, but it doesn't know what it is saying. We can simply mimic the actions of Jesus and it will be of great benefit to the world, but Jesus is looking for more than that. We are not parrots or robots. We are disciples who love God with all our heart, MIND, soul, and strength. We can be smart about the things of God and make some important decisions in situations Jesus never mentioned. By imitating the life of Jesus, and thanks to the Holy Spirit, we develop the character and the mind of Christ. That means we begin to think like Jesus thinks and that's good, because we will find ourselves in all kinds of situations that Jesus never faced. How would Jesus respond to nuclear weapons, Internet pornography or global terrorism? There are no stories in the gospels where Jesus deals directly with these things, so there are no concrete teachings for us to follow. How do we know what to do?

This is where character comes in. Jesus healed sick people because Jesus is compassionate. Jesus focused so intently on people who are poor, rejected, and unpopular because He knew the poor and vulnerable have a special place in the heart of God. Jesus forgave the guys who pounded nails into his hands and feet and teaches us to turn the other cheek and love our enemies because Jesus is merciful. Jesus refused violence and insisted on making peace because Jesus believed that offering salvation was more important than punishing and humiliating people for their sins and mistakes. He shared everything He had with anyone who needed it because He was generous. Not only that, He was meticulously unselfish, seeing a fascination with pleasing ourselves as the source of all sin. These qualities explain a lot of the decisions Jesus made. The better we understand and develop a Christ-like character that is shaped by Christ-like values, the easier it becomes to confidently respond with Christ-like clarity to the situations that are shrouded in shades of grey. Because Jesus is compassionate, we will choose to make time for people who are struggling and help them any way we can. Because Jesus refused violence, we will choose to forgive our enemies and love them instead of retaliate. Because Jesus valued and defended the poor and powerless, the poor will be a central concern in our lives and ministry together. But these choices do not come naturally to us. They must be learned, practiced, and encouraged in others. We learn it best the way the Twelve learned it: in a group of fellow disciples led by a mature teacher.

Discipleship Is a Team Sport

We live in an age of self service. If you plan it right, you could take care of almost everything in your life without having to deal with another human being face to face. You can work from home via the Internet. No more having to deal with other people at the office. You can pump your own gas at the gas station then pay at the pump so you don't have to talk to a cashier. You can purchase most things online and have it delivered right to your house. You can even bag your own groceries at the self-checkout line. If we are dealing with stress and anxiety we visit the self-help section of the local bookstore. We may have to visit the doctor face to face when we are ill, but we don't have to go to the pharmacy to have our prescription filled. It can be sent through the mail. "DIY: Do It Yourself." That's us. We may be more comfortable with DIY, but we are not created to face the uncertainties of this life alone. Sometimes, we need others to accomplish what we never could on our own. People trying to break the power of addiction over their lives have greater success in recovery when they join a group like Alcoholics Anonymous or Celebrate Recovery. Many people enjoy much greater success losing weight when they join a group like Weight Watchers. Athletes, even at the top of their game, rely on a team of coaches and trainers to keep them at their best. World renowned opera singers never outgrow the need to work with a vocal coach. Why, then, would we ever think that we can break our addiction to sin and grow to full maturity as disciples of Jesus Christ without the help and support of others?

The most important work of our new lives is done for us by Jesus. By His death and resurrection our past is buried, our sins are forgiven and we are reborn into a brand new eternal life. The rest of this work is accomplished in us by the Holy Spirit. Our heart begins to crave the holiness of God as we lose our taste for the old sins and temptations. The Spirit changes us from the inside out to become more and more like Christ. But, Jesus won't save us against our will. The Spirit won't transform us against our will. We have a part to play. Too often, when things get hard, or the novelty of salvation wears off, we lose interest and quit. That's when we really need somebody else. Addicts in recovery have a sponsor who they call when they need help and are tempted to drink. Athletes lift weights in the weight room with a spotter who keeps them from getting hurt by overdoing it and keeps them from giving up to soon by pushing and encouraging them. God knows that we are weak. God knows that we can be distracted. God knows that we need to pace ourselves. God knows that we often give up too easily. We need someone to turn to when we are feeling weak. We need someone to turn to when we are tempted to stray from God. We need someone to help us when we are getting lazy and start giving up. We need someone to push us when we lose the fire of our passion for God. The devil will throw everything in his arsenal at us to tear us away from God. We all need someone to watch our back and refuse to let us go without a fight. That is why God created the Church because "Discipleship is a team sport."

But not everything we do as a church provides this kind of help and protection. Take worship for example. We gather into the sanctuary with 200 other people, maybe we know some of them, maybe we don't. But because we are so busy worshiping, we can't really connect with each other personally or talk one on one. That is why many healthy churches are made up of small groups of 8-15 people who can talk, pray together, study and learn together in ways that are impossible in worship. It can be argued very easily that the Church of Jesus Christ was born as a small group when our savior invited twelve people to travel with Him, learn with Him, serve with Him and grow with Him. That small group of twelve disciples has remained the basic building block of the Kingdom of God ever since. In the early Church, recorded in Acts and the letters of Paul, Peter, James and John, individual churches were small groups that met in each other's homes. They were very personal, and met regularly to comfort each other, encourage each other, challenge each other, and to watch over each other. They were involved in each other's lives to keep moving closer to God together. Just like the first twelve disciples, we continue to meet together in small groups to allow God to shape us into obedient servants who are equipped to help

God change our world. Together we learn and practice the obedient life of a disciple. In small groups, we learn to love and care for each other through accountability and caring for each other's needs. Like addicts and athletes, we need spotters and sponsors. We need someone to encourage us, push us, and comfort us. We also need someone who will challenge us, and confront us with the hard truth when we cross the line or begin to stray. Sometimes we'd rather just do it on our own. That is why we all need someone to watch our backs and refuse to let us go without a fight. Remember: "Discipleship is a team sport."

As we gather in small groups to learn to follow Jesus together, like Jesus' first disciples, we will practice living out this new life together in many ways. We call them "The Disciplines of Learning":

I. Group Prayer
II. Group Study
III. Group Service
IV. Mutual Care
V. Mutual Accountability

I. Group Prayer
Jesus' disciples admired His prayer life. They asked Him one day to teach them how to pray. The result was what we now call the Lord's Prayer. The early Church spent much time together in prayer, sometimes praying all through the night. Prayer has always been a major part of our life and work together as the Church. As disciples, we pray together. Prayer is a basic skill in deepening our love relationship with God and binds us closer together as God's followers. But it is more than that. We pray for each other and with each other. A group that learns to follow Jesus together prays together. (See the earlier section on prayer for guidance on how to pray together as a group.)

II. Group Study
We learn together. Study was easy for the original disciples. They learned the words of Jesus by listening to Jesus as he taught. They imitated the life and character of Jesus by being around Him. For us, it takes a bit more research and effort. We pray as a group to stay open to the teaching of the Holy Spirit revealed through our study. We read and study the Bible. We read and study about our Triune God. We read and study how to live the "Jesus Way of Life". We imitate the life and character of Jesus which is a radically different way of life that provides an alternative to the accepted ways of the world. Disciples are strange and subversive people who undermine the ingrained values of power and prestige with humble and

loving kindness. It is a life of strange contradictions in which we gain by giving, win by losing and live by dying. We help God change lives and make the world a better place. It is our primary purpose and our most necessary skill and we cannot pass on a way of life that we are not already living to the fullest. We have a lot to learn. We are acquiring "holy knowledge" and "holy know how." A group that learns to follow Jesus together studies together. What exactly should we study together? Again, we will let Bill Hull be our guide. Forgive the repetition, but this is a foundational teaching. At its core, a disciple learns the following:

1. A disciple submits to a teacher who teaches how to follow Jesus.
2. A disciple learns the words of Jesus.
3. A disciple learns Jesus' way of ministry.
4. A disciple imitates Jesus' life and character.
5. A disciple finds and teaches other disciples who also follow Jesus.

The best way to learn this is by studying the biblical stories of Jesus purposefully. Reading books that further explain how to imitate Jesus are very helpful but can never be a substitute for reading the Bible. (See the earlier section on self-study and reading as a means of grace).

III. Group Service

We serve together. What we learn in our study is not just knowledge to be stored in our heads to make us smarter about the ways of God. It is a way of life to be practiced. After enough time, Jesus sent his disciples out two by two into the surrounding villages to serve as Jesus served. They were to heal the sick, care for the poor, confront demons and share the Good News that Jesus is changing lives and making the world better. I'm sure they learned by trial and error. I'm sure they made mistakes out there. But we are also sure that the Spirit worked in them and through them and good things happened. There comes a time for every follower of Jesus to take off the training wheels and learn to serve as Jesus serves. We learn to ride a bike by riding a bike. Reading books and talking about how is not enough. We learn to pray by praying. We learn to serve by serving. A group that learns to follow Jesus together serves together. As you will see in our upcoming section on service, there are a billion different ways to serve Jesus in the lives of other people.

IV. Mutual Care

We care for each other. There is a strange expectation in the Church of the modern era that the pastor is hired to provide "pastoral care." There have been many documented cases over the years of hospitalized parishioners who received multiple visits from fellow church members but complained bitterly that "the church didn't visit me" because the pastor did not stop in. The CHURCH did visit multiple times and the fact that this care lovingly given by fellow brothers and sisters in Christ somehow didn't count is a sad dismissal of the work of Christ and the Holy Spirit in us all. We are called to care for the world, lovingly meeting the needs of others. That is part of the mission of the Church. If we do not allow each other to care for us within the church, then we are sending out servants who are not equipped to care for the rest of the world. Like nursing students who practice taking each other's blood pressure, followers of Jesus practice caring for others by caring for each other. There are 59 different verses in the New Testament that include the words "one another." Love one another. Bear one another's burdens. Forgive one another. Encourage one another. This is that "friendship of a truly supportive family" that is one of the reasons we choose Jesus in the first place. We learn to care by caring. A group that learns to follow Jesus together cares for each other.

V. Mutual Accountability

When athletes are in the weight room, they work with a spotter. The spotter's job is to assist the athlete with the weight to keep them from being injured when they push their muscles to exhaustion. It is also the spotter's job to push and encourage his partner to keep them from giving up too easily. In Alcoholics Anonymous, every person on the road to recovery is paired with a sponsor who holds them accountable. To be held accountable means that someone else will call us on our failures, encourage us in our struggles, and push us when we need to be pushed. We tend to go easy on ourselves and make excuses to justify our failures. As disciples growing in Christ, we want to keep moving forward in our walk with Jesus rather than sliding backwards. We need someone who refuses to give us permission to quit. We need someone who refuses to allow us to fail. We need someone who will speak the truth in love and tell us what we need to hear rather than what we want to hear. A group that learns to follow Jesus together holds each other accountable.

6
CHALLENGES TO GIVING AND SERVING

The Greatest Obstacle: Sin

Before we explore the heart and life of a servant of God, we will take a quick look at the obstacles that hinder generosity and service. There are plenty of obstacles in the world around us. But the most significant barriers are inside us all. *"All have sinned and fall short of the glory of God."* (Romans 3:23) In the New Testament, the Greek word *hamartia* that we translate as sin refers to an archer trying sink an arrow in the center bullseye of the target. Instead we miss the mark. Have you ever played darts? I have and am not ashamed to tell you that not only have I missed the bullseye, I have often missed the board altogether and sank a dart into the wall. It does not belong there. Hitting the mark in our lives together is living in such a way that our actions and thoughts are compatible with God's expectations for us. Anything we do or say or think that is outside of God's desires for us misses the mark. We can take our eye off the goal of serving God's plan for our universe and can even make it harder to communicate with God in prayer. As we move ahead into ways we serve God through Giving, Serving, and Encouraging Others to take their next step closer to God, we will need to be on the same page and communicating on the same frequency with God as much as possible. There are a lot more than just seven ways to sin, but what we have come to call "The Seven Deadly Sins" are seven common drives and desires that give rise to all kinds of problems. Let's consider them before we discuss God's remedy and alternatives.

1. Pride
2. Envy

3. Gluttony
4. Lust
5. Anger
6. Greed
7. Sloth

1. Pride

Pride is the worship and elevation of self above all else and is the source of all other varieties of sin. From birth we are in a triangle of relationships between God, other people, and ourselves. The question at the heart of our existence is: "Who is at the center of the universe? Around whom does the world revolve?" Pride is the elevation of self over God and other people. It is the insistence that we are at the center of the universe and that the world and everything in it (including God) revolves around us and exists to serve our needs and wants. God is reduced to being a waiter standing by our table ready to take our order. We too often assume that our wish is God's command which is why we often feel betrayed by unanswered prayers. Other people are seen as either our competition, our servants, or irrelevant. Life is about what we want, what we need, and what we prefer. The opposite is also true. We attempt to block what we don't want, what we don't need, and what we don't prefer. Pride is the conviction that we deserve to always get our way in all things and that something is wrong and unjust in the universe if we don't get it. Pride claims the first Undeniable Truth as all the justification it needs to run rampant. Watch a two year old throwing a tantrum and we see how ugly this utter selfishness can be. Pride is the mortal enemy of the fourth Undeniable Truth that life is not fair. Life is unpredictable because anything can and does happen to us. It is our pride that pouts that life's random setbacks are "unfair."

2. Envy

Envy is the ugly thing that creeps up in us when we don't get what we want but see someone else enjoying what we don't have. We become jealous, which is our pride inflamed at the perceived injustice. We become bitter and resent the person who has what we want. This leads to all manner of theft, violence and murder. That is why envy is addressed as the last of the Ten Commandments: *"Thou shall not covet"*. It is the smoldering ember inside of us that catches flame leading to the breaking of so many other commandments like lying, stealing, killing, and adultery. It is not only about things. Envy is also the desire for others' traits, status, abilities, or situation. The grass is always greener on the other side of the fence. When we zero in on the unfairness of life, it is oftentimes true injustices that we name. But other times, if we are honest, it is the resentment and envy we feel when others seem to have a better time of life than we do.

We counter this envy several ways, but start with self-examination. Have we truly taken responsibility for our own lot in life? Everything costs something. Is it possible that the person we are envying has taken more personal responsibility and was more willing to pay the price? Or must we seek the Spirit to help us accept the things we cannot change? We also seek contentment, appreciating what we do have with gratitude.

3. Gluttony

Gluttony is not just eating too much. *Gluttony is an inordinate desire to consume and use up more than we require.* It is a lack of self-control that can have damaging effects on our body, mind, and the world around us. The Greek philosopher Aristotle taught about this in a concept he called "The Virtue of the Mean." Simply put, it states that too much or too little of anything is harmful to us. "All things in moderation" was his guide. Aristotle did not corner the market on this wisdom. God taught very clearly that we find joy in trusting God for what we need and being content with enough. God instructed the Israelites wandering in the desert to collect only as much manna as they needed each day. Anyone who tried to gather up extra, whether through a gluttonous desire to gorge themselves on a feast or the opportunistic instinct to profit by selling it, were frustrated to find their extra manna rotting and filled with worms.

The writer of Proverbs seeks this moderation in prayer:

7 Two things I ask of you;
    do not deny them to me before I die:
8 Remove far from me falsehood and lying;
    give me neither poverty nor riches;
    feed me with the food that I need,
9 or I shall be full, and deny you,
    and say, "Who is the Lord?"
or I shall be poor, and steal,
    and profane the name of my God. (Proverbs 3:7-9 NRSV)

This "over the top" self-indulgence leads not only to our damaged health, and damaged finances, but also contributes to a level of waste in the world that fills up landfills around the globe. In Jesus, we seek contentment, self-control, and a sustainable lifestyle that is good for us and the world around us.

4. Lust

Lust is an out of control craving for the physical pleasures of the body. Of course we naturally think of sex, but lust extends to include a wide range of sensual and physical pleasures to the exclusion of intellectual and spiritual pursuits. Lust often inspires gluttony and envy as we crave the pleasure we desire and all common sense and self-control goes out the window. We develop a dangerous tunnel vision where nothing matters but satisfying that desire burning within us. It seems to reason that the best way to satisfy a temptation is to give in to it, but when we do we surrender responsibility and control of ourselves to the thing we crave which makes it even harder to resist in the future. When it comes to sexual lust, we find we are playing with fire. We are not sexual prudes. God created sex as a powerful force of attraction to bring us together as husband and wife. God's first command ever was "be fruitful and multiply" and God hard wired sexual attraction into us to make sure that we do just that. Sexual desire can be a powerful glue that leads to an unbreakable emotional and spiritual bond between two people. It can also burn the house down.

Many lives have been destroyed by an out of control craving for sex. Pornography turns fully living children of God into two dimensional objects of sex that exist not to assist God in changing lives and making the world a better place, but to gratify our cheap desires. Promiscuity is sex without limits. We feel we can have sex anywhere, anytime, with anyone we want with no consequences. God created sex to create unbreakable bonds. But sex with anyone without taking these potential bonds seriously uses others to gratify our urges but does little to encourage our sexual partner to take their next step closer with God. You will read more about this in a later section. People are not meant to be used. The Dalai Lama once said:

"People were created to be loved. Things were meant to be used. The reason why the world is in chaos is because things are being loved and people are being used."

Adultery is breaking these emotional and spiritual bonds with the person we are committed to in order to use someone else for our sexual gratification. The sexual act is over in minutes, but a committed emotional and spiritual bond can last for eternity. Throwing that away for a few moments of excitement and endorphins is as dumb as Esau giving up his birthright to inherit his father's estate for a bowl of soup.

Paul wrote that celibacy and singleness were best because they enable us to focus our entire life on God. But let's get real. Very few people can suppress this natural biological urge to be a more dedicated Christian. Paul writes that those who are unable to resist these temptations should marry, enjoy each other physically as God intended, but let that grow into a concern for each other's spiritual wellbeing as well. Just as we are lifted above the animals and are not slaves to the instinct of survival of the fittest, as those created in the image and likeness of God we are created for more than just biological urges for pleasure and reproduction. Resisting temptation is difficult which is why we train for obedience and self-control through the spiritual disciplines of fasting and self-denial.

5. Anger

James sums up everything we've already shared and shows that when every other desire is out of control anger is inevitable.

"What causes quarrels and what causes fights among you? Is it not this, that your passions are at war within you? You desire and do not have, so you murder. You covet and cannot obtain, so you fight and quarrel. You do not have, because you do not ask." (James 4:1-2 NRSV)

Everything costs something and according to Jesus our anger comes with a hefty price tag.

"You have heard that it was said to those of old, 'You shall not murder; and whoever murders will be liable to judgment.' But I say to you that everyone who is angry with his brother will be liable to judgment; whoever insults his brother will be liable to the council; and whoever says, 'You fool!' will be liable to the Hell of fire. So if you are offering your gift at the altar and there remember that your brother has something against you, leave your gift there before the altar and go. First be reconciled to your brother, and then come and offer your gift." (Matthew 5:21-24 NRSV)

Anger is a strong violent feeling of hostility directed toward another person or situation. It is a natural survival mechanism designed by our Creator to equip us to respond to danger. The problem is, it is easy to trigger this response even when we are not in any real danger. Anger and resentment are emotions so by definition they do not make rational sense. Also, remember that because we are responsible for ourselves, we refuse to be controlled by our emotions and feelings. Anger may pretend to lay out a "rational case" against another like a prosecutor in a court of law, but its conclusions cannot be trusted. Anger traffics in feelings masquerading as irrefutable facts. When we are angry, our brain releases adrenaline into the bloodstream preparing us for "fight or flight". We become defensive and sensitive to any perceived threat and are ready to strike. We too often perceive even innocent words or actions as attacks and strike back, escalating the conflict. It can start small with bitterness and resentment and grow through hatred to explode in violent rage. It is destructive when acted upon and destructive to we who carry it around inside of us. Again seeing the wisdom of God expressed around the world, Buddha once said that

"Holding on to anger is like drinking poison and expecting the other person to die." Proverbs agrees by asking:

> *27 Can a man carry fire next to his chest*
> *and his clothes not be burned?*
> *28 Or can one walk on hot coals*
> *and his feet not be scorched?* (Proverbs 6:26-28)

Anger is a desire to destroy which is completely opposed to the Way of Jesus which is a way of healing, repair and improvement. We join Jesus in building people up. Whether through our thoughts, words or actions, tearing down the people Jesus died to save is opposed to everything God is doing in the world and is quite literally "anti-Christ." It is important to remind ourselves that anger, like all our emotions, is natural. Just as physical pain alerts us that we are in danger of injury our God given emotions alert us when something is wrong in our relationships. So simply feeling anger is not necessarily wrong but if we carry it around too long it will grow. If you don't learn to control your anger, your anger will soon control you. You can say that about all the Seven Deadly Sins. We are responsible for ourselves. We are in charge of ourselves. Anger is not in charge, but often takes charge and leaves a lot of wreckage in its wake. We can lose control and say things we don't really mean and damage a relationship beyond repair. Anger has burned more bridges than fire.

As followers of Jesus we learn to deal with our anger constructively which means seeing it as an opportunity to build something that brings God glory in the Kingdom of God rather than to destroy something in the here and now.

6. Greed

If gluttony is the out of control desire to consume more than we need, greed is the relentless pursuit to acquire and possess more. Greed is the desire to accumulate material wealth or gain, ignoring the realm of the spiritual. Greed is never satisfied and seeks to gain more by any means necessary. It's hard to explain the source of this desire. Perhaps we tie our self-image and success to how much we achieve or gain. Maybe some of us see everything in life as a competition to be won and use material wealth to keep score. With greater wealth comes greater power, greater access to opportunity, and greater influence and control over others. Whenever we see life as a competition and those around us as competitors the second Undeniable Truth of sharing the planet with others goes out the window. Greed is about gaining, keeping, and increasing. Generosity is about giving, sharing and sacrifice. All three lead to having less stuff and run counter to the goals of greed.

7. Sloth

Sloth is the avoidance of physical or spiritual work. It is the refusal to take responsibility for oneself and denial that everything costs something. Sloth is wanting something for nothing, refusing to put in the effort required by life. Laziness rarely results in the life we want. How often we are envious of those who have what we don't and complain that life is not fair, as if we are the victims of a cosmic conspiracy denying us the good things in life! Everything costs something. Life takes effort. Our choices have consequences.

7

THE DISCIPLINES OF GIVING

Giving covers a lot of ground beyond simply money. As said above, it is generously sharing whatever we have with God and with others. If you've spent any time at all in a local church, you may be tempted to skip over this section, dismissing it as a cynical attempt to pick your pocket, fill up an offering plate, or meet an overtaxed church budget. *Don't skip this!* It is about the example of Jesus and Jesus gave a lot of stuff to a lot of people. Like Jesus, we choose to offer what is ours to others. In order to truly understand giving as a disciple of Jesus, we need to take a closer look at our relationship with our possessions:

I. STEWARDSHIP
II. GENEROSITY
III. COMMITMENT
IV. CONTENTMENT
V. SACRIFICE

I. STEWARDSHIP

A steward is a manager of the king's household who is afforded great authority and trust to manage the king's property and wealth. It was a great trust and a great responsibility because in all matters the steward was expected to manage those resources according to the king's priorities and interests. As followers of Jesus, we begin all discussion about earning, owning, saving, and spending by describing this responsibility as stewardship. Stewardship is rooted in the deeply biblical belief that everything that exists has been created by God and therefore belongs to God. We may be tempted to disagree, citing that by our hard work and discipline we have earned everything we have. There is truth in this assumption. We are responsible for ourselves. We stated earlier in our discussion of the "Five Undeniable Truths" that we can have anything we want in this life if we are willing to pay the price. The price paid by most of us for the money in our pocket and the roof over our heads is hard work and that hard work is both admirable and encouraged. This close connection between what we have and how we earned it causes many to feel rubbed the wrong way by this idea of stewardship. It doesn't sit right with us to hear that the things we have worked for are not really our own, but God's. God did not create the house that we make thirty years of mortgage payments to own, but God made the trees to mill into lumber as well as every other natural resource needed to build. We human beings have figured out how to use these resources to make all kinds of things, then invented rules like exchanging money to trade God's resources back and forth. It is according to our human rules that we trade our labor and goods for money that we can trade for other goods and services, but none of it would be possible without God providing everything needed including our human creativity. Remember, everything that exists in this world was created by God, belongs to God, and is given to us to further God's pleasure and plans for this world.

God blesses us with resources in this life for three purposes:

1. To meet our needs.
2. To meet the needs of others.
3. To support God's work in the world through the Church.

We are free to responsibly use everything that naturally exists in this world for these reasons. God knows our needs better than we do and has purposes that are beyond our full comprehension. Let's take a closer look at stewardship to better understand our dependence on God.

A. My Life Is God's.

Dr. Frankenstein tried, but only God can create life. We can't take credit for being alive. Life is a precious gift that we have each received at birth. God created life. God gave us life, and we answer to God for how we use that life. Life is given to us for the same reasons everything was created in this world, for God's pleasure (because God likes having us around) and to help further God's plans for our world. Life is not to be wasted or destroyed.

B. My Time Is God's.

Time is how we humans measure the passing of our lives. We are learning to accept the undeniable truth that nothing lasts forever, including life, so the way we use the time we do have is of great interest to God.

C. My Talents are God's.

God gives us natural abilities and the capacity to develop skills and talents through practice and hard work. I may be born with a giftedness for numbers or a musical ear, and am free to use these gifts however I choose. We are responsible for ourselves, so we are free to choose. Because they begin with God, we know God has a purpose for every talent and ability. We can use them to meet our needs, meet the needs of others, and to support God's work in the world.

D. All Treasure Belongs to God.

As we've already stated, everything we own belongs ultimately to God. Our cars, our cash, our homes can and must be used according to God's purposes to change lives and make the world a better place. But this goes far beyond just the things we own. To say that everything exists for us to use is not accurate. They may exist to meet our needs, but that is not to say that everything in creation can be bought and sold, mined or refined. Sometimes we are so busy trying to make money off of nature we overlook that sometimes it exists just to be beautiful. We need beauty. We need peace and simplicity. We need to spend time surrounded by God-made things rather than human-made things to be reminded that God is creator, not us. We are stewards of creation, too.

E. We Manage According to God's Purposes, Not Our Own.

We have now come full circle in our discussion of stewardship. The steward is entrusted with the wealth and property of the King and is expected to care for it all according to the king's purposes and priorities rather than his or her own. This is a radically different view of what we earn, own, save and spend than that held by the world around us. The world teaches a different philosophy: "What's mine is mine. If you need, get your own." The idea that God is trying to pick our pocket to take what is ours is not biblical and certainly not of Jesus. There is a humility that comes in knowing that someone else has helped to provide for us which inspires gratitude. Recognizing that God is partly responsible for our success acknowledges that God is a shareholder in what we own and has a say in what we do with it. Money and things are not evil if kept in their proper place. It is the love of money that is the root of all evil, not money itself. It is out of step with the heart of God to use money solely for our self-interests rather than investing in God's ongoing adventure to change lives and make the world better. Investing in God and others is another way of saying that God gives through our generosity. Once you've met your needs, we all must decide for ourselves, "How much do I keep to spend on my wants rather than God's purposes?" The Holy Spirit works in us over time to want what God wants, which makes it easier to give as God needs us to give. We will look at these ideas below under "contentment."

II. GENEROSITY

Let's keep this from being complicated. Every kindergarten student knows that generosity is about being willing to share. We can be more complicated if you want: "to partake of, use, experience, occupy, or enjoy with others" (Merriam Webster). It is the willingness to give what is ours to others.

A. Obstacles to Generosity

There are many things that get in the way of generosity and sharing.

1. Greed Gets In The Way of Sharing With Others.

Some people are never satisfied and constantly want more. Greed is the drive to acquire more than we need and is never content with enough. Giving is seen as losing what we have worked so hard to gain. Giving is moving backwards in our quest for more. Greed can even grow to dangerous levels where, not only are we not willing to share, but are driven to squeeze, grasp, and take what we want from others by any means necessary.

2. Self-Gratification Gets In The Way of Sharing With Others.

Life is short and must be enjoyed. We believe that as followers of Jesus, but for many the pursuit of pleasure and avoidance of pain become the total purpose of life. We want to have nice things, go nice places and have fun. Our own comfort, pampering, and entertainment are all we work for and all we care about. The bigger house, nicer car, and newest phone are all part of treating ourselves well. This life is expensive because there is no shortage of places to spend money. Many call it "living the good life" but it ensures that our money is always spoken for leaving little to none left to give to God or others. More precisely, giving to God and others isn't even on the radar.

3. Idolatry Gets In The Way of Sharing With Others.

Pardon the old fashioned Bible word, but it is still the best word to use. God forbids worshipping idols in the Ten Commandments. These were handmade statues that were worshipped as if they were real gods. The meaning has evolved to include an unhealthy commitment or attachment to human made things rather than a loyalty to God and other people. We are practicing idolatry when we assign an inappropriate and unhealthy meaning to things that we own. Our possessions do not determine our status or worth as a human being. It is a trap to constantly compare ourselves to and compete against other people. There will always be someone better off than us that will inflame our jealousy and someone worse off than us that will feed our arrogant sense of superiority. Sometimes we turn to the things we buy to make us feel better about ourselves because we never found the love we need from other people. No matter how much we spend, our clothes and furniture cannot love us back. We want to invest our resources in things that can love us in return, like God and people. Again, remember what the Dalai Lama once said: *"People were created to be loved. Things were meant to be used. The reason why the world is in chaos is because things are being loved and people are being used."* That is what idolatry is.

4. Fear of Scarcity Gets In The Way of Sharing With Others.

Churches are more guilty of this mistake than anyone else. How many times have we turned away from an opportunity to change somebody's life and make the world better because we didn't think we could afford it? When we succumb to the fear that there isn't enough to go around we fail to trust in the God who provides. We aren't talking about being reckless, but stepping out in faith. If we as stewards use what we have according to God's desires and direction, then isn't God obligated to provide? If a congregation only budgets what it knows its members will give in the year to come, then we are trusting in our own power and abilities. If God is calling us to a level of generosity and service beyond what we know how to fund, we trust God to work it out. As followers of Jesus do we trust God to provide as we give according God's purposes?

5. The Dark Side of Self Reliance

In the United States, one of our founding myths is that of the self-sufficient loner. We embrace the first Undeniable Truth (that we are responsible for ourselves) to be the only one that matters. Success is attributed to hard work where we take responsibility for our own needs and improvement. It is an important factor. But when the virtue of self-reliance turns to resentment of anyone who accepts the help or charity of others it turns its back on Jesus. Political systems based on the virtue of self-reliance too often bring with them a scorn for altruism and generosity as somehow causing harm to society and to the people who are benefiting from it. I will never forget a conversation with an elderly woman who was highly regarded as a leader in her congregation. She asked me if I didn't think giving so much to the local shelter and food pantry was causing more harm than good. She was afraid that we were rewarding laziness which damages character and causes people to become dependent on handouts. I asked her what Jesus might have meant when he said *"Give to all who beg from you"*

(Luke 6:39). "God helps those who help themselves," she replied. I then reminded her that this shows a stronger loyalty to Ben Franklin (who actually wrote those words) than to Jesus. Christ followers do not verbally attack someone in the checkout line for using food stamps. Christ followers do not answer everyone who begs with the words "Get a job." We are responsible for ourselves, but don't ever forget that life is not fair. Not everyone is born with the same abilities or advantages which is why we are not all equally capable of pulling ourselves up by our own bootstraps. We do share the planet with other people which is why we need to learn how to share. Offering and accepting help actually heals our society according to Jesus which is why generosity is one of the five disciplines of the Christian life.

B. What Generosity Is

We have just discussed some of the things that keep us from being truly generous. Most of it is found in the struggle to make room in the world and in our heart for others. Generosity is holding onto things loosely because we know we are going pass them on. Generosity is knowing that God's blessings come to us on their way to someone else. If you think about our national economy we see that it is important for money to keep changing hands. If the money stops moving, then the whole system grinds to a halt. Without our spending, those who manufacture and sell the things we need have no one to sell to and no money coming in. Everything grinds to a halt. Several years ago, I received a check in the mail from the federal government because the president wanted to jump start the economy. People with money will spend it and move it around. I did my patriotic duty and bought a couch. Likewise, God blesses us to meet our needs, meet the needs of others and to support God's work in the world. God's blessings are intended to continue blessing us as they are continuously shared and passed on. We hold on loosely because we expect to pass them on.

Here is how Moses explained it in Deuteronomy 15:

7 If there is among you anyone in need, a member of your community in any of your towns within the land that the Lord your God is giving you, do not be hard-hearted or tight-fisted toward your needy neighbor. 8 You should rather open your hand, willingly lending enough to meet the need, whatever it may be. 9 Be careful that you do not entertain a mean thought, thinking, "The seventh year, the year of remission, is near," and therefore view your needy neighbor with hostility and give nothing; your neighbor might cry to the Lord against you, and you would incur guilt. 10 Give liberally and be ungrudging when you do so, for on this account the Lord your God will bless you in all your work and in all that you undertake. 11 Since there will never cease to be some in need on the earth, I therefore command you, "Open your hand to the poor and needy neighbor in your land."

III. COMMITMENT

Now that we have made the decision to open our hand and give to God and others, we might as well make it a bigger priority in our lives. It is time to develop a plan to make sure it happens on a regular basis. Giving is a spiritual discipline through which we deepen our love relationship with God. We have already discussed developing a plan to make sure we are taking enough time apart with God to pray and study every day. We encourage taking just as much care in planning our giving.

A. Promise

We believe in "Promise Giving". Some people prefer to call it tithing, but either way, it involves setting aside a portion of what we earn and own and promising to give it to God on a regular basis. It could be as simple as deciding what you want to give to, how much you want to give, and how often. For example, I may promise to give $75 dollars every week to support God's work through my local church. I may also choose to give a ten dollar grocery card every week to a neighbor who is looking for a new job after being laid off. The spiritual discipline is similar to that of fasting and self-denial. We make a promise to God, then reorient our life and priorities to keep our promise. That is how trust in relationships are strengthened, by making and keeping promises.

B. Percentage

How much should we promise to God? It was the practice in ancient Israel to establish ten percent as the tithe. For that reason, it has become common practice in Christian congregations to teach giving ten percent of our earnings to God as a reasonable goal. However, it was the practice of the Jerusalem Church in Acts chapter two to sell their possessions and give one hundred percent to the apostles and share all things in common. So because your decision of a giving promise can be anywhere between one dollar and everything you have, it is important to talk to God about it in prayer. Make your giving promise part of your regular prayer life.

C. Priorities

The Church has been struggling to answer this question: "How does God expect us give, until it hurts or until it feels good?" We encourage the latter. Generosity places us in the center of God's will and that is a very good place to be. Being a part of the good God is doing to change lives and make the world better brings us joy and pride. We will begin to change our priorities in order to continue to enjoy the privilege of joining God at work. We are happy to invest in changing lives and in improving the world. This is also where personal testimony comes in. When we know where our giving goes and the difference it is making, we are anxious to give more.

John Wesley used to teach that we should *"Earn all you can, save all you can, so you can give all you can."* A generous life is not just one that holds things loosely but actively seeks opportunities to give, taking great joy in blessing others. He chose to wear his hair unfashionably long and unwigged because he would rather give his money to the poor than to a barber or wig maker. Everything costs something For Wesley, increasing the amount he could give away was paid for by spending less on niceties and personal comforts. Giving was a higher priority for him than keeping up with the Joneses.

D. Trust
Rearranging our financial life to keep a promise to God is not always easy. We sometimes find ourselves in a season where money is tight. Life is not fair and we live in a world where anything can happen and usually does. Medical bills happen. Car repairs happen. Unemployment happens. Sometimes it seems impossible to give anything to God because there isn't even enough to pay our bills. We may not give much, but we still try to give something because we trust God to provide. Even giving a single penny is a sign of great trust in God to see us through.

E. Gratitude
We have established earlier that everything ultimately belongs to God. Our ongoing commitment to give is also fueled by our gratitude for God's generosity. Our regular giving through weekly promises or a "spur of the moment" gift to someone in need are excellent ways of thanking God for all the ways God has blessed us. Imitation is the sincerest form of flattery. If we are thankful that God has given to us, the best way to express it is to do likewise and pay it forward to others.

IV. CONTENTMENT
The opposite of greed is generosity. Greed is the uncontrollable desire for more. Contentment is being satisfied with enough. Contentment allows us to be happy with less which frees up more that we can give, just like John Wesley's long hair.

A. Appreciation
Sheryl Crow sang in her song "Soak Up the Sun": "It's not getting what you want. It's wanting what you've got!" How true! When we truly appreciate what we already have we feel less urge to replace it with a newer model. We've shared above that the value of our possessions is found in their usefulness not status. My car is valuable to me because it runs and

reliably gets me where I need to go. It may be a few years old. It might have some dents and scratches. It might not be as shiny as it used to be, but it is good enough.

B. Sustainable Lifestyle

Simply put, our earning, owning, saving, spending and giving have to be kept in balance so that there is enough money to go around. "Sustainable" means that we are able to maintain something at a certain level continuously over time. There are three options related to maintaining a sustainable lifestyle:

1. Living Beyond Our Means

When we spend more money than we make, we find ourselves in debt. It is very difficult to live a truly debt free life because there are different kinds of debt. Certain major investments in our life and future are out of reach for most of us without borrowing money. Student loans, car loans and home mortgages must be applied for responsibly but are acceptable ways to invest in yourself. Many find themselves in debt because life is not fair. Accidents, illnesses, layoffs, medical bills can wipe us out and put us in the hole. The worst debt is when we have no self-control and just keep funding everyday purchases with a credit card that we never pay off. As the balance continues to grow, we are vulnerable to high interest rates that can make paying the debt impossible.

2. Living Within Our Means

This is what most of us strive for. Unlike Congress, we try to maintain a balanced budget, spending no more than what we earn. This requires doing some planning and setting of priorities. Our budget includes everything we need, everything we are obligated to pay, and should include what we set aside to save and give.

3. Living Below Our Means

Like John Wesley, if giving is a high enough priority, we can learn to survive on less in order to free up enough to give more. That will require us to focus on needs instead of wants, appreciate what we already have, and to be content with living more simply.

V. SACRIFICE

Choosing to live with less in order to give to God and others is the kind of sacrifice that God honors. Sacrifice means choosing to lose so that others might win. It is also choosing to lose so that others may gain. Sacrifice is one of the holiest and most noble acts we can commit.

8
THE DISCIPLINES OF SERVING

Imagine you are swimming in the community pool and you begin to have some trouble. You are struggling to keep your head above water and it's too deep to touch bottom. You're not sure, but this could be serious. You look up and see…the lifeguard….sitting high above the pool on her really big chair with that really great tan, spinning her whistle around on her finger all day. You feel a little bit better knowing the lifeguard is there, keeping an eye on things. But by now, you are really struggling. You just accidentally inhaled some water the last time your head slipped under and now you are choking and coughing and gasping for breath. You're starting to panic now. You're not swimming any more, you're just flailing your arms around blindly. Your heart is racing, your lungs are burning. You are starting to go under. You begin to fear the worst. Just about that time, the lifeguard finally notices you and begins to move into action. She stops spinning her whistle, stands up and begins shouting at you. You can barely hear her, but you're pretty sure she's saying: "Hey you! Stop drowning!"

She means well, and you'd like to obey her, but seeing as you are already in the process of drowning it's kind of hard to stop. The life guard is shouting louder now. She is giving clear instructions on what you should never do in the pool. She then gives more step by step instructions on how to swim and she's getting a little frustrated with you, too. Her instructions were perfectly clear to everyone else standing around the edge of the pool. She's not sure why you are having such a hard time with it. Her words are muffled now that you are sinking deeper and you are finding it hard to concentrate as your lungs fill up with water. I can assure you that everything she has been saying is accurate, truthful and to the point. She was saying all the right words, but we need something more than words at a time like this. That's not the kind of guardian you want when your life is actually on the line. The life guard has three options when there is someone in the water in distress:

Option One:
Assume they brought this on themselves by doing something stupid and let them drown.

Option Two:
Give them instructions on what they shouldn't do in the pool and instructions on how to swim.

Option Three:
Get down in the water with the people who are in trouble and bring them out.

If you are in the water, and you're in trouble, which one do you want? Option One is common among those who think the first Undeniable Truth is the only one that matters. We are responsible for ourselves. You got yourself into this mess. It's your job to get yourself out. We forget the second Undeniable Truth that we share the planet with others. When we are drowning, we don't need long speeches. We don't need somebody to quote a bunch of scripture verses at us. We don't need somebody to browbeat us with a lot of criticism and judgment. We don't need to be told what we "shoulda" or "coulda" done better. We don't need to feel worse about ourselves than we already do. We need help. We need somebody to jump in and rescue us, to put an arm around us and hold us up because we are too tired to go on. We need somebody to encourage us by letting us know they are here and that everything is going to be alright. We need somebody to tell us which way we're going to go to be safe. We need somebody to hold onto us with one hand and swim with the other. When we are drowning, we need somebody who is willing to risk their own life by joining us in the water to bring us safely out.

The God of Heaven, who is high and lifted up in the Kingdom of Heaven has jumped in to save us. Born in a manger in Bethlehem, God has joined us in the danger and death to bring us to safety and life. There will be time for God to tell us what we did wrong. There will be plenty of time for us to learn how to do things right the next time. But that time will never come if we don't survive. God has come to us, just as we are, with just what we need most, to save us. This baby in a manger spent His entire life seeking out the people who were struggling, nasty, broken, wounded, and lost. Jesus fed the hungry, healed the sick, encouraged the despondent. He swam in deeper where most folks wouldn't want to go in order to bring out the ones abandoned as too far gone. It was risky. It was dangerous. It cost Him His life, but that was OK, you know why? You're worth it. You are worth saving. Christ is willing to die a thousand deaths to reach us, but it only took one.

Christ is still with us in this world just as He was two thousand years ago. He's not lying in a manger or healing the blind, or dying on a cross. He is in this world in a thousand places at once through the mysterious power of the Holy Spirit. He is present in this world through the Body of Christ, His Church, who also exists to join the struggling and the hurting out in the waves and bring them to shore. I know that too often the Church has forgotten what life guards are supposed to do. Too often we as Church have spent more time working on our tans than diving in to help those who are struggling. We've spent more time decorating the life guards' lounge than saving lives. (When we spend more time discussing the color of the carpet in the sanctuary than we do feeding hungry people in our town, we are lifeguards who have missed the point of our existence.) We've gotten really good at twirling our whistles around our fingers while people are dying out there. Because we've learned how to pray, we want to spend all our time sitting on God's lap, feeling good about ourselves rather than getting our hands dirty.

To you who've been let down by the Church, I am truly sorry. But I assure you, we are learning how to swim again because Option One is not an option. With Christ at our side, we know this is not the time for criticism and judgment. This is not the time to browbeat or lecture. This is not the time to stuff people full of a lot of scripture verses. There will be time to learn lessons later. Now is the time to swim out to where people are and save lives. Now is the time to find a need and meet it. Now is the time to put an arm around hurting people and let them know they are not alone. Now is the time to swim by their side for as long as it takes, encouraging them and telling them that everything is going to be alright. When they are lost and confused and don't know which way to turn, now is the time to tell them which way we can go to be safe. We help them swim toward Christ. It's been said that if you want to spend time with God, then you need to go where God is. God is in the world, searching the waves for those who are going under, and we, the disciples of Jesus, are there to help. That is what the Disciplines of Serving are all about. It is loving our neighbor as we love ourselves, doing what needs to be done in order to help, even if it means getting our hands dirty and tracking up that sanctuary carpet with muddy footprints. We are called to this by Christ.

Consider this powerful quote by William Booth, founder of the Salvation Army:

"'Not called!' did you say? 'Not heard the call,' I think you should say. Put your ear down to the Bible, and hear him bid you go and pull sinners out of the fire of sin. Put your ear down to the burdened, agonized heart of humanity, and listen to its pitiful wail for help. Go stand by the gates of hell, and hear the damned entreat you to go to their father's house and bid their brothers and sisters, and servants and masters not to come there. And then look Christ in the face, whose mercy you have professed to obey, and tell him whether you will join heart and soul and body and circumstances in the march to publish his mercy to the world.'"

Our mission is Jesus' mission. We deepen our love relationship with God to draw strength as we serve. We learn together how to better follow Jesus in order to better serve. We give generously in order to help others, so let's take a closer look at how we serve.

I. A SERVANT'S HEART
II. A SERVANT'S LOVE
III. A SERVANT'S CALLING
IV. ACTS OF MERCY
V. ACTS OF JUSTICE

I. A SERVANT'S HEART

Before we talk about what God wants us to do, we must realize that it is possible to do the right things for the wrong reasons. The motives with which we serve are just as important as the things we do to serve. If I pursue a leadership position in Christ's Church out of personal ambition, to promote myself in the eyes of others, I am not serving God. I am serving myself. Jesus warned the disciples against giving and praying in order to impress others. That is not serving the purposes of God. We are told to speak the truth in love, rebuking each other when we go astray. We may be all too eager to point out each other's faults in order to knock each other down to size. This self-serving attack tears others down rather than build them up. The motives with which we serve can make all the difference. A key question to ask ourselves regularly in our Prayer of Examen is this: "Am I serving God by doing this or am I serving myself?"

John Wesley preached about the possibility of "Christian Perfection" which was a controversial idea. Many thought it meant that we can be error free. But John was referring to a Christ-like heart. We experience Christian Perfection when everything we do, say and think is done with the singular motive of love of God and love of neighbor. It is the work of the Holy Spirit whose job is to conform us into the likeness of Christ. Here are some non-negotiable qualities of Jesus' heart:

A. Humility

According to Paul in Philippians 2, humility is regarding others as better or more important than ourselves. It is attending to the interests of others as well as our own. We too often think of humility as being a passive doormat that is willing to be used and abused by the whims of others. That is not what Christ-like humility means. It means that we live as if other people matter. It takes the second Undeniable Truth very seriously and is necessary to share the planet with others. It is a repudiation of the idea that the world revolves around us. Without taking a genuine interest in the wellbeing of others, nothing else in the disciple's life is possible. Without putting others first, generosity and service are impossible for us. Humility is a foundation upon which everything else built.

B. Submission:

Once we are able to consider others as more important than ourselves, it is possible to place ourselves under the authority and direction of another. As Bill Hull teaches, we become disciples by "submitting ourselves to the authority of someone who can teach us how to follow Jesus." As disciples we submit to the authority of God the Father, Son, and Holy Spirit. We submit to our spiritual leaders. We submit to one another. It may seem like weakness but it is anything but. It is a powerful expression of respect and trust to let someone else come first and chart our way. I've noticed over the years that "control freak" drivers make lousy passengers. They cannot relax in the back seat and let someone else drive. Allowing someone else to take the wheel requires trust. We do not constantly second guess, criticize, or argue. No one likes a back seat driver. Submission is about extending trust and yielding control which are challenging for many. Submission is also yielding to the needs of others rather than our own personal interests.

C. Obedience

Jesus said "*a tree is known by its fruit.*" You know it is an apple tree when you see apples on it. Likewise, you know when someone is truly submitted when they obey. This is a word few of us are comfortable with because we live in an age of independence. Obedience brings to mind images of tyranny and slavery that impose domination and humiliation. Humiliation is when we belittle others. We force others to feel less than us. Humility is when we choose to lift others above ourselves. Quite simply, once we submit to others by accepting and recognizing their authority with respect and trust, obedience is following their direction. We submit to God and obey God's call. Obedience is humility and submission with boots on.

D. Grace

This is a word every believer has heard but too few can adequately define. It is framed and hung on the wall as part of Grandma's cross stitch. It inspired one of our most beloved hymns. But for too many people it expresses a "vague niceness" of God. Grace is the English translation of the Greek word "*charis*" meaning gift. It has been defined by the theologians as "unmerited favor" or a gift we did not earn or deserve. This brings us a little closer to my favorite definition which takes the word from sounding like a greeting card to something far more radical. *Grace is treating others better than they deserve.* Let that sink in for a moment. We are saved by grace which means God has treated us better than we deserve. We don't deserve forgiveness. We don't deserve Jesus' death. We don't deserve a second chance of eternal life, but God treats us better than we deserve. Why? Simply because God has chosen to. How do I treat the guy in the station next to mine at work? Better than he deserves. How do I treat the guy that just stole my wallet? Better than he deserves. This is why Jesus can have the audacity to expect us to love and care for our enemies. It is absolutely consistent with the heart of Jesus who treats everyone better than they deserve.

E. Sacrifice

We said above that humility is attending to the needs of others as well as our own. Sacrifice is a bit more costly. Sacrifice is attending to the needs of others INSTEAD OF your own. It is being willing to lose so that others might win. It is choosing to struggle so that others might thrive. It is choosing to lose so that others might gain. It is a true gift. We see this most clearly in Jesus' agony upon the cross. Jesus did not agree to the cross because it was going to be good for him. No soldier ever dove onto a live hand grenade asking "what's in it for me?" Or as Jesus said, "*Greater love has no man than this, that he lay down his life for his friends.*" What about someone who lays down their life for complete strangers? Whenever I teach on sacrifice I often remember the winter day in 1982 when an Air Florida passenger jet with ice on its wings lost altitude, crashed onto a bridge, then sank in the Potomac River. What I remember most was the one man swimming strongest in the freezing river helping other, more wounded, passengers into the harness to be lifted by helicopter to safety. Time after time he would grab someone else and shove them into the harness to save their lives. Before he could be rescued, he slipped under the water and drowned. He was one of the strongest swimmers out there after the crash. If anyone had the strength to survive it, he did. He chose to give that last ounce of strength to save others. That is love. That is sacrifice. That man's name is Arland D. Williams, Jr. and I have remembered his sacrifice all these years. That is Christ-like love.

II. A SERVANT'S LOVE

The heart of service is love. *"Love your neighbor as yourself."* We know Jesus said it but we sometimes we get this one wrong. Love is not a feeling, but an action. It is a choice. The word "love" has been hijacked by greeting card companies to mean a sweet warm fuzzy romantic feeling. That's why loving our enemies seems like such a crazy idea. I don't have positive warm fuzzy feeling for my enemy. But that is not what "love" means. Love is a way we treat people. I can love someone even if I don't like them because *love is a choice to treat someone with kindness, compassion, and respect.* I Corinthians is one of the best explanations of what love is and isn't. Let's take a closer look.

A. What Love Is and Isn't: I Corinthians 13

1. "Love is Patient"

Patience is the ability to wait peacefully. I don't know about you, but patience was never my thing. Maybe that's why I've never enjoyed fishing or gardening. Both require too much waiting. You put seeds in the ground but you have to wait to eat watermelon. I can get frustrated at my seeds because they aren't yet watermelons, but no amount of emotion will speed things up. There is a disconnect for us between the way things are and the way we feel things ought to be. When I compare my seeds in the ground to the pictures on the packets, I am disappointed every time and I blame my seeds for not being perfect. When we compare our spouse and families to the beautiful perfect looking people on TV, we may be disappointed. When we compare those around us with the biblical ideal of how people should act, we will always be disappointed and often blame them for not being perfect. We are waiting for our kids to become the kids we want them to be. We are waiting for our spouse and coworkers and president to be the people we want them to be. We are frustrated about it and that's why we boil over. We have compared them, criticized them, and judged them. We are so busy comparing, criticizing and judging others, we don't have any time left to love them just the way they are. In the basement of the first church I ever served was a small poster that hung on the wall of one of the Sunday School rooms. It was the picture of a toddler whose shoe was untied, hair was uncombed, room was a mess with what looked like the leftovers of ravioli all over his face. The caption read: "Be patient with me…God's not done with me yet."

There it is. Every single one of us is a work of God, and every single one of us is a work in progress. This is why Jesus commands us to love enemies as well as friends. Because despite the evil, violence and nastiness we see in them now, God isn't done with them yet, and neither should we be. Through the Spirit, God enables us to see in them, not the nastiness that is, but the grace and beauty that will be. I know that sounds hopelessly idealistic to many of us, but it is what God promises and what God expects. Patience is the ability to wait. Love is patient.

2. "Love is Kind"

Kindness is the decision to help and not harm. It is the firm commitment to treat all others as we ourselves would like to be treated. It is the willingness to build others up and never, EVER tear them down. Kindness is an unwillingness to join in the fun if someone else is being hurt by it. It is a thousand thoughtful and generous gifts that provide just what is needed most. Kindness is about care and protection, healing and comfort. It is not about cutting our neighbor and watching them bleed. Rather, it is about taking the shirt from our own backs and tearing it into strips and using them to bandage the wounds of our neighbor so the bleeding may stop. Kindness is doing what is necessary to help someone else thrive. It is not about competition but about cooperation. It is also about forgiveness and understanding and patience, especially when we are extending kindness to someone who is very cruel. Kindness makes us safe to be around and makes the world a better place, too.

3. "Love is Not Envious, Arrogant, Boastful, or Rude"

Envy, arrogance, boasting, and rudeness accomplish the same thing. They are used to build ourselves up by tearing others down. Envy is resenting people who have what we want. Arrogance is puffing ourselves up by belittling others. Being boastful is singing your own praises and rudeness is speaking in a way that is hurtful and unkind. Author P.M. Forni, leader of the Johns Hopkins Civility Project defines rudeness this way:

"When we are polite, we confer regard. The original meaning of regard is "to look," "to notice," and "to keep in view." To disregard, then, is to look elsewhere, to withdraw attention—and, with it, respect and consideration. Rudeness is disregard. It diminishes and demeans. By treating others curtly, we put them in their place, which is a way of controlling them and thwarting their attempts at controlling us. Through rudeness we show off, dominate, intimidate, coerce, threaten, humiliate, dissuade, and dismiss. Rudeness is control through invalidation." ("Choosing Civility" St. Martin's Press 2002).

All of these put together make other people feel worse about themselves because of our insistence that we are better. In order to love someone as Jesus loves we must go out of our way to make other people feel important.

Remember humility? Humility is considering others as more important than ourselves. In order to love them, we instead make them feel appreciated, accepted, and valued. We don't give them time to brag or boast or fish for compliments, because we are already telling them what we admire about them. We don't struggle against them to claim the credit because we've already given them credit loudly, warmly and publicly. They don't have to dominate the conversation, because we've decided to simply listen. They don't have to tear us down to build themselves up because we've already lifted them up on our shoulders. According to Jesus, if anyone loses, we all lose. We win when we all win. We do not build ourselves up by shoving the rest back down. We all rise together. Life is not a contest or a competition but a cooperation because we are all in this thing together. Therefore we encourage each other, we listen, we appreciate, we compliment, we praise. We give someone else the spotlight, the gold medal, the standing ovation.

So we ask ourselves, even with the people we like the least, what can I admire in this person? What can I genuinely appreciate and praise? For some people it will be hard to find, but it is there in all of us. Tell people how great you think they are. Show people how great you think they are, not because they've done amazing things, broken world records, or have accomplished much, but simply because they are created in the image of God. We are all worth infinitely more than we can ever imagine. When we are arrogant and rude, calling each other names, we take away their humanity and when we take away their humanity, violence and cruelty are easier. It's harder to hate an enemy you admire and appreciate. It's harder to destroy a member of your own team. Love is not envious, boastful, arrogant or rude.

4. "Love Does Not Insist on its Own Way"

My daughter and I were sitting at a red light recently and quite frankly I was tired of waiting. "Watch this," I told her then clapped my hands twice. By sheer coincidence, the light turned green, and my daughter pretended to be impressed with my amazing powers. If only it really worked like that. If only we had the power to make the world turn exactly the way we want it to. There would be no more red lights, slow traffic, or long checkout lines at the grocery store. No more taxes, TV commercials, or bills to pay. Everything would be free…for us at least. No more people who disagree with what we do, or complain or criticize. Wouldn't that be nice? We all have things we don't like. We all have people that rub us the wrong way. What if we could just make it all go away so that the only things left in the world are the things we like? What if we could make it so that everyone agreed with us, and liked us, all the time? Wouldn't that be nice? Richard Foster in his book "Celebration of Discipline" (HarperColliins 1998) describes it this way:

He speaks of the *"terrible burden of always needing to get our own way. The obsession to demand that things go the way we want them to go is one of the greatest bondages in human society today. People will spend weeks, months, even years in a perpetual stew because some little thing did not go as they wished. They will fuss and fume. They will get mad about it. They will act as if their very life hangs on the issue. They may even get an ulcer over it."*

We create a lot of heartache for ourselves by always insisting on our own way. We try to enslave the people around us by forcing them to think what we think, like what we like, and do what we want them to do. The only person we can ever control in any situation is ourself...but that never stops us from trying and we create a lot of damage in the process.

According to the Bible, this fascination and obsession with the self is the root of all sin. Adam and Eve's temptation had nothing to do with fruit. It was the desire to grasp God's power and abilities for themselves. To do what only God can do...and only God has the power to have whatever God wants. But who ever said that God gets God's own way? God created a world in which people should love God, but they don't. God created people to love each other and treat each other well, but they don't. God created us to take care of this world, but we don't!! God allows us to be who we are, even when God disagrees with us. God respects our right to make our own choices, even when they are bad choices. God teaches us, commands us, invites us, endures us, but God does not control us. God has decided that we should think and choose for ourselves, hoping all the while that we will choose to love God in return. This freedom is part of what it means to be created in the image of God. We are never fully human until we have learned to control ourselves and allow others to do the same. Remember the first Undeniable Truth: you are responsible for yourself. Even if we disagree, we let others decide for themselves. We love by making room in the world for other people to be themselves.

5. "Love Is Not Easily Angered and Keeps No Record of Wrongs"

Our second Undeniable Truth asserts that we share the planet with other people. We are connected whether we want to be or not. Because our wellbeing is tied to the wellbeing of others, we must cooperate to achieve what is best for the greatest number of people. Because we are all connected...Because what happens in our life affects every other life...We all have the power to create damage for everybody or healing for everybody. Which one it will be depends on whether or not we can stay connected. Now there are thousands of ways that we humans can break this connection. Some of them are subtle, like misunderstandings, careless words, or accidents. Others can be huge, like betrayal, insults, violence and intentional nastiness of every sort. All it takes to break this connection is for one person to get angry with another person. We want to move farther away from them. To make that easier, we slap a label on them. Jerk. Hothead. Selfish pig. Terrorist. Criminal. Enemy. But once I've convinced myself that you are a jerk, I don't have to treat you as a human being anymore with hopes, and dreams and feelings. As a matter of fact, you don't even deserve the right to talk to me anymore. I push you away even further. Next we blame. We decide who is responsible for this conflict and place the blame and punishment squarely on the other. If you are to blame, then you are responsible to fix things, not me. But that gets harder and harder if we are not talking. And even when we do talk, we fight, because if you are to blame, then I am going to punish you for it every chance I get. If I retaliate enough, maybe you won't even want to come near me anymore, and we are even further away. But I want to make sure that you stay further away, so I will keep us from ever coming back together by holding a grudge.

Addressing the church at Corinth Paul writes that *"love is not easily angered and keeps no record of wrongs."* We control our anger instead of letting our anger control us. We decide that repairing the damage is more important that rehashing how the damaged occurred in the first place. We also hold onto our common humanity instead of our grudges, and let the past go. Paul is talking about forgiveness. Forgiveness is not about giving somebody a pass they don't deserve. Forgiveness is not about ignoring the hurt and injustice and moving on without consequence. Forgiving is not even about forgetting. *Forgiveness is the process by which we make our past hurts irrelevant to our future.* Forgiveness is simply the refusal to throw each other away and to work toward a greater healing and wellbeing for all involved. It is the willingness to stay connected. Blame disappears as we must cooperate to heal our conflict. In the act of forgiveness, we both have something to let go of. We are willing to be stripped of our grudges as well as our guilt. We cannot move forward together unless both are left behind. The uneasy question is who must let go first? To love as Christ loves means to be willing to be the first one to let go. I will let go of my hurt and blame first to make it safer for you to move closer and lay down your guilt.

At the cross of Christ, God strips away our guilt and sin, removing it completely. God buries our guilt with Christ and raises up a future with new possibilities. But God also buried God's anger and blame against us, too. Long before we ever recognized our sin or confessed it, God took the first step and made healing possible. God desires our healing far more than our punishment. God doesn't want to be our prison guard who punishes us every single day but wants to be our friend, who lays aside the blame to make it safe for us to come back together again. Love is taking the first step to make it safe for us to come back together again.

6. "Love Does Not Rejoice in Wrongdoing but Rejoices in the Truth"

a. Honesty

"Thou shalt not lie" is one of the Ten Commandments. Complete honesty with God is one of the hallmarks of effective prayer. Honesty in our dealings with one another is equally important to our life together as followers of Jesus. We cannot trust one another if we cannot trust what we say to each other. Dishonesty ruins trust and destroys relationships. Paul K. Chappell, in his book "The Art of Waging Peace" (Easton Studio Press, 2013) offers the brilliant observation that war and violence depend upon deception. If a boxer can fake out an opponent with the left hand it may be easier to land a solid punch with the right. Wars are fought by trying to mislead the enemy as well. Disinformation, propaganda, keeping secrets and psychological tactics are all part of the process. Healthy relationships require trust. Deception and dishonesty erode trust faster than just about anything else.

b. Speak the Truth in Love

We may be tempted to avoid the truth sometimes in order to spare someone's feelings, but it is important to say what needs to be said. We have shared earlier that as disciples we need someone who will tell us what we need to hear not just what we want to hear. But sometimes the truth hurts. We practice "assertive communication" which is the refusal to avoid issues, sugarcoat the truth, and withholding information. Little white lies may seem compassionate but they can hinder our personal growth as a disciple. We help each other confront our sins and mistakes. We help diagnose each other's strengths and shortcomings. The 5x5 discipleship process depends on determining where we really are in our walk with Jesus (warts and all) so we can determine the most productive next step. We would never want our doctor to sugarcoat a diagnosis or keep bad news from us in order to spare our feelings, but we appreciate a good bedside manner. Speaking the truth with love is truth-telling with an excellent Christ-like bedside manner.

Paul's letter to the Church at Ephesus is addressing this same difficult balancing act. The church at Ephesus was filled with brand new Christians who want to do the right thing. They want to speak the truth and act the truth and insist upon the truth. They want to hold one another accountable, but they didn't know how. Some were pointing out every tiny little insignificant fault to try to make each other more holy, but that got very irritating. Others used this new found accountability as an excuse to attack each other and build themselves up. Others were tempted to avoid the whole mess and began lying more to keep the peace. Sound familiar? It was time for Paul to teach them and us how to find the middle ground that is just right. Truth is not an optional ingredient in our life together, so avoidance and living the lie is out. But how are we to share the truth so that it does not wound us either? According to Paul, we have to mix it with love. We are to speak the truth with love, but the recipe has to be just right. Truth without love is cruelty. Love without truth is deception.

The first step is to ask ourselves: "Why am I really speaking up in the first place?" What is my true motive? Paul writes that we are to speak the truth as a way of protecting our salvation, healing our relationships, and defending the dignity of all human beings. Am I speaking in order to heal our relationship or to restore our friendship? Am I doing this to protect a brother or sister in Christ from sin? Am I doing this to protect and advocate for the wellbeing of others? Or has anger and bitterness crept in and I am speaking just to give that jerk a piece of my mind? Am I just trying to get my digs in but hide it under the guise of respectable Christian love? *If this word of truth burning on my lips will not protect anyone's salvation, build someone up, heal anyone's relationships or defend anyone's human dignity then it is not necessary.*

III. A SERVANT'S CALLING

We said earlier that God invites us to help God change the world. We have a part to play in the coming Kingdom of God. It is our real purpose in life and that purpose in life begins with God. How do we know what God wants us to do? God calls us, which means God gives us special assignments to be carried out on God's behalf. Henry Blackaby, in his book "Experiencing God" (B&H Publishing, 2008) shares that God is already at work in the world around us and God saves us in order to join in this work.

A. God Invites Us to Help Change the World.
1. God is at work around us.

If we think of God as being far away in Heaven, we might be tempted to think that we are the only hands and feet God has. We might think that God sends long distance messages giving us work to do on God's behalf. The problem is we can assume then that we are the only ones accomplishing things in this world because God is so far away in Heaven. NOT. TRUE. God is not only present with us but God is at work all the time. We remind mission teams when we commission them to never think that they are "taking God" to a place where God is needed. We do not "take" God anywhere. God is already there waiting for us to catch up. We join a story that is already in progress. We join God already at work. It may sound like an archaic word, but we teach what we call "Prevenient Grace" which is everything God does long before we even know God exists. God created the world once long ago, but the fact that the world keeps turning is the result of God's decision to let it continue. The earth is a colorful life giving oasis floating in the cold blackness of space. We continue to exist by the Providence of God, which is everything God provides to make things exist and live. God is also knocking on doors and whispering in the ears of people who do not know or refuse to believe God exists. God is actively trying to communicate with everyone on earth to begin a love relationship that is personal and meaningful. Our triune God is also working together to repair our broken world.

2. God saves us to join God's work.

By the death and resurrection of Jesus, we are made new which is great for us. Our salvation is a gift, but there is something in it for God. God has chosen to include human beings in the effort to repair and transform the world. We are saved to join God in this work. God is recruiting and building the workforce through which lives are changed and the world is getting better. We are baptized into the work that Jesus began.

3. God invites us to join God at work.

We may be saved by God to join in this healing work, but God does not force us to figure that out on our own. Throughout the Bible, God takes the initiative to involve us in God's activity. God invites us to join in by doing specific things at specific times with specific people in specific places. That's a lot of detail. How exactly can we know exactly what God wants? Many people believe that God is calling them to serve but struggle to figure out how. God does communicate, but the messages can come in different ways.

B. The Call We All Share

We are all called. As a follower of Jesus, we already have our marching orders found clearly in the following scriptures:

1. The Great Commission: Matthew 28: 19-20

"19 Go therefore and make disciples of all nations, baptizing them in the name of the Father and of the Son and of the Holy Spirit, 20 and teaching them to obey everything that I have commanded you. And remember, I am with you always, to the end of the age."

2. The Great Commandment: Matthew 22:37-40

"You shall love the Lord your God with all your heart, and with all your soul, and with all your mind.' 38 This is the greatest and first commandment. 39 And a second is like it: 'You shall love your neighbor as yourself.' 40 On these two commandments hang all the law and the prophets."

3. *The Great Requirement: Micah 6:8*

"...What does the Lord require of you but to do justice, and to love kindness, and to walk humbly with your God?"

4. *The Great Surrender: Luke 9:23*

"If any wish to become my followers, let them deny themselves, take up their cross daily, and follow me."

We don't require a Voice from Heaven or a burning bush to hear and respond to the call God places upon all who follow. We love God. We love our neighbor as ourselves. We dedicate ourselves to justice and kindness. We think of being called as those personal moments when God speaks dramatically and intimately to us giving specific orders for our lives. We will look more deeply into this kind of personal call in a moment when we consider "special assignments." But if you haven't experienced one of these supernatural moments with God, don't fret. You are called to Worship, Learn, Give, Serve and Encourage others to take their next step closer to God. That is what discipleship is all about: living out our call to serve God's plan for creation by following Jesus.

C. Receiving "Special Assignments" from God

1. God Speaks.

Moses heard God through a burning bush. Samuel heard God's Voice in the temple. Joseph heard from the Angel Gabriel through a dream. Elijah heard God in silence. God speaks and is still speaking. Sometimes it is powerful and audible. Other times it is a vague feeling, a nudge by our conscience that doesn't go away. Sometimes it is God inspiring the words of others. Through a daily discipline of prayer we become more sensitive to the leading of God and thus better able to discern what God is asking us to do. Through the scriptures, we see a pattern forming for those whom God recruits for a special assignment.

2. The call must be heard.

Young Samuel heard a voice calling his name in the middle of the night (I Samuel 3). He thought it was the priest Eli, but Eli was sound asleep. Sometimes we hear something stirring, but have no idea what it is.

3. The call must be recognized.

Only after young Samuel woke Eli up several times did the priest recognize what was actually happening. It was God who was calling the boy. Sometimes we need the perspective of other people recognize God at work in us.

4. The call must be claimed.

Only after Samuel knew that God was calling, and that God was calling HIM could a real conversation take place. If someone calls collect, you have to accept the charges. If someone hands you the telephone you have to decide whether or not you are going to take the call. When you claim a call from God, you choose to give God your undivided attention.

5. The call demands our response.

In the original "Mission Impossible" television show, the secret assignments were delivered by way of a tiny tape recorder. After the voice on the tape outlined the mission it always said "the mission, SHOULD YOU CHOOSE TO ACCEPT IT..." It may be God asking, but we are not slaves. We are free to choose whether we will accept the mission or not. We can refuse or we can get busy accomplishing God's will, but some response is required.

6. Noticing God

There are other ways to pick up on a call. Henry Blackaby, in his book "Experiencing God" (B&H Publishing, 2008) brings such welcome clarity to the idea of call. "*For Jesus, the revelation of where the Father was working WAS His invitation to join in that activity. When you see the Father accomplishing His purposes around you, that is your invitation to adjust your life to Him and join Him in that work.*" Here are several questions we can ask ourselves to determine where God is at work around us:

a. "Where do I see lives changing for the better?"

God changes lives. So when you see it happening you know God is behind it. Go help.

b. "Where do I see the world becoming a better place?"

God makes the world a better place. Maybe you see the homeless getting off the street. Maybe you see the drug addicted getting clean. Maybe you see wounded soldiers being helped back into a normal life after combat. Maybe it is feeding the hungry and assisting the poor. God makes the world better. So when you see it happening you know God is behind it. Go help.

c. "What unmet needs burden me?"

If the last two questions point us towards the things that warm and inspire our hearts, this question asks what troubles them. What suffering do we see? What is unfair? What is being overlooked? Who is being neglected? What causes you to say "Someone ought to do something about that?" Several years ago my brother in law Michael began a new job as a high school chemistry teacher. He joined a local church but began to be frustrated that there were no classes or groups for people his age. He had recently graduated college and chose this church because there were younger people in worship, but no one had ever gathered them together in a group to learn to follow Jesus together. Finally I said "Perhaps the reason this bothers you so much is because God is calling you to lead it." Michael had been very active in Navigators Campus Ministry at Penn State for six years and even attended a national training event in Colorado. I doubt there was anyone else more qualified than him. What frustrates you? What offends your sense of right and wrong? What do you find yourself constantly complaining about? You may be a spiritual canary in the coal mine. The canaries were more sensitive to poisonous gas and would be overcome long before the miners. Their sensitivity saved the lives of countless miners. You may be more sensitive to a particular problem or injustice than anyone else. Act on that with God and you too may save more lives than you can count.

d. "What blessing am I most grateful for in my life?"

Gratitude is a powerful motivator, too. One of the ways we can express our gratitude for the greatest blessings in life is to pay it forward in a way that allows others to enjoy the same blessings in their lives. A woman who has dreamed of owning a home her whole life is not just thrilled to move in, but volunteers tirelessly for Habitat for Humanity to help others achieve the same dream. A former addict who thanks God every day for life saving sobriety leads recovery groups. A mom, whose greatest joy is her children, dedicates herself to promote adoption.

D. God equips us to join God at work.

1. Gifts of the Spirit

The Spirit gives different gifts or abilities to us as the Spirit chooses. They are practical gifts, meaning they are given to be used for the common good and to build up the Body of Christ.

a. Discovering Your Gifts

You can discover your gifts through a spiritual gifts inventory. By answering questions, you are given a glimpse into which gifts are most active in your life at that moment. Keep in mind that these inventories are a modern invention which means they may be discovered the old fashioned way: through prayer, call, and service. By trying to serve in different ways we begin to get a knack for what kinds of assignments are best for us. When you are serving outside your gifts, you will most likely experience frustration and anxiety. Keep in mind also that God may call us into a new area of service in order to develop a new gift in us. Many are taught to use the results of the inventory to choose the area of service to which they should dedicate themselves. Henry Blackaby in "Experiencing God" gives us a healthy reminder that these inventories may tempt us to put the cart before the horse:

"If God merely provided us with a gift, we would tend to place our confidence in the gift rather than in Him. But since the Holy Spirit does the work through us, we must continually rely upon our relationship with Him if we are to be effective in the ministry He gives us. Conversely, if we refuse to obey what God asks us to do, the Holy Spirit will not equip us. We don't need to be equipped for something we refuse to do. Our divine enabling always comes as we obey what God tells us to do—never before our obedience. Focus your attention on hearing God's call to an assignment which is His invitation for you to join Him. When you adjust your life to Him and obey Him, the Holy Spirit will work in you, enabling you to accomplish what God desires."

As you will see below, each gift corresponds to a role or task necessary to help the Church help God to change lives and make the world a better place. We do not choose these for ourselves like choosing food from a menu. The Holy Spirit chooses for us according to the Father's plan for us. We are indebted to Erik Rees for his explanation of these gifts. You can find them in his excellent book "S.H.A.P.E." (Zondervan 2006) which offers a variety of ways of understanding how God has shaped your life to serve.

I Corinthians 12:8-10
Wisdom

The God given special ability to serve and strengthen the Body of Christ by making wise decisions and counseling others with sound advice, all in accordance with God's will.

Knowledge

The God given special ability to serve and strengthen the Body of Christ by communicating God's truth to others in a way that promotes justice, honesty, and understanding.

Faith

The God given special ability to serve and strengthen the Body of Christ by stepping out in faith in order to see God's purposes accomplished, trusting God to handle any and all obstacles along the way.

Healing
The God given special ability to serve and strengthen the Body of Christ by healing and restoring to health, beyond traditional and natural means, those who are sick, hurting, and suffering.

Miracles
The God given special ability to serve and strengthen the Body of Christ through supernatural acts that bring validity to God and God's power.

Prophecy
The God given special ability to serve and strengthen the Body of Christ by offering messages from God that comfort, encourage, guide, warn, or reveal sin in a way that leads to repentance and spiritual growth.

Discernment
The God given special ability to serve and strengthen the Body of Christ by recognizing truth or error within a message, person, or event.

Tongues
The God given special ability to serve and strengthen the Body of Christ by communicating God's message in a special language unknown to the speaker.

Interpretation of Tongues
The God given special ability to serve and strengthen the Body of Christ by understanding, at a specific time, God's message when spoken by another using a special language unknown to the others in attendance.

I Corinthians 12:28
Apostle
The God given special ability to serve and strengthen the Body of Christ by launching and leading new ministry ventures that advance God's purposes and expand God's kingdom.

Prophet
See definition above.

Teacher

The God given special ability to serve and strengthen the Body of Christ by teaching sound doctrine in relevant ways, empowering people to gain a sound and mature spiritual education.

Miracles
See definition above.

Healing
See definition above.

Helping
The God given special ability to serve and strengthen the Body of Christ by offering others assistance in reaching goals that glorify God and strengthen the Body of Christ.

Administration
The God given special ability to serve and strengthen the Body of Christ by effectively organizing resources and people in order to efficiently reach ministry goals.

Tongues
See definition above.

d. Romans 12:6-8
Prophecy
See definition above.

Serving
See definition for "Helping" above.

Teaching
See definition above.

Encouragement
The God given special ability to serve and strengthen the Body of Christ by helping others live God-centered lives through inspiration, counseling, and empowerment.

Giving
The God given special ability to serve and strengthen the Body of Christ by joyfully supporting and funding various kingdom initiatives through material contributions and the tithe.

Leadership
The God given special ability to serve and strengthen the Body of Christ by casting vision, stimulating spiritual growth, applying strategies, and achieving success where God's purposes are concerned.

Mercy
The God given special ability to serve and strengthen the Body of Christ by ministering to those who suffer physically, emotionally, spiritually, or relationally. Their actions are characterized by love, care, compassion, and kindness toward others.

Ephesians 4:11
Apostle
See definition above.

Prophet
See definition above.

Evangelist
The God given special ability to serve and strengthen the Body of Christ by sharing the love of Christ with others in a way that draws them to respond by accepting God's free gift of eternal life.

Pastor
The God given special ability to serve and strengthen the Body of Christ by taking spiritual responsibility for a group of believers and equipping them to live Christ-centered lives. Shepherding is another word used for this particular gift.

Teacher
See definition above.

2. Fruits of the Spirit
We shared earlier that the Spirit moves in and dwells in us to conform us into the likeness of Christ (Romans 8:29). That means that the longer the Spirit works within us, the more we not only imitate the life and character of Jesus, we also genuinely share the same qualities. Fruit grows on a healthy tree as it matures. The "Fruits of the Spirit" are evidence that the Holy Spirit is making progress in us and we are growing to maturity. We call this work of the Spirit "sanctification" which means growing in holiness. As seen earlier, a growing life begins to make the world better by adding more love, joy, peace, patience, kindness, goodness, faithfulness, gentleness, and

self-control. As we practice self-examination, from week to week, we ask ourselves: "Am I more loving? More patient? More kind? More self-controlled?" Let's take a closer look at these qualities:

Galatians 5:22-24
Love
A caring commitment, in which choose to treat others with kindness, compassion, and respect. It is what we do as well as what we feel.

Joy
James writes "*count it all joy when you face trials*" (James 1:2). That seems odd to us that we would be joyful about bad things happening. But that is because we don't understand what joy really is. Joy is different from happiness. If happiness depends on what happens to us, joy depends on what is going on inside of us. Joy is an unshakable feeling of hope that despite what I am facing now, my life is in a good place with God and heading in the right direction where it will only get better. THAT is joy.

Peace
Peace as Jesus speaks of it is more than just the absence of conflict. It is wholeness, health, contentment. In Hebrew we use the word "Shalom" which is often translated as "peace" but it is a much bigger word than that. It means "the fullness of all that God desires for you" which results in serenity and tranquility of mind.

Patience
Patience is the quality of self-control which shows itself particularly in a willingness to wait upon God and his will. Believers are called upon to be patient in their expectations of God's actions, and in their relationships with one another.

Kindness
Earlier we defined kindness as being motivated by a desire to help and not harm. It is the countless thoughtful, generous things we do for others to ensure their wellbeing and happiness.

Gentleness
Gentleness is an expression of our compassion. It is marked by tenderness and care, the opposite of roughness and force.

Generosity
Generosity is the willingness, openness, and desire to give and share with God and with others.

Self-Control
Self-control is exactly what the word implies. It is the ability to control ourselves physically, spiritually, and emotionally even in times of great stress and temptation. We practice self-control through prayer and self-denial.

3. Guidance of the Spirit
The disciples had to panic when Jesus told them in the upper room that he was leaving them. There was so much they still had to learn. He sent the Holy Spirit who would continue to teach them and remind them of everything Jesus had ever taught them. They were also told not to worry when arrested and brought before kings and magistrates to defend the faith. They had no need to worry about what they would say because the Spirit would place the right words on their lips. The Spirit guides us as we follow Jesus into uncharted waters.

4. Encouragement of the Spirit
The Spirit was called the "Comforter" who soothes us in our fears and grief and strengthens us in our struggles.

5. Power of the Spirit
Starting with Pentecost, the Spirit came with power to proclaim the Good News in every language. This power makes the unlikely likely and the impossible possible.

IV. ACTS OF MERCY
There are 59 different verses in the New Testament that include the words "one another." Love one another. Bear one another's burdens. Forgive one another. Encourage one another. This is that "friendship of a truly supportive family" that is one of the reasons we choose Jesus in the first place. We learn to care by caring. A group that learns to follow Jesus together cares for each other. (See "Mutual Care")

We treat others as we would like to be treated. We love our neighbor as we love ourselves. We help. We care. We pitch in. We protect. We comfort. We join people in their moments of need and we remind them that because we share the planet with others we don't have to struggle alone. The Church was created to point the world toward God. The things we do reveal to the world who God is, which is why we help, care, provide and forgive. God helps, cares, and provides. God invented grace which is why we treat people better than they deserve. Kindness is never limited to those who "deserve" it. That is why we welcome everyone, help everyone, and share what we have with everyone. God does not ration out kindness with a teaspoon and neither do we. God is extravagant in kindness and so are we. On one hand, ministry in Christ's name is simply helping others to meet their needs, such as:

A. Physical Needs

Jesus fed the hungry, healed the sick, and raised the dead. We do likewise helping people to survive. It may include providing food or medical care but might also include helping someone with their rent, electric bill, repairing a leaky roof or building a handicap ramp. Helping people in a moment of need is always the right thing to do but they also point us toward God and the coming kingdom where no one is hungry, sick, or in need.

The Christ-like formula for giving and helping others generously and compassionately without weakening character and personal responsibility is this: *"We bear one another's burdens so each can carry their own load."* We help one another in the crises of our lives that threaten to harm us and destroy us so that we can help people get back on their feet and take care of themselves. As shared in an earlier section, we distinguish between a burden and backpack, the crisis that could crush us and our daily obligations of life.

B. Emotional Needs

Emotions are natural warning signals that alert us when something is out of balance in our relationships. Feeling anger, jealousy, fear or worry is natural but BEING angry, jealous, worried or afraid is a choice to allow these emotions to take control and make bad decisions for us. When we are angry we can use someone to help calm us down. When we grieve we need comfort. We all need someone to talk to who understands. We all need a shoulder to cry on. We all have issues in our past that cling to us and destroy our joy in the present. We talk. We listen. We pray. We may even sit with someone in silence because there is nothing to say other than "You are not alone." Care, prayer, and conversation can go a long way to restore our emotional health, but sometimes we need professional care. We support mental health care providers with the same confidence and gratitude that we support doctors and surgeons. As a congregation we not only refer hurting people to counseling but help pay for it when the cost is beyond reach. We offer one another compassion, the willingness to share each other's pain.

C. Relational Needs

Sometimes our problems are with other people. A feud breaks out between two siblings. A husband and wife are considering divorce. A conflict erupts between two people in the congregation. We sometimes find it difficult to forgive and reconcile and we help each others to make peace. Conflict is actually an opportunity to make and strengthen friendships but it must be handled with care. Jesus clearly teaches that repairing conflicts is the work of the church in Matthew 18: 15-17.

15 *"If your brother or sister sins, go and point out their fault, just between the two of you. If they listen to you, you have won them over. 16 But if they will not listen, take one or two others along, so that 'every matter may be established by the testimony of two or three witnesses.' 17 If they still refuse to listen, tell it to the church; and if they refuse to listen even to the church, treat them as you would a pagan or a tax collector."*

1. Mutual Grace

Grace is treating others better than they deserve which covers a lot of ground. "Mutual Grace" is a broad way to speak of all the ways we choose to treat one another better than we deserve. We don't really stop to ask whether someone deserves our kindness when we are happy with them. Grace is required when kindness is hard to give. We are entering a challenging set of teachings in which Jesus requires us to love, pray for, and care for our enemies as well as our friends. It is no credit to us if we treat our friends well. Even non-believers do this. What should separate Followers of Jesus from the rest of the world is how we keep God's big picture in mind and treat our enemies.

2. Forgiveness

Nothing ruins our relationship with God quite like our sins and mistakes. If God kicked us out the door for good the first time we told a lie, or were cruel or selfish, then God would be all alone. God wants to fix what is wrong in our relationship and put our mistakes behind us because God wants to be with us. Forgiveness is the willingness to get over the anger and resentment, to cancel the grudge and punishment. It is the process by which our past becomes irrelevant to our future. Anger drives two people farther away from each other and resentment keeps them apart. We have to choose to let go of both the anger and the resentment in order to come back together. Forgiveness is letting go. Forgiveness opens the door to allow us to come back together and stay together. We hold grudges for all kinds of insults and slights, both minor and major. We hate each other for being different, such as being of a different color, different religion, or different country. Human beings just don't trust or like each other all that much. It breaks God's heart, because God wants us to get along with each other and enjoy each other as much as God enjoys us. There is only so much of this repair work God can do for us. If they are our mistakes and our grudges, then only we can set them aside. Why is it so important to us? There are several reasons.

a. Forgiveness releases us. First, forgiveness is not just letting the other person off the hook. It is a release and a healing to us. We are free from carrying the burden of the hurt. We can free our mind from rehearsing the countless wrongs we've endured. We can stop rehearsing all the angry things we want to say when we see that person next. We can stop looking in the rear view mirror all the time and be free to live again in the here and now. By carrying the grudge, we are giving another power over us. We are allowing them to control our happiness. Forgiving releases us from carrying the weight of anger, bitterness and resentment. Proverbs 6:27 asks *"Can a man carry fire next to his chest and his clothes not be burned?"* We are burned by the fire of anger that we want to throw at someone else. For our own sake, it is time to put out the fire.

b. Forgiveness requires God's help. Second, forgiveness is not easy to do without staying close to God. It is a God sized task that is often too big for us to accomplish on our own. By attempting it, we draw on God's grace and power and grow closer to God in the process. We will need that grace and power every moment of every day. Prayer becomes even more of a lifeline to us. The best way to keep that help coming is to stay fully connected to God all day long. (See "Practicing the Presence of God")

c. Forgive to be forgiven. Lastly, and maybe the most importantly, God will not forgive us if we refuse to forgive other people. Jesus couldn't say it any more clearly when he said: *"...so will my Father do to you if you do not forgive your brother from your heart."* He taught the same thing in the Lord's Prayer. We ask God to *"forgive us our sins as we forgive those who sin against us."*

He teaches further that *"If you are willing to forgive others their trespasses, your Heavenly Father will also forgive you. But if you do not forgive others their trespasses, neither will your Father forgive you."* If you want to be forgiven, then forgive someone else. Our peace comes from giving peace to someone else. Our life comes from giving life to someone else. Pretty clever of God to tie our wellbeing to the wellbeing of others. It's a pretty good incentive, isn't it? It is good news that we can have all the forgiveness we want from God, and we know exactly how to receive it. Confess your sin to God and ask for forgiveness while at the same time forgiving someone else. Never ask for forgiveness in prayer without also telling God who you are forgiving as well.

d. How to Forgive

Understanding why forgiveness is important is easier than actually forgiving. When we take seriously everything we have learned so far and add them together, forgiveness becomes inevitable.

e. The Chain of Forgiveness

A chain reaction is a series of events set in motion by an initial step. Push over the first domino and as it falls it knocks over the second, which in turn knocks the third. Forgiveness is a chain reaction in which we commit fully to the first link in the chain (humility) which makes grace possible, and so on.

Humility + Grace + Love + Obedience + Sacrifice = Forgiveness

Humility is always the first step. If we struggle with humility, forgiveness will be impossible. Pride gets in the way. We begin to forgive by meditating on humility first. We consider others as more important than ourselves. Grace is humility in action. It is treating others better than they deserve. Meditate upon Grace. Love is Grace applied in a million different specific ways through kindness, compassion, and respect. Meditate upon Love. As we've seen above, Forgiveness is a currency we trade constantly among ourselves that makes life together possible. God has chosen to forgive us but makes forgiving others a requirement for claiming our forgiveness. This is often overlooked. Forgiveness is not just a matter of whether we feel like it or not, it is a crucial matter of obeying the will of God. Meditate upon obedience. Sacrifice requires giving something up. When it comes to forgiveness, we give up our insistence on being right. We give up our desire to punish. We give up our desire for revenge. We give up our insistence that God judge between us and prove once and for all that we are righteous and our opponent is evil. That is required to seek the wellbeing of all involved. By being willing to let go we are taking a risk that we might be hurt again. That is a Sacrifice, being willing to lose so that all might win. This is why forgiveness is difficult for us. Too often we try to jump from hurt to forgiveness in one step and fall short. Forgiveness is a process that must be taken step by step. Do the math. Take the steps.

3. Reconciliation

If forgiveness is clearing away the obstacles between us, reconciliation is the process of moving back together again, restoring a broken relationship to health. Forgiveness is rarely once and done. Like grief, resentment can sneak up on us and come flooding back in with no warning. Reconciliation requires constant forgiveness because as we move closer together to someone we resent the original conflict can reignite. That is the risk we spoke of earlier. Forgiveness can be one sided. We can forgive someone who will never give us an apology. But reconciliation takes two. As said above "At the cross of Christ, God strips away our guilt and sin, removing it completely. God buries our guilt with Christ and raises up a future with new possibilities. But God also buried His anger and blame against us, too." When burying the hatchet, we both help to dig and we both must throw something into the hole. Forgiveness is an ongoing process of dousing embers inside of us with Living Water. Reconciliation is also a process:

a. The Chain of Reconciliation

As shared above, a chain reaction is a series of events set in motion by an initial step. Push over the first domino and as it falls it knocks over the second, which in turn knocks the third. Reconciliation is a chain reaction in which we commit fully to the first link in the chain (forgiveness) which makes confession easier, and so on. Because Reconciliation begins with Forgiveness, it begins with Humility. Humility is always the first step in anything we do as followers of Jesus.

Forgiveness + Confession + Repair + Repentance + Patience + Trust = Reconciliation

i. Forgiveness (see above)

ii. Confession is telling the truth about the problem between us, particularly our role in it. We take responsibility for what we have done to cause harm to others whether it be our words or our actions. Many arguments consist of accusations and denials. We defend ourselves against accusations of wrongdoing even when we have done wrong. The refusal to even admit what has happened can be infuriating and will turbocharge the emotion and frustration, escalating the conflict while solving nothing. Once we confess, we can stop wrestling over blame and begin repairing the damage.

iii. Repair: It is not possible to right every wrong. Some things can't be undone, but to the degree we are able, we take the responsibility to clean up the mess that we've created. As we slowly put things back together, it is wise to learn from our mistakes and never do this again. This is also about Justice.

iv. Repentance is making a change that will hopefully prevent this kind of conflict in the future. Repent means to "turn" or to go another way. It is charting a different course in a new direction. Repentance is a new way of living, a midcourse correction.

v. Patience is required because this process takes time. Our relationship is not repaired overnight. We are a work in progress and our progress will be sporadic and irregular. We will have our good days and our bad days.

vi. Trust The relationship is not fully restored until trust is re-established. Rebuilding Trust also requires patience. Trust is a strange commodity because it really cannot be demanded. It must be earned. The good news is, trust can be rebuilt. Stephen M. R. Covey, in his landmark book "The Speed of Trust" (Free Press 2006) offers thirteen behaviors that can build trust:

1. Talk Straight: Say what is on your mind. Don't hide your agenda. When we talk straight, we tell the truth and leave the right impression. We spend entirely too much time trying to decipher truth from spin. Straight talk needs to be paired with tact. There is no excuse for being so blunt that you hurt feelings and destroy relationships. Tact is a skill that can be learned and when coupled with straight talk, will build Relationship Trust.

2. Demonstrate Respect: The principle behind demonstrating respect is the value of the individual. The behavior is acting out the Golden Rule. Almost every culture and religion recognizes the value of the Golden Rule. We should treat people the way we want to be treated. Our actions should show we care. They should be sincere. People will notice if an action is motivated by a lesser reason or an impure value. Respect is demonstrated in the "little" things we do daily.

3. Create Transparency: Tell the truth in a way that can be verified. Transparency is based on principles of honesty, openness, integrity and authenticity. It is based on doing things in the open where all can see.

4. Right Wrongs: To right a wrong is much more than apologizing. It involves making restitution. It is the principle of going the extra mile. Some will justify their wrongful behavior while others will try covering up their misdeeds. Both of these attempts will not only fail to make deposits in trust accounts, but are certain to make substantial withdrawals.

5. Show Loyalty: First, give credit to others. As a leader you need to give credit to the individuals responsible for success. Giving credit to others is the right thing to do. It will foster an environment where people are encouraged to be creative and innovative. It will increase trust and have a direct impact on the bottom line.

Second, speak about others as if they were present. Some people think it builds relationships to talk about others. The opposite is true. Talking about others behind their back will decrease trust with your current audience.

6. Deliver Results: Results give you instant credibility and trust. Delivering results is based on competence. *"This behavior grows out of the principles of responsibility, accountability and performance. The opposite of Deliver Results is performing poorly or failing to deliver. The counterfeit is delivering activities instead of results."* Delivering results converts the cynics, establishes trust in new relationships, and restores trust that has been lost due to lack of competence. It is also the first half of Covey's definition of leadership: getting results in a way that inspires trust.

7. Get Better: In today's ever changing environment one must continue to improve or become obsolete. You cannot learn a skill and ride that one skill for 30 years. You have to constantly be improving. When others see you continually learning and adapting to change, they become more confident in your ability to lead into the future. Be careful not to become a life-long learner that does not produce, or one who sees only one way to improve self and others.

Covey suggest two ways to get better. First, seek feedback from those around you. Second, learn from your mistakes.

8. Confront Reality: We cannot close our eyes to the tough realities we face. If we are honest about the difficult issues and are addressing them head-on, people will trust us. We have to avoid the temptation to avoid reality or act as if we are addressing the difficult issues while we are actually evading them.

9. Clarify Expectations: It is important to focus on a shared vision of success up front. This is a preventative measure. When expectations are not clearly defined up front, trust and speed both go down. A lot of time is wasted due to leaders not clearly defining expectations.

Failure to clarify expectations leaves people guessing. When results are delivered they fall short and are not valued.

10. Practice Accountability: In a 2002 Golin/Harris poll, "assuming personal responsibility and accountability" was ranked as the second highest factor in building trust. Great leaders build trust by first holding themselves accountable then holding others accountable.

Holding yourself accountable includes taking responsibility for bad results. It is often our natural response to blame others for failure. When we fail, we need to look in the mirror.

Holding others accountable allows performers to feel good about the job they are doing. It also increases trust by assuring performers that slackers and poor performers will not pull them down.

11. Listen First: Listening before prescribing, builds trust. Trying to give advice before knowing all the facts is a waste of time and simply not fair. You need to be careful not to learn the mechanics of listening and leave the impression you are listening when you really are not. Remember that communication is more than just words so you will have to   listen to nonverbal messages as well. If a person is displaying a high level of emotion, they don't feel understood. Keep listening. Also, a person is not likely to ask for advice until they feel you understand all the pertinent information. Don't give advice too early.

12. Keep Commitments: Covey refers to this as the "Big Kahuna" of all the trust behaviors. When you make a commitment you build hope. When you keep a commitment you build trust. Be careful when making commitments. Make only the commitments you can keep. Also, don't be vague when making commitments.

There are implicit and explicit commitments, and violating either is a huge withdrawal from the trust account. Be aware of the expectations to a commitment i.e. Some companies are strict with internal meeting times and others are more flexible. Also, remember family commitments are just as important if not more so than work commitments.

13. Extend Trust: The other behaviors help you become a trusted leader; this behavior helps you become a trusting leader. We should extend trust to those who have earned it. Be willing to extend trust to those who are still earning it. Be wise in extending trust to those who have not exemplified a character worth trusting.

Too often we want to skip over the process of Confession, Repair, Repentance, and Trust and get right to Reconciliation. We want something for nothing. Trust is earned, not demanded. Unlike forgiveness, reconciliation is a two way street. It takes two people doing their part who are committed to coming back together in a healthy way. We can decide to act is if nothing happened but without clearing the air, without taking out the trash, without repairing what has been damaged, without rebuilding the bridge the embers are still smoldering deep down inside waiting to ignite again. Everything costs something. German pastor and theologian Dietrich Bonhoeffer speaks out against the dangers of what he calls "cheap grace" in his work "The Cost of Discipleship" (A Testament of Freedom.

HarperCollins 1995):

"Cheap grace is the grace we bestow on ourselves. Cheap grace is the preaching of forgiveness without requiring repentance, baptism without church discipline, Communion without confession...Cheap grace is grace without discipleship, grace without the cross, grace without Jesus Christ, living and incarnate."

"The essence of grace, we suppose, is that the account has been paid in advance; and, because it has been paid, everything can be had for nothing...."

But we know that it is an Undeniable Truth that "Everything Costs Something" and as Thomas Paine once said: *"What we obtain too cheaply, we esteem too lightly: it is dearness only that gives everything its value."*

A Warning About Reconciliation

It is important to note that while forgiveness is always right, reconciliation is not. Reconciliation is not best in every situation. In cases of abuse or deep betrayal it may not be safe or appropriate to come back together. We can choose to forgive in order to release ourselves from the burden of bitterness and resentment. We can extend grace to forgive those who have neither asked for it nor deserve it. Jesus forgave his executioners. A woman can forgive her abusive ex-husband, but it could be fatal to move back in. Putting a conflict behind us to make it irrelevant to our future is good for all of us. We bless each other without malice to go our separate ways.

D. Spiritual Needs

We all have our doubts and hang ups when it comes to God. We all need our "spotters and sponsors" who can help us to keep taking steps closer to God (See "Mutual Accountability" in the section on the Disciplines of Learning).

V. Acts of Justice

God changes the world one life at a time. If you change enough lives you can begin to turn the tide of selfishness, corruption, abuse and greed. That is where the idea of justice comes in. Sin is not just the individual disobedient acts we commit. Sin is also weaved into the very fabric of society that is larger than all of us. It is a system that we find ourselves trapped in. Acts of Mercy are the little kindnesses we give to each other, like feeding the hungry. Justice asks why people are hungry in the first place. Mercy cares for the poor while Justice strives to eliminate poverty. Just as the ancient prophets served to warn and guide the kings of Israel, the Church exists to be the conscience of the nation around it. Justice may require us to confront the powerful and speak up in the halls of power. It may require us to defend the powerless, question authority, and open our eyes to the unfairness around us that we overlook and accept. We work for justice to ensure the greatest good for all.

Peace Making

Jesus said "*Blessed are the peacemakers for they will be called children of God.*" In the simplest terms possible, peacemaking is assisting others to forgive and reconcile. Forgiveness and reconciliation require rational choices to overrule our destructive emotions that come so naturally to us. Forgiveness is not a thoughtless reflex, but a chosen, measured response. It can be a struggle to make an informed choice instead of a knee jerk reaction. Sometimes we need help with that. When discussing "Mutual Accountability" we introduced the concept of "spotters and sponsors." Spotters help when lifting weights in the gym. They stand by to help take the weight when arms get tired to prevent injury. Spotters also push and encourage to keep the lifter motivated. Those on the road to recovery, as in Alcoholics Anonymous, are assigned a sponsor who encourages, listens, reminds the person in their care about the principles of recovery, and holds them accountable in moments of weakness. We need to keep the big picture in mind that in the midst of temptation our goal is sobriety.

Peacemakers are "spotters and sponsors" who work with people in conflict, struggling with forgiveness and reconciliation, and attempt to decrease anger, hatred, and violence. They can work with friends who welcome their assistance or they can take a prophetic stance and intervene in a situation without being welcomed or invited. Consider the risks taken by faithful priests during the unrest in Kiev, Ukraine in January 2014.

"For three months a volatile crowd of protesters, swelling at one point to some 300,000 people, camped in the bitter-cold streets of the city. Among the tumult were numerous priests. Wearing the vestments of their office and carrying crosses and icons, they were highly identifiable amidst the chaotic clash of people. Photos show them blessing both police and protestors, tending to the wounded, ministering to the dying, and praying among the dead. They set up prayer tents, and a cathedral's nave served as a temporary hospital and shelter. The most striking photos show them — some alone, some with one or two others — standing between the lines of police and the angry mobs. One photo shows a resolute bishop who alone served as a human shield to quell the violence. Another shows two priests with votive candles burning and crosses in hand doing the same."

("This Restless Sea: Contemplative Practice and Prophetic Witness Amidst Violence" by FR. James Krueger, (www.onbeing.com) December 26, 2015)

Sometimes the first step of peace making is getting in between two sides to prevent any more violence, like a referee stepping in between two out of control boxers. Referees in the ring have a dangerous job. Just by being so close to the fighters, they have accidentally been stepped on, punched, and even knocked out. Peacemaking is equally risky because we are involved in a conflict, not as a combatant, but as a referee attempting to ensure safety and order. Collateral damage happens. Sometimes the peacemaker becomes the target of the violence. In 2014 Croatian boxer Vido Loncar was so angry at losing a match he attacked the referee, beating him furiously. Then there is the tragedy of Kent State University in 1970 when members of the National Guard opened fire on unarmed peaceful student protesters.

Understanding Anger and Conflict

The reason conflict is dangerous is because it can escalate so quickly. What starts out as a minor misunderstanding can end in violence and murder if not handled well. Speed Leas describes **Five Levels of Conflict** that show how anger grows out of control.

Level One begins as a Problem to Solve.
We have a difference of opinion or different needs and values. It's not personal it is just a problem. If we are not able to solve the problem the situation develops.

Level Two is marked by a Disagreement.
The problem begins to take a back seat as things get personal. We begin to focus more on the person disagreeing with us than on solving the problem. Distrust and hurt feelings begin. We begin to confuse a difference of opinion with a personal slight. If we cannot turn our attention back to solving the initial problem things will deteriorate rapidly to Level Three.

Level Three is a Contest to be won.
Nobody likes to lose. Pride (remember Pride?) gets in our way and now we care only about winning. Personal attacks become more painful. Sides form, each seeking allies to form opposing factions. This is where anger distorts our perception of reality. Everything we see and hear is colored by our anger.

Level Four is where the war breaks out into Fight or Flight.
We begin to see the world and each other in black and white. Our opponents are now our enemies who are evil while we are righteous in every way. It is here that initial problems are long forgotten and we indulge in fantasies of good versus evil which make compromise impossible.

Compromising with evil is turning your back on God. Level Four is about the absolute defeat of the enemy.

Level Five is the Nuclear Option.

It is an intractable situation and cannot be solved as both sides are committed to the absolute destruction of the other.

Leas also identifies a Level Zero: Depression.

Depression is defined as "anger turned inward." The best response to anger according to Leas is to try to walk back to a lower level. We must refocus on the initial problem and solve it. (There will also need to be forgiveness and reconciliation to repair the personal damage done.)

Controlling Our Anger

Perhaps the best way to control our anger is to prevent it from catching fire in the first place. We tend to act as if our anger is automatic, but as we learned earlier, our emotions are a result of our own choices. Remember that quote by Viktor Frankl from earlier?

"Between the stimulus and the response, there is a space. In that space is our power to choose our response. In our response lies our growth and our freedom."..."*Everything can be taken from a man but one thing: the last of the human freedoms—to choose one's attitude in any given set of circumstances, to choose one's own way."*

He also said:

"Forces beyond your control can take away everything you possess except one thing, your freedom to choose how you will respond to the situation."

Or, as Roman emperor Marcus Aurelius explained:

"If you are distressed by anything external, the pain is not due to the thing itself, but to your estimate of it; and this you have the power to revoke at any moment."

"You don't have to turn this into something. It doesn't have to upset you. Things can't shape our decisions by themselves."

"Choose not to be harmed, and you won't feel harmed. Don't feel harmed and you haven't been."

"Reject your sense of injury and the injury itself disappears."

Irrational Beliefs

Our response depends on how we think about the situation. It is possible to choose patience and reason even when we are mistreated. Psychologist Albert Ellis taught that mistakes in our thinking about the way things should be are the cause of all our anxiety. He created a list of "11 Irrational Beliefs" that we all seem to believe. They are why we get defensive, offended, frustrated and insulted by events around us. Be completely honest with yourself as you read through each of these beliefs. How many do you believe? Are these beliefs rational or irrational (make no sense)? Will they be helpful or unhelpful?

Irrational Beliefs Challenged by Albert Ellis

1. I must be loved by everyone or I am not lovable.
2. I must do everything well or I am incompetent.
3. I must damn others if they do not treat me well.
4. I must damn life if things do not go well.
5. I must control events and people because they control how I feel.
6. I must worry about anything fearful or risky.
7. I must avoid responsibilities and problems in order to be comfortable and content.
8. I must depend on other people or else my life will fall apart.
9. I must be controlled by my past and disturbed by anything that once disturbed me.
10. I must damn other people's problems and be disturbed by them.
11. I must damn life if I cannot find the perfect answers to human problems.

You can imagine how unhappy we will be if we expect all of these to be true for us all the time. As disciples, we reject these irrational beliefs as fairy tales we tell ourselves and face life as it really is. It takes honesty and courage to do that and diplomacy and compassion to help others to do that as well.

Moralistic Judgements: Observing vs. Evaluating

Psychologist Marshall Rosenberg in his book "Nonviolent Communication" (PuddleDancer Press 2003) teaches a second human tendency that gets us in trouble. We evaluate everything. When we see another person, we tend to evaluate everything about them in terms of what is good or bad, right or wrong, righteous or evil, etc. These black and white evaluations help us decide whether a person is a friend or an enemy and whether he or she deserves reward or punishment. If reward, we treat them well. We offer patience. We offer kindness. We give them the benefit of the doubt. But if the person is an enemy, we are all too happy to offer punishment through harsh words, insults, cold shoulder or physical violence. These harsh actions will come easily to us because we believe the person is getting what they deserve. This skewed view of justice, getting what one deserves, fuels the escalation of conflict documented by Leas and is antithetical to a Christian teaching of grace, which is treating people better than they deserve. When we make moralistic judgements we categorize others according their worth as a human being. Jesus commanded us to never judge another. When we judge, we are determining the worth of another human being which is something only God can do. We might judge the actions and choices of other people, but never the people themselves. We learn then to observe without evaluating.

Fight of Flight

The human brain was designed for more dangerous times. When our ancient ancestors were out foraging for food and were attacked by a lion, they needed to react quickly. Our brains are designed to respond as the amygdala or threat center of the brain starts dumping stress hormones into the blood stream which power us up to either fight for our lives or run for the hills. It turbocharges our brain with enough palpable fear to drive us to safety or enough anger and rage to fight to the death. The problem with this is that our lives are much safer now. We don't run into lions and bears in the office. What our brains perceive as threats are the actions and insults of others which may not be pleasant but are far from life threatening. We however automatically react with the same intensity of adrenaline, anger, and fear as our ancestors which is overkill and causes situations to escalate. This comes from the less rational and more instinctual parts of our brain. We are not at our smartest when we are angry or afraid. We do not think clearly, which is why we choose to opt out of anger altogether.

Dr. Rick Brinkman and Dr. Rick Kirschner, in their excellent book "Dealing With People You can't Stand" (McGraw Hill 1994) state that:

"Everybody responds to different situations with different levels of assertiveness. During times of challenge, difficulty, or stress, people tend to move out of their comfort zone, and they become either more passive or more aggressive than their normal mode of operation. When challenged, a highly assertive individual might make his or her presence known by speaking louder or taking action faster. An individual of low assertiveness might be increasingly reticent about the same activities. You can recognize how assertive people are by how they look (directing their energy outward or inward), how they sound (from shouting to mumbling to being silent), and what they say (from making demands to offering awkward suggestions)."

In other words, when upset, people will respond either aggressively (fight) or passively (flight). We can however choose to stay actively engaged in a constructive way without blowing up or run away. This might sound impossible to you, but the Bible offers multiple encouragements to do just that:

"Know this, my beloved brothers: let every person be quick to hear, slow to speak, slow to anger; for the anger of man does not produce the righteousness of God." (James 1:19,20 NRSV)

"A gentle answer turns away wrath, but a harsh word stirs up anger." (Proverbs 15:- NIV)

Frankl Reconsidered

So how, you may ask, do I avoid getting angry? To answer that question, we will have to double back to some of the material we covered under the Five Undeniable Truths. We agreed that because we are responsible for ourselves, we will no longer allow ourselves to be controlled by external events, other people or our emotions. The 11 Irrational Beliefs begin to make less sense once we've made this decision. We can't control what other people think so it is of absolutely no concern to us what they think about us. We do not need the approval of others so we no longer seek it. We see that the opinions of other people are just that, opinions, not facts, so they mean very little to us. Our wellbeing is our responsibility and is not dependent on sunny skies and kind people. We simply make the decision to need less from other people and allow other people to take responsibility for themselves. Because there is a space between the stimulus and our response, our anger is not automatic. We think things over and choose how we will feel about it. We choose to be angry or we choose not to invest the energy in anger. No one can ever make us angry, or afraid, or happy or sad. My anger is my problem.

The opposite is also true. We are not responsible for how other people are feeling. If someone is angry with me it is never my fault. It is their choice to be angry. Granted, perhaps I said or did something unhelpful. I may be guilty of making a mistake, having an accident, or being unkind. I am responsible for my actions but I am never responsible for someone else's anger because that is the result of their choice. There are things in life that we can control and things we can't. Our thoughts, choices, and feelings are inside of us and thus only we can control them. Here is a truth handed down from ancient times that might leave your head spinning: *When we take full responsibility for our thoughts, feelings, and actions we experience absolute freedom, courage, and tranquility.* We are untouchable. Nothing bothers us without our permission. Remember Epictetus the abused Greek slave? His life was painful and humiliating but he knew that it's not what happens to you, but how you react to it that matters. Granted it will take more time than we have here to master this "ninja level" thinking. For now, it is important to assert that it is possible. Begin by studying and challenging the irrational beliefs and see how your own thinking changes. Take another look at the section on the Five Undeniable Truths and let these ideas grow in your brain. Reject your sense of injury and the injury itself disappears.

This is doubly important to us as we serve the interests of God. There is always a higher goal in mind as we interact with the world. We are to help draw the world toward God. We are seeking to turn strangers into friends who then become friends of God. With that goal in mind, it becomes easier to overlook the ugly, prickly, painful words and actions of others because we want to become friends who can help make life better rather than punish them for perceived unkindness. Marshall Rosenberg liked to say that there are two very different games we can choose to play in life. The first is a game called "Whose Right?" That's when we evaluate, judge, punish and reward. We focus on what people deserve. The second game is called "Make Life More Wonderful for Everyone." It involves focusing on what we have in common rather than our differences and contributing to the greater good. It requires a willingness to look past unhelpful behaviors to help each other meet our needs and solve our problems. In the first game we tend to treat others as competitors and obstacles while in the second we are all on the same team. Thus, there are no losers because we all win. That sounds a lot like Kingdom of God to me. As followers of Jesus we learn to deal with our anger constructively which means seeing it as an opportunity to build something that brings God glory in the Kingdom of God rather than to destroy something in the here and now. Now that we've made the decision to avoid getting angry, let's discuss steps we can take to constructively deal with the anger and conflict coming from others.

Every Behavior Has a Function

Brinkman and Kirschner teach that all behavior is the result of the positive desire to get things done. Psychologist Marshall Rosenberg agrees. Every behavior has a function. Our anger and outbursts are always misguided attempts to meet some positive needs. We need to be loved. We need to be accepted. We need to be understood. We need help. Regardless of whether our needs are rational or irrational, every insult, criticism, or angry outburst is actually an ineffective way to ask for help. We can choose to focus, not on the anger coming at us, but on deciphering the need trying to be met. We ask ourselves "What is the function of this behavior?" If we can focus on the needs and intentions behind the difficult behavior, we can meet the need and end the conflict. We don't read minds though. How do we know what people really want when they are screaming insults at us?

Brinkman and Kirschner simplify the process by breaking every human need and intention into four distinct categories. Granted, that may seem like a huge oversimplification, but remember, in a tense situation we don't have much time to diagnose an endless list of possible motives. We are either focused on tasks or focused on people. We are either trying to get something done or done right or we are trying to get along with people or get appreciation from people. They write:

"Every behavior has a purpose, or an intent, that the behavior is trying to fulfill. People engage in behaviors based on their intent, and they do what they do based on what seems to be most important in any given moment. For our purposes, we have identified four general intents that determine how people will behave in any given situation. While these are obviously not the only intentions motivating behavior, we believe that they represent a general frame of reference in which practically all other intents can be located. As an organizational framework for understanding and dealing with difficult behaviors, these are the four intents:

- *Get the task done*
- *Get the task right*
- *Get along with people*
- *Get appreciation from people"*

"When people's intents are not met, their behavior begins to change.

When people want to get it done and fear it is not getting done, their behavior naturally becomes more **controlling**, *as they try to take over and push ahead.*

When people want to get it right and fear it will be done wrong, their behavior becomes more **perfectionistic**, *finding every flaw and potential error.*

When people want to get along and they fear they will be left out, their behavior becomes more **approval seeking**, *sacrificing their personal needs to please others.*

When people want to get appreciation and fear they are not, their behavior becomes more **attention getting**, *forcing others to notice them."*

Again, this takes more time and explanation than we are going to offer here, which is why I highly recommend Brinkman and Kirschner's book "Dealing With People You Can't Stand." As we learn to recognize the intent behind the behavior, we can offer cooperation to those wanting to get something done. We can offer a greater attention to detail for those wanting get things right. We offer friendship to those wanting to get along and praise and appreciation for those seeking it. We tend to judge ourselves by our good intentions but judge others by their behavior. We will choose to assume that everyone's intentions are good at heart regardless of how misguided their attempts may be. Repeat it to yourself a thousand times: *Anger directed at me is never really about me. Every behavior has an underlying function. Ignore the behavior and the angry words and focus on the function and we can respond to anger and conflict without feeling any anger at all.* I also recommend the book "De-Escalate: How To Calm an Angry Person in 90 Seconds or Less" (Beyond Words Publishing, 2017) by Douglas E. Noll which offers a new gold standard in effectively engaging the negative emotions in others in a way that helps bring them back to their senses. His technique is about effectively listening to others which may sound mundane but it has great power for peace.

1. How Do We Make Peace

Author Paul K. Chappell is an advocate for peace and a practitioner of the skills and tactics necessary to achieve it. He writes in his book quoted earlier, "The Art of Waging Peace":

"... There are two major differences between waging war and waging peace...Waging war tries to turn human beings who oppose you into corpses, while waging peace tries to turn human beings who oppose you into friends."

So how then do we make friends? Imagine the Ukrainian priest standing between the police and the protestors. How can this priest, placed in an impossible situation, make friends of both sides?

Do Not Choose Sides.

First, peacemakers do not choose sides, but seek to become friends with all involved. There is a risk to this, as peacemakers are often accused of being "too friendly with the other side." For a peacemaker there are no sides.

Be a Non-anxious Presence.

Second, peacemakers do not join in the animosity or get caught up in the excitement, but rather strive to be a calming, non-anxious presence. We've just learned how that is possible.

Give Respect

Third, peacemakers excel at giving respect. Chappell tells the story of how a fight once broke out in a restaurant because someone took someone else's fork. Once cooler heads prevailed, apologies were given and all was well. But as he reflected on the incident, something crucial became clear. There was no harm done. There were more forks available, but "*a mini-war was almost started just because people felt disrespected...Why do martial arts teach us to respect everyone, including our opponents? The reason is because the majority of human conflict comes from people feeling disrespected.*"

He continues: "*The first step in waging peace is respect. Realizing how dangerous disrespect can be and becoming skilled at giving respect are the most effective and essential methods of waging peace.*"

Jesus called it "loving our enemies" but since that word "love" is sometimes problematic the word "respect" may be more helpful to us. Paul described love as patience, kindness, humility, and grace (I Corinthians 12). These are concepts we already know and are practicing. They are the same ways we show respect, de-escalate conflict, and show our acceptance and interest in even the nastiest enemies. We treat them like they are already our best friend despite how they are treating us at the moment. If my friend is having a bad day and takes her frustration out on me, I can take it graciously because I know her and know that she respects me. Instead of getting offended and defensive, I place myself in her shoes and support her as a friend. We can do the same with everyone on the planet even if they are complete strangers. After all, in Christ, strangers are just friends we haven't met yet. Enemies are future friends who are having a bad day. We choose not to take it personally. Many a person in pain has cursed at the emergency room doctor who is simply trying to help. Hurt people often hurt people. It's not personal. We remain calm and focused on our goal in this situation: to make a friend. Remember two helpful quotes from Marcus Aurelius that we keep repeating:

"*Choose not to be harmed, and you won't feel harmed. Don't feel harmed and you haven't been.*"

"*Reject your sense of injury and the injury itself disappears.*"

This why the "examined life" is so important, to be constantly aware of the state of our soul. This is why training in self-control through spiritual disciplines is so important. We are not controlled by the actions of other people or our emotions. We choose to override our feelings of anger and treat an enemy as our future friend who is having a bad day. We know how we treat our friends. We look out for them. We want what's best for them. We look past their rough edges and rough moments because we are on the same side. Actually, there are no sides. That's why Jesus said "*Love your neighbor as yourself*" and "*Do unto others as you would have them do unto you.*"

Respect is a way to defuse the bomb when we are in conflict. By giving respect, we protect ourselves from the anger and ugliness of others and protect others from our potential anger and ugliness. "An eye for an eye" comes naturally to us. We tend to give back what we've been given. Call this the dark side of Reciprocity. When we respond with courtesy and respect regardless of how we are being treated, we help prevent dangerous situations from escalating. The three skills that compromise this "shield" seem almost embarrassingly simple.

Three Elements of Respect by Paul K. Chappell

Listening
Speak to the Goodness of Others
Don't be Hypocritical

Listening
As Douglas E. Noll writes:

"How many times have you heard voices become angry or louder as an argument ensued? The conflict is escalating because neither person believes that he or she is being heard. The easiest, but least effective way, to be heard is to raise one's voice. But then the other person doesn't feel heard and raises his voice in response, and so on. Sometimes out of shear frustration violence erupts."

I am amazed at the number of times someone within the church was furious with me about something and just the act of listening to whatever they have to say before commenting, defending or explaining allowed us to become real friends afterward. I respected them enough to listen to everything they were wrestling with, and in many cases they felt so much better after sharing their thoughts there was no longer a problem to address. We must learn to listen with empathy, listening to not just the words being spoken but appreciating the emotions and values being expressed through those words.

Speak to the Goodness of Others
When people speak to us with respect, they always talk to us as if they know that deep down we are good people even when we are behaving badly. We recognize and speak to the dignity, goodness and worth of others as human beings, even if it is not deserved. Disrespect makes us feel worthless while respect recognizes our enormous human potential.

Don't be Hypocritical

"Do as I say, not as I do" is a morally corrupt standard. We must lead by example, holding ourselves to the same standards we impose on others. (Again, reciprocity in action establishes a sense of justice and fairness.) We must practice what we preach. The Army's Drill Sergeant Creed states: *"I will lead by example, never requiring a soldier to attempt any task I would not do myself."* This why Jesus said *"Why do you look at the speck of sawdust in your brother's eye and pay no attention to the plank in your own eye."* Earlier we learned that reconciliation is a two way street requiring mutual effort.

Nonviolence

Fourth, peacemakers choose Nonviolence. Martin Luther King, Jr. said: *"Nonviolence is a powerful and just weapon. It is a weapon unique in history, which cuts without wounding and ennobled the man who wields it. It is a sword that heals."* Jesus clearly teaches nonviolence in the Sermon on the Mount and leads by example during his arrest, trial, and crucifixion. If our goal in every situation is to make a friend then violence is never helpful to our cause. Certainly there are those historical situations where violence was a necessary last resort because making a friend was impossible and we needed to defend ourselves and others. But we too often use these rare occurrences to depend on violence as a first resort. Remember, if we are pushed into this corner and are forced to defend ourselves, we still lose. Even if we win the fight and save ourselves from harm, we have most likely lost the opportunity to make a friend.

The General Rules of the Methodist Societies as retold by Bishop Reuben Job were:

"Do no harm. Do good. Stay in love with God."

We do no harm because violence divides us and drives us further apart. Violence and harm do not tend to inspire friendship. It inspires revenge. In doing all manner of good, we are demonstrating our good will and best of intentions for this other person, which can be confusing and disarming when they have treated us poorly. Our entire life of worship in which we deepen our love relationship with God will be necessary to keep our resolve to return evil with good.

Chain of Forgiveness and Reconciliation.

Fifth, peacemakers teach and practice the Chain of Forgiveness and Chain of Reconciliation. As shared above, this is how relationships are patiently pieced back together.

9

THE DISCIPLINES OF ENCOURAGING OTHERS

Jesus was very clear: *"Go therefore into all the earth and make disciples, baptizing them in the name of the Father, Son, and Holy Spirit, and teaching them to obey all that I have commanded you."* (Matthew 289-20) These generous gifts of God that we enjoy are not something we keep to ourselves. God's best gifts always come to us on their way to someone else. We tell others about God. We invite others to get to know Jesus. We introduce others to His Church. We offer others the opportunity for a life, for a fresh start, for the friendship of a truly supportive family, for a purpose worth living and dying for. We call this act of giving God to others "evangelism." For far too long though evangelism has been a word that inspires anxiety and guilt. We feel anxiety because too few people feel comfortable sharing the gospel with others. We feel guilt because we are constantly told we should.

According to D.T. Niles *"Christianity is one beggar telling another beggar where he found bread."* If we go to a great restaurant and have a great meal, we tend to tell others all about it. If we go to the theater and see a great movie, we tend to tell others all about it. Actually, the better the dinner or the movie is, the harder it is to keep quiet about it. We can't help but talk about it. Because of our enthusiasm, it just pours out of us, and often our excitement is contagious. Why then would we not share our freedom in Jesus Christ just as passionately? I don't mean to step on any toes, but maybe it's because we really don't have a personal experience of Jesus to talk about. Maybe we went to the restaurant but sat at the table while others ate. Maybe we went to the theater, but slept through the movie. Maybe I went to church, but I never actually met Jesus Christ. Maybe I've heard a lifetime of stories about Jesus, but really don't know Jesus personally. Deep down, we may not be truly convinced that Jesus changes lives because he hasn't yet changed ours. God desires a personal love relationship with us. Ask yourself: "Do I have a personal love relationship with God?" If not, you now know how to experience God in every part of your life. We cannot give what we do not have. The good news is that we cannot save anyone. That is God's job. We are, after all, saved by grace. It does not depend solely on our ability to "close the deal." We are distrustful of any efforts to teach evangelism through sales tactics designed to maneuver a target into saying yes. Discipleship is a lifelong relationship. We don't talk a future spouse into marriage through well-rehearsed tactics, convincing arguments, and polished rhetoric. The Church is not an aggressive used car lot that closes the deal by any means necessary. We don't sell Christ through manipulative banter. We are offering a real relationship with a real person with all the tenderness, intimacy, and respect you would hope for in any relationship. It is not about being convinced by artful debate. It is about falling in love.

I am convinced that the "Jesus Way of Life" is a comfort and healing for our world. I have seen God do wonderful things in the lives of those who truly follow. We have seen depression replaced by joy. We have seen marriages strengthened. We have seen doubt replaced with purpose and meaning. By watching over each other with love...by deepening our love relationship with God...by learning how to follow God together...by generously sharing what we have with God and others...by loving God by loving others...we are seeing lives change and the world is becoming a better place, even if it is only one life at a time. As a member of several 5x5 Groups, I find myself inviting people to join one every day because it works.

Here is the answer to all that anxiety and guilt associated with sharing Jesus: When you are experiencing God, deepening that love relationship every day, and you have a ready to go method that works to help others do the same, you can't help but offer it to other people.

What we mean by "method" is not a sales tactic but a way of life. By learning and living the Jesus Way of Life through something like a 5x5 group, you are experiencing a life changed by God. You know how you learned to talk and listen to God. You know how others encouraged you. You know better than anyone else what a tremendous difference God is making in your life. You will have no hesitation welcoming someone onto the Path beside you so you can walk with Jesus together. Be clear, we feel no pressure to convert anyone. That is God's job. The Spirit is constantly surrounding us and speaking to everyone on earth to begin a new relationship. Our job is simply to encourage everyone to take their next step closer to God. *"Draw near to God and God will draw near to you."* (James 4:8 ESV). We call it evangelism when the next step is actually the first step, but regardless of how long you have been in a relationship with God, there is ALWAYS a next step to take to move us closer to God. If "evangelism" makes you nervous, let's use a different "E" word: "Encouraging." *We encourage each other to take our next, logical baby step closer to God.* Evangelism may feel like trying to sell something but encouraging is focused on helping someone else. We focus more on where other people are and what other people need than on what we want for them. What we want doesn't matter at all. As followers of Jesus, we are concerned more with what God wants and God wants a personal love relationship with each of us that lasts forever. That's why God has been patiently standing beside them their whole lives. They never heard the quiet whisper or felt the gentle tap on their shoulder. Most people don't realize that God is already so close to them and that meeting God really doesn't take all that much. Just a baby step in the right direction. That's what we encourage them to do.

I. Who Do We Encourage?
II. Friends With God
III. Friends With The Church
IV. Next Steps and Leaps of Faith
V. Staying Connected

I. Who Do We Encourage?

Good question. It was Jesus who first used the image of fishing to describe the idea of evangelism and disciple making. It is important to remember that the fish we enjoy on our dinner table usually come from two sources: FARM RAISED or CAUGHT IN THE WILD. Disciples are made in similar ways. Every congregation should dedicate itself to teaching the gospel to the children born and raised within the congregation. Just because we enter church life as an infant does not mean that we automatically have a mature saving relationship with God through Jesus Christ. Those "CAUGHT IN THE WILD" would be the people of all ages that we meet in the world around who have no real relationship with God. Martha Grace Reese in her book "Unbinding the Gospel" (Chalice, 2008) identifies the people around us that we can teach. It begins with the safest and most convenient and works its way through the community to the ones that require the most risk. What follows is based on her discussion of the variety of people who require our focus and attention in order to share Christ with them.

We can begin with our children.

Of all the kingdom building ministries we can take part in, few are as demanded of us by Jesus as teaching our own children to follow Jesus. That happens at home and it happens within the congregation.

We can also teach our children's friends.

Parents tend to follow their children's interests these days, so if our children's friends join us in our ministry, their parents will most likely check us out too. That is why we also teach people who regularly attend our church but have yet to really commit to following Jesus full time.

We can teach those who attend regularly but have not committed to Jesus.

That may be those who were born in the church or those transferring into our church from a church similar to ours as well as those coming to us from churches that are very different from ours.

We can teach ex-Christians.

We branch out and talk with people who were raised in the church but drifted away. There are a lot of those in the world around us. There are also too many people who were raised in the church who were hurt by the church.

We can teach those who have no experience of God at all.

We work a little harder to connect with people who were not raised in church who are similar to us in other ways, like living in the same town, or work at the same job. Then there are folks that we feel we have nothing in common with at all. This last category covers a lot of ground and often is the category that makes us the most uncomfortable. It is a strange thing to be approached by a complete stranger who is worried about our eternal salvation. Maybe we should get to know each other first. Our first step is not to "sell Jesus" but to become friends. That's what we are encouraging them to do, become friends with God and friends with God's Church.

II. Friends With God

Regardless of where people are in their relationship with God, we all grow through the same stages on our way to maturity in faith. These phases of spiritual growth were identified by Greg L. Hawkins and Cally Parkinson the authors of the book "MOVE" which shares the insights of the Willow Creek Community Church REVEAL Study (Zondervan, 2011). They lay out several predictable phases that we mover through in establishing a relationship with Jesus. We explore the challenges and opportunities of each in turn. The predictable phases are:

A. Meet Jesus

B. Explore Jesus

C. Grow in Jesus
D. Close to Jesus
E. Jesus Centered

A. Meet Jesus

You can't have a relationship with someone you've never met. That goes for God, too. If you've ever tried to fix one of your friends up on a blind date, you know how difficult it is to play match maker. You can't force someone to fall in love. Neither can we force someone to agree to a first date. So how do we encourage someone to take that first step closer to God? Very rarely will someone blurt out that they want God, but they gladly share other things they want that God can help with. People who are tired of the chaos they make of their lives wish they could get things under control. Self-control was never their strongest gift. They might ask aloud if it is possible to fix mistakes and stop making things worse. God teaches self-control. It is a fruit of the Spirit. It is something to which we hold each other accountable. Long before people are interested in God they may be interested in the disciplined life that is free of the constant self-created drama. They want peace. They want purpose. They want life to make sense. They can have that. They may not be ready to grab onto God just yet, but they may be able to see something in you that they wish they had. That is our opportunity to introduce them to our very best Friend. It is an opportunity to introduce them to the "Jesus Way of Life." It is an opportunity to let them know that God is all around them and trying to get in if they would just open the door. We can also offer to pray for them to meet God and find what they have been looking for all along. The mystery is this: If God is calling everyone on earth by name, inviting them to know God, why do only some people hear and respond? As we learned in the introductory chapter, God wants three things for us:

- God desires an intimate love relationship with us that lasts forever.
- God wants to help us love and care for each other.
- God invites us to help God change the world.

There are some obstacles that get in the way:

1. Barriers to Knowing God

a. Ignorance

Some people have never heard about God. In the United States, it is nearly impossible to find someone who has never ever heard of the idea of God. Whether people believe or not, Heaven, Hell, God and Jesus are in the culture around us. Some people have heard the word "God", but know very little about who God really is. Some people have heard all about God but really don't understand and need to have it explained. Some people have heard, and understood, but need to see faith lived as well as explained. Evangelism begins with telling, explaining, and showing the Good News of God in everyday life. Bad examples of the Christian faith abound, from television and movie caricatures, to overly judgmental congregations that insult and condemn. Many people who tried church earlier in their lives have drifted away for a variety of reasons. Remember, just because we are in church, it does not mean that we are in Christ. The world desperately needs to know what a real experience of God is all about.

God's Response to Ignorance

God has revealed everything we need to know about God through the holy scriptures and through the Church. It's not enough to just hear the ancient stories. People need to see and experience the daily miracles of changed lives. The most persuasive stories are our own stories of what God has done and is doing in our lives. If the promises of God in scripture are not real in us here and now, then they aren't real anywhere. The supernatural becomes super practical in our everyday lives. That is why, as said before, we don't just share God with people by giving them a Bible of their own (which is great place to start). We share our lives with people because that is where God is most real.

b. Sin

Romans 3:23 states that *"all have sinned and fallen short of the glory of God."* Sin is all the ways we miss the mark. It is all the ways we fall short of God's Way of Life that make us incompatible with and drives us farther away from God. The root of all sin is a fascination with ourselves. The more we focus on our own wants, needs, and selfish desires (see the Seven Deadly Sins) the more closed off we are to God and other people. It gets harder to tune in and recognize the Voice of God. Romans 6:23 states that *"The wages of sin is death, but the gift of God is eternal life in Christ Jesus our Lord."* Sin results in death, not just in a punitive way but in a natural cause and effect way. Perhaps we should consider this a sixth "Undeniable Truth." Sin can be forgiven, but it requires a costly price to be paid. In our sin, both the idiotic and rebellious things we do and the imperfect nature that we are all born into, we earn death because "everything costs something ." This is a debt that absolutely must be paid.

This is where all that scary preaching about Hell and damnation comes in. In 1741, New England preacher Jonathan Edwards wrote a famous sermon entitled "Sinners in the Hand of an Angry God." God has since been cast in the role of an angry, vindictive and abusive overlord who is angry enough with us to build a torture chamber called Hell in order to punish us with excruciating pain that never ends. That doesn't sound like the kind of person you can have a healthy loving relationship with, does it? Too many people carry the deep inner and outer scars of abusive parents or spouses. They will have no desire whatsoever to risk placing themselves in the hand of an angry God. Does God get angry? Of course. The scripture clearly reveals that. God invented emotion and God is an emotional God. Every married couple who love each other deeply has gotten angry with each other. That is natural. Remember, emotions are an alarm system alerting us that something in our relationships is out of balance and needs attention. Violence and abuse inflicted in anger is sin. God condemns it, so there is no way God would indulge in it.

The debt created by sin must be paid and that creates an enormous problem for God. God is just so the cost of sin must be paid. Accounts must be settled. But God is loving and merciful. What's a loving and just God to do?

God's Response to Sin
This helps explain the necessity of the cross. The debt is a human debt and must be paid by us. God became a human being and volunteered to pay it with his life. But because Jesus is more than just an ordinary human being, because Jesus is God, the debt has been overpaid. It was not just one ordinary human death but God's death. Surely that satisfies the debt with much to spare! It's a poor analogy, but imagine buying a cup of coffee at a local diner and paying the check with ten billion dollars. It only cost you three dollars, which leaves a staggering amount left over. You tell the manager to keep it and use it to pay for anyone else who comes in and can't pay. Because God is just, the debt was paid. Because God is merciful, God volunteers to pay it for us. We are saved by grace. Grace is a gift.

By Jesus' death on the Cross, we are forgiven of our sins and imperfections and given a fresh start. This is another reason why trying the "Jesus Way of Life" makes it easier to recognize and experience God. Not only are we being forgiven of the damage and guilt in our past, we are learning to live in a healthier way that is more open to and cooperative with God and other people. Remember the "Chain of Forgiveness" and the "Chain of Reconciliation?" These practical steps to restoring a broken relationship with another person are useful in restoring broken relationship with God too. They are part of our daily walk. That is also why God pours the Holy Spirit into our lives to rewire our desires and decision making, and to encourage us to open ourselves yet more to God.

c. Death

This may not seem like something that could get in the way of meeting and starting a relationship with God, but remember, nothing lasts forever. We will all die. That means with each passing day we have less time available to fall in love with God. Let that sink in. Every day, time is running out. The fact that the clock is ticking adds some urgency to meeting God before we run out of chances. We arrogantly believe we have plenty of time. We assume we will live to the ripe old age of 103 which means there is plenty of time. Is there? We've established that life is not fair, that we live in a world where anything can happen and usually does. Tomorrow is not guaranteed. Life can end unexpectedly at any time. Our death is also a problem for God because God desires an intimate love relationship with us that lasts forever. We don't naturally last forever. As soon as God establishes a relationship with us, we die and disappear. Compared to God our lives are over literally in the blink of an eye. Life is short. We know how we weep and grieve when loved ones die. Imagine how God feels! Remember, God created us to be with us. God really loves us and weeps at every death that ends a relationship. When you consider the number of people who die every day around the world without knowing God, every one loved and longed for by God, it begins to dawn on us that our God of eternal joy is also deeply grieved and unhappy too.

God's Response to Death

This helps explain the need for the resurrection of Jesus where, for the first time, human flesh is made immortal. The Way of Jesus is the Way of the Cross but is also the Way of the Empty Tomb. Jesus offers us eternal life. He is changing us but our eternity does not come easy. Everything costs something, remember? Our eternal God, who is Three Persons in One God, surrendered one member of the Family to the grave. Jesus died, which means GOD died...for us. Let THAT sink in. God is so desperate to spend more time with us than our mortal life allows that God chose to join us in real death because that was the only way to bring us out of death into resurrection. The only way to save a person from a burning building is to enter the burning building and carry them out. It seems the only way to save us from death was for Jesus to enter the grave and carry us out. This Kingdom of God that Jesus speaks so highly of will become real in a New Creation, a "Heaven on earth" that also lasts forever.

d. Apathy

Even if we hear the Word of God, sometimes we just don't care. We aren't interested. We ignore it and move on. There are a lot of reasons why we don't care to listen, many of which are listed below. Apathy is a tough nut to crack. It is not the same as cynicism or hostility. It might sound odd to say but people who are hostile to God and the Church are emotionally tied to God and the Church. We talked earlier about how forgiveness frees us from carrying the burden of a grudge. When we carry a grudge against someone we are choosing to give them some power over us and a place in our life. But apathy is just nothing. No feelings one way or the other. No thoughts.

God's Response to Apathy

How do we matter to someone who doesn't care? We first have to get their attention. God has to get back on the radar. Something needs to change to get our attention. Sometimes, the tragedies and hardships of life are enough to get our attention. We may notice the person stepping up to help us when everything falls apart. There is a positive way to upset the apple cart too: inspiration. God breaks through our apathy by speaking and inspiring by the Holy Spirit. As human beings, we can't control this one. Sometimes the Holy Spirit just moves in on us and we experience something powerful and unexplainable. Maybe it is while listening to a piece of music or watching a movie. Perhaps it is while attending the funeral service of a friend. Saul of Tarsus met God while riding a horse to the next town. I once experienced it waiting in my pew to take communion. John Wesley attended a small group meeting at a house on Aldersgate Street in London. He was going through a particularly rough season and didn't really want to hear from God, but he went to the meeting any way. While the leader was reading something kind of boring to most of us, God moved John. This is how he described it in his own words:

"In the evening I went very unwillingly to a society in Aldersgate Street, where one was reading Luther's preface to the Epistle to the Romans. About a quarter before nine, while he was describing the change which God works in the heart through faith in Christ, I felt my heart strangely warmed. I felt I did trust in Christ, Christ alone, for salvation; and an assurance was given me that He had taken away my sins, even mine, and saved me from the law of sin and death." (Journal of John Wesley, May 24, 1738)

This experience changed the course of John's life. Notice that he did nothing to "make" this happen. It just happened on God's timing, but it was more than enough to put John on the Path.

e. Competing Beliefs

Countless people hear the Word and invitation of God and it doesn't jive with what they already believe. Perhaps we are rational minded scientists who believe in human reason and things that can be measured and proven. Perhaps we already hold faith in another religion. There is just no room in our heart and mind for a different idea. There is no room at the inn for Jesus unless we evict another tenant and we may not be ready to do that.

God's Response to Competing Beliefs

God neither condemns nor ignores those with competing beliefs. God scatters the seed everywhere and engages in conversation to compare and contrast our beliefs as a way that eventually leads to Jesus. We see the apostle Paul doing this in the Greek city of Athens in Acts 17. Noticing the countless temples and shrines to the many gods of the Athenian people, Paul engages in a conversation with those gathered at the Areopagus, a courtyard where great thinkers and philosophers gathered to talk and debate. Paul does not denounce the Athenian gods but claims they are pointing the people toward the God of Israel. Paul begins by engaging what he has in common with people of other beliefs. The first scientists studied Creation as a way of better appreciating the Creator. We can certainly engage science at that level. We may disagree with someone who worships a different god, but at least we can appreciate a common belief in spiritual realities. Not everyone believes there is a God. Some of the cynicism about religion comes rightly in the fact that people have been fighting and killing for thousands of years over whose god is the true god. Encouraging others to take a step closer to God begins with friendship with God and friendship with the people of God's Church. Telling someone how wrong they are is an attack against everything they are and everything their family raised them to be. It is insulting, and insults rarely lead to friendship. We always love with kindness, compassion, and respect.

We said before that it doesn't matter whether you gave your life to Jesus and now are beginning a new way of life, or whether you begin a new way of life that builds the trust necessary to give your life to Jesus. This Jesus Way of Life heals the world and we can finds parts of that Jesus Way of Life being lived by Buddhists, Muslims, Hindus, Sikhs, or countless others. There are similarities that we have in common. For example, as we shared in our discussion of reciprocity, most world religions contain a teaching similar to what we call "The Golden Rule."

BUDDHISM:
HURT NOT OTHERS WITH THAT WHICH PAINS YOURSELF.

CHRISTIANITY:
DO UNTO OTHERS AS YOU WOULD HAVE THEM DO UNTO YOU.

HINDUISM:
TREAT OTHERS AS YOU WOULD YOURSELF BE TREATED.

ISLAM:
DO UNTO ALL MEN AS YOU WOULD WISH TO HAVE DONE UNTO YOU.

JUDAISM:
WHAT YOU YOURSELF HATE, DO TO NO MAN.

NATIVE AMERICAN:
LIVE IN HARMONY, FOR WE ARE ALL RELATED.

SACRED EARTH:
DO AS YOU WILL, AS LONG AS YOU HARM NO ONE.

We will most likely meet people of other faiths who are walking a way of life that is similar to ours. We begin there. We believe in love, faith, service, sacrifice, and justice. Like Paul in Athens, we build friendships with others at these places where our paths cross. In matters of peace, nonviolence, kindness to the poor, protection of life, freedom to worship as we choose, and the daily experience of the divine, we can talk and become friends who treat each other with kindness, compassion and respect. As many Christian missionaries who serve around the world can attest, taking an interest in the faith of another opens a door for them to take an interest in our faith in Jesus. By simply talking and explaining our faiths to each other as friends, we leave room for the Holy Spirit to move. Remember, we feel no pressure to convert anyone. That is God's job. The Spirit is constantly surrounding us and speaking to everyone on earth to begin a new relationship. Our job is simply to encourage everyone to take their next step closer to God.

f. Cynicism

Many people do not trust the things of God and are motivated to defend against them. Perhaps we blame faith for all the bloodshed in the world. Perhaps we think faith is foolish superstition and fairy tales that keep people from thinking for themselves. Perhaps we have been hurt by the Church and are ready to fight back. Whatever it is, the walls are up, the "no trespassing" sign is on the front door, and they are loading the shotgun to get God off their front porch. Let's take that very seriously for a moment by acknowledging some history. In the Middle Ages, the Church sent armies into the Holy Land to conquer and "reclaim for Christ" the lands held by Muslim leaders. The Inquisition practiced a gruesome strategy of imprisonment, torture and execution of non-believers. "Convert to Christ or die" was the only choice given. We have seen churches that supported slavery and racial segregation during and after the Civil War. More recently, sexual abuse of children by clergy and the attempt of church hierarchy to cover it up has grabbed the headlines and eroded the trust people have in God's Church. Traditional biblical teachings on homosexuality have contributed to parents and churches treating young people struggling with their identity with hostility rather than kindness, compassion, and respect. For two thousand years, the imperfect walk of imperfect Christians has caused harm to some. We meet people every day who, for legitimate reasons, do not believe God or God's Church are safe.

Another factor contributing to this growing cynicism is what the world calls "hypocrisy." Our Jesus teaches one thing, but people observe us behaving in very different ways. We actually expect that. We are sinners in recovery which means we will stumble now and then. We will lose control of our emotions. We will give in to our lower temptations as we are learning how to better control ourselves and resist our temptations. We are not perfect. No one, on this side of Heaven, is perfect. Certainly we can try harder and do better. Our stumbles can destroy our witness. People may not trust us as we invite them to step onto the Path with us.

God's Response to Cynicism

God is patient with cynical hostility knowing it is rarely defeated by direct assault. God tends to show tenderness, patience, and kindness towards the cynical, knowing that cynics need to experience the goodness that comes from obedient faith to realize how beneficial God really is. Cynicism is rooted in a fear that God and God's Church are not safe, honest, trustworthy, or good. It is impossible to earn someone's trust by simply saying "trust me!" (I tend to strongly distrust anyone who says "trust me" without giving a real reason to trust.) God, and God's Church know that words are cheap and that this is a time to show more than tell. A cynical person needs to experience real kindness, humility, generosity, and respect from God and God's Church with *no strings attached*. It requires gentle patience. God does not smash our cynicism but lovingly engages it by surprising us with patience and showing the love we reject. Love is always the right answer. It may also require some reconciliation on our part. Like we said, there has been harm. We must be honest about that. We are not proud of these darker moments in our history when the Church has been led by people who were clearly not living the Jesus Way of Life. We have to own that. Again, remember the Chain of Reconciliation. Despite these moments of failure, though, the Church has been very, VERY good for this world in ways that cannot be counted. Sacrificial love is shown every day in feeding the hungry, rebuilding storm damaged homes, adopting orphaned children, giving homes to refugees, loving addicts through their addiction, rescuing women and children from human trafficking, and living in the streets loving the poorest of the poor and comforting the dying. When the Church "walks the walk" cynicism shrinks.

g. Comfort

Sometimes life is so good without God, we have no reason to change anything. Who needs God when life is already so very satisfying? Comfort is a good thing, but too much comfort makes us spoiled and lazy. Remember the words of Seneca shared earlier:

"If we coddle ourselves, if we allow ourselves to be corrupted by pleasure, nothing will seem bearable to us, and the reason things will seem unbearable is not because they are hard but because we are soft."

Ouch!

God's Response to Comfort

Seneca is right! Too much comfort makes us lazy and soft. God challenges us and stretches us out of our comfort zone. God offers us a purpose worth living and dying for. God also allows a great deal of adversity to enter our lives and is always ready to use these instances to help us gain a new perspective. Few things wake us up like suffering, loss and pain. God can use that to get our attention. Chicago journalist Finley Peter Dunne, when speaking of the roll of the press in society said it was to *"comfort the afflicted and afflict the comfortable."* Over time, the Church saw that as a good way to describe the role of God and the Church. There are two diseases which destroy humankind, the disease of poverty and the disease of wealth. You can say it another way: the diseases of comfort and suffering, which are the diseases of having it too easy and having it too hard. Aristotle taught that too much or too little of anything is harmful to us. Consider Proverbs 30:8: *"Give me neither poverty or riches, feed me with the food that I need or I will be FULL and deny you saying "Who is my Lord?...Or I will be poor and steal and profane the name of the Lord."* The disease of wealth turns us not into desperate criminals, but spoiled children who are good for nothing. God has a Kingdom to build and that takes work!

h. Suffering

As just mentioned, Suffering covers a lot of territory. It can be anything from physical pain to poverty, to emotional pain. Whatever the cause, relentless pain and constant disappointment keep us focused on our own survival. They also have a way of wearing us down. We can lose hope.

Worse yet, too much pain and suffering can cause us to doubt that we are worthy of anything good. It can also make us angry enough at God for not doing something about it that we too shut God out of our lives.

God's Response to Suffering

God offers us comfort and healing in our suffering. Yes, sometimes God does choose to heal us of our pain. But even if the immediate healing does not come, God provides comfort, help, and companionship through the Holy Spirit and the Church. That is why we visit each other when the chips are down, when we are sick, grieving, in prison, hungry, and struggling. When we know we need help, we may be more open to the help God provides.

i. Distractions

There are so many things competing for our attention, from work, to problems, to fun, that God gets crowded out like seeds choked off by the high weeds. There are only so many hours in the day. There are only so many days in a week, and quite frankly there are more interesting ways to spend what time we do have than trying to hold a conversation with a God we cannot see or hear. There are too many other things, from television, to sports, to deadlines vying for our attention, that we just never get around to God.

God's Response to Distractions

God deals with our distractions much the same way God deals with our apathy and comfort. Distractions may come from the "good life." I don't have time for worship, or a group or a service project because we are traveling, we have more vacation, our kids have a game, etc. Distractions are about priorities and opportunities. We may have so many opportunities it requires a hard look at our priorities to choose how to best spend the rapidly dwindling days of our very short life. That big picture perspective is something God does well. God tends to stir up in us deep questions in the middle of the night about the meaning of life. We may begin questioning what life is all about. Our distractions might also be led, not by our pursuit of pleasure, but by the demands of our own ambition. Work, achievement, and success may eclipse everything else. We may be distracted by our pain and suffering too, which is about the loss of opportunities. Again, it all boils down to how our priorities shape the choice of the opportunities around us. God can use these times of suffering, dissatisfaction and soul-searching to help us focus on what is most important to us. God focuses on us so we can focus on God.

j. Inoculation

This one requires some explanation. Inoculation and vaccination are pretty much the same thing. A vaccine, which protects us from a dangerous disease, contains a tiny bit of weakened virus that is injected into our system. Because it is weakened, our immune system can defeat it right away, making antibodies that protect us from ever catching the disease again. This little bit of disease may be in us but it has no power to make us ill. Likewise, we sometimes accept God's invitation to come into our lives, but feel a little God is enough. We are satisfied with a little bit of God, an hour on Sunday, a few seconds of prayer before we eat, but refuse to let God have any more of our life than that. God is in our lives, but we don't permit God to really change us. We can get numb to God...immune. A lot of the reasons outsiders call us hypocrites is because of the actions of inoculated Christians who claim to have God in their lives, but are completely lacking in God's grace and transforming power. These people then encourage the CYNICISM in others and keep making God's job harder. John Wesley referred to these people as "Almost Christians." We will take closer look at them in the next section.

God's Response to Inoculation

By definition, inoculated Christians need more God. The best way to allow that is more involvement. One hour on Sunday is never enough. Jesus' disciples lived with Jesus full time and learned from him constantly. We are to love God with all of our heart, mind, soul, and strength. Inoculated Christians need the accountability to read the "gas gauge" that measures our heart, mind, soul, and strength. How much of our heart does God have all, some or none? How much of our time? Inoculation results from many things already mentioned above. God provides plenty to break through the impasse and get people moving again. God calls and inspires. God offers the encouragement and accountability of other disciples. An inoculated church is one in which people are given permission to quit and fail. Make no mistake: this group is very difficult to reach. Antibodies make us disease resistant. A little bit of Jesus can actually make us Jesus resistant.

B. Explore Jesus

However we meet God, it is time to get to know God up close and personal. These are people who are searching for God, looking for answers to a thousand questions. People in this phase are interested in the things of God but have not yet fallen in love and made a commitment. Believe it or not, the Exploring Christ segment is composed of two distinct groups of people—those who are active explorers and those who are passive attenders. The first group (the active explorers) includes those individuals who are genuinely seeking to resolve their doubts about the reality and character of Jesus. These are the people we most commonly associate with the description "Exploring Christ." But there is also a second group of people in this segment who are not really "seeking" at all. These are churchgoers who seem content with a shallow spiritual life marked by minimal faith-based beliefs, relationships, and activities. We've already called them "inoculated Christians." They may have a nominal faith, but they fail to show any signs of active growth. The combination of these two kinds of "explorers" makes the Exploring Christ segment a mixed bag of nonbelievers. Again, Hawkins and Parkinson write: *"While many are actively searching for answers to their spiritual questions, others attend church mostly out of habit or for reasons of social acceptance—and they demonstrate little or no interest in pursuing a relationship with Christ."* ("Move." Zondervan, 2011.)

Three important things to remember are:

- They attend church regularly but have no personal relationship with Christ.
- Their pace of spiritual growth is sluggish
- The longer they attend church, the less likely they are to become Christ-followers.

Hopefully we don't get stuck in this phase. It is a sobering warning that the longer people attend church with no real commitment to Jesus, the less likely they are to go any further. 5x5 was created not only to disciple those brand new in the faith, but to equip those in this category who are stuck.

C. Grow in Jesus

Some keep searching and seeking and fall in love with God and are open to God. They have made a decision to follow Jesus, but they have a lot to learn. As we have seen in the 5x5 process so far, there are things we need to know and things we need to know how to do. In this phase we try everything and learn as much as we can. Here we are learning to move beyond an acknowledgment of Jesus Christ to having a personal relationship with Jesus Christ. We submit ourselves to the authority of another who can teach us how. The church becomes very central to this growing life of new found faith. We rely on pastors, small groups, classes, worship services and spiritual mentors. We are anxious to grow and need to be guided and encouraged to keep taking next steps. We are cautioned by Hawkins and Parkinson to never let a passion to serve eclipse a commitment to personal spiritual disciplines. Many feel that simply helping new people connect with a ministry or serve on a committee guarantees Christian growth. It does not. It might be helpful to make a church member but does not grow a disciple.

D. Close to Jesus

These disciples are on personal terms with God. As we keep growing, we begin to take ownership of our faith. We take full responsibility to live for Jesus and to represent God in the world. Again, I quote Hawkins and Parkinson: *"Unlike those in the previous segment, the faith walk of those who are Close to Christ is not dependent on spiritual mentors, dynamic preaching, or compelling Bible studies. While most of them believe that belonging to a church is essential to their ongoing spiritual growth, they take on much of the responsibility for advancing their own relationship with Christ."* They allow Jesus to join them in every part of their lives. They know how to pray and do so regularly. Remember Brother Lawrence who chatted with God all day long while working in the monastery kitchen? He was close to Christ allowing Jesus to be a part of his life every day.

E. Jesus Centered

We can keep growing closer to Christ to the point that, instead of Jesus being a larger part of our life, our life only has meaning in God's. These disciples are fully surrendered to God. They have yielded control of their lives to God. The Great Commandment instructs us to love God with ALL our hearts, minds, soul and strength. It is a constant struggle to decide whether God gets some, half, most, or all. Hawkins and Parkinson remind us:

"Christ-Centered believers emerge from a battle between two sets of values—the secular values that define personal identity, happiness, security, and success for much of the world, and the spiritual values of selfless love and dedication to others that characterize a life centered on Jesus. In every other segment of the spiritual continuum, the values scale tips in favor of the secular. Even those who are Close to Christ have worldly aspirations that constantly compete with Jesus to influence the direction of their lives. But the men and women who make up the Christ-Centered segment have, in large part, relinquished those secular values and worldly aspirations and yielded that control over to Christ. The sacrifice this lifestyle requires is magnified by the daily nature of their commitment. More than a one-time decision, those who live the Christ-Centered life regularly face their struggles and must choose each day to follow Jesus rather than giving in to the pull of the secular world. They learn by habitual practice to deny themselves, pick up their cross, and follow Christ." ("Move." Zondervan, 2011.)

PHASES OF CHRISTIAN MATURITY

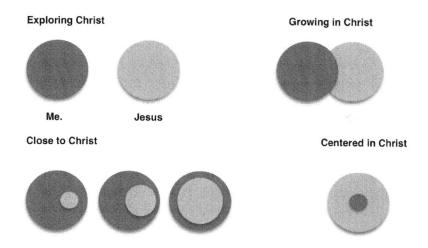

Exploring Christ

Growing in Christ

Me.   **Jesus**

Close to Christ

Centered in Christ

II. Friends With God's Church

In his landmark book "The Purpose Driven Church," Rick Warren describes five levels of commitment to God and the Church (Zondervan, 2011). He explains these levels of commitment in terms of how much commitment we are willing to make in order to experience God among the people of God's Church. He moves from those with the least amount of commitment to the greatest. They are: *Community, Crowd, Congregation, Committed,* and *Core.* We will look at which through the lens of turning strangers into friends.

A. Strangers (Community)

When Jesus arrived in a new town, the only relationship he had with the people around him was that they were all in the same geographic area at the same time, but they weren't connected in any way. Our churches are surrounded by countless numbers of people who are strangers to God and God's Church. They don't know God. With the exception of weddings and funerals, they've never visited a church. They have no experience with us, no knowledge of us, and no interest in us. The first step is to turn strangers into friends.

B. Friends (Crowd)

Once Jesus started speaking or healing, a crowd would inevitably gather. Some people took the initiative to turn aside from what they were doing to listen. Those who take the time out of their week to join us in worship, have made more commitment than most people in the neighborhood. Our churches contain lots of folks who attend worship fairly regularly, but that is about as far as it goes. It is important to strengthen these casual friendships into strong relationships. How do we strengthen friendships? We use "The Friendship Five."

"The Friendship Five
1. Everyone Needs to Be Known

This goes deeper than simply knowing someone's name, but let's not skip over that. Taking the time to learn someone's name shows that we have taken an interest in them. They matter. Never underestimate how important it is to learn and remember names. But making a friend goes much deeper than just a name. How much do we know about the people sitting around us in Church? How much do we know about our closest friends and family members? If we are going to become friends and family together we have to really take the time to get to know each other. This is just a sample of how well we will get to know each other:

"Where do I live? What do I do every day? Who's my family? Where did I grow up? What is the best thing happening to me this month? What is the worst thing happening to me this month? What are my favorite things in the world? What are my least favorite things in this world? What is my greatest hope and dream? What is my deepest regret or fear? When is my birthday?"

2. Everyone Needs to Be Remembered

What does it mean to be remembered? To paraphrase the theme song from "Cheers" we are remembered when somebody knows our name and remembers it as weeks go by. It means that someone is always thinking about me. If I am not in worship, someone will miss me. Because they miss me, they will get in touch with me to make sure all is well. Being remembered means I will never fall between the cracks, be overlooked, or forgotten. Depending on the size of a congregation, that takes some real effort to ensure for everyone.

3. Everyone Needs to Be Loved

We've already spent time defining what love is and what love is not in an earlier chapter. We've defined love as choosing to treat others with kindness, compassion, and respect. If we are not treated kindly, or compassionately, or with respect, we will have no desire to stay. We all desire to be accepted, valued, and treated with the dignity worthy of one who is created in the image and likeness of God.

4. Everyone Needs to Be Connected

We know we are connected when we are involved in the lives of other people, and they are involved in our life beyond Sunday morning. In short, I know I'm connected with other people in this congregation when my phone is ringing, my door is knocking, my mailbox is bursting, and my seat is being saved for me by someone who can't wait to see me.

5. Everyone Needs to Be Cared For

We watch over one another with love, but how do we do that? We care for one another in every kind of need: emotional, physical, spiritual, and relational. Do you have someone to watch the kids while you see the doctor? Do you have someone you can call in the middle of the night who will simply listen to you pour out your troubles? Do you have someone to help you get through life? We all need that. We also need a balance of positive encouragement and accountability. Encouragement is vital to keep us going through the difficult times. Accountability is needed to question us when we have gone astray in sin or error. It also is needed to push us to keep growing in our faith. See again what we had to say about "Mutual Care" in our chapter on "Disciplines of Learning."

C. Family (Congregation)

A some point, there were people who gave Jesus more than a few moments' attention. They left what they were doing and followed Jesus from town to town. Together they became a strange little family that we call the disciples. In our congregations, there are those who take the next step and become family. They make their relationship with God and the Church permanent, not just through a promise or vow, but in a committed life that accepts responsibility from God for the Church. *This is the difference between making church members and making disciples.* Members say a vow then have their name recorded in a membership roll. They are then free to participate as much or as little as they choose. Disciples begin living the Jesus Way of Life every day with the encouragement and accountability of other Jesus followers.

D. Followers of God (Committed)

Among those who followed Jesus, there were twelve who were closer to Jesus than anyone else. They did the heavy lifting among the followers of Jesus and were clearly being trained by Jesus to continue His work after His death. Not only did Jesus give them responsibilities, but also held them accountable for their performance. In our congregations, we are surrounded by those who are drawing closer to God every day and are becoming dependable servants of the coming Kingdom. These are people who are beginning to take on leadership roles within the church and investing their lives in other would-be disciples.

E. Full Grown Servants of God (Core)

Among all who followed, Jesus had three who were His closest confidants: Peter, James, and John. They were the only disciples to accompany Jesus on the Mount of Transfiguration and were also given the task of watching over Jesus while He prayed in the Garden of Gethsemane. They were leaders among the rest of the disciples. In our congregations, we rely upon those mature disciples who put God first in all things, who base their decisions upon the will of God rather than personal preference, and who lead the Church into greater obedience.

In many congregations, the leaders chosen to lead are those who have been part of the congregation the longest. Too often these longtime members are inoculated members rather than mature disciples. As we've already shared, being in a congregation for many years does not necessarily ensure spiritual maturity. Intentionally drawing closer to Jesus over time does.

IV. Next Steps and Leaps of Faith

A. Baby Steps

Regardless of where we are on the Path, there is always a next step to take. We are becoming more like Jesus every day, which means there are an infinite number of incremental steps to be taken as we become more like our infinite and eternal Savior. Encouragement and accountability are necessary to keep us constantly identifying and taking our next step closer to God. Most of the time, these are baby steps. But don't let their tiny size fool you. They are crucial. Sometimes the tiniest steps yield the greatest rewards. A surprising number of 5x5 participants confess early on that the biggest problem they have in prayer, reading the Bible, or listening for God is failing to take time for God every day. We zero in on that. We work very hard to encourage and hold each other accountable for taking a daily quiet time with God. It seems small, but once this is accomplished, prayer increases, and Bible Study is rich and transforming. None of it was happening before we took that first baby step of carving out time every day.

B. Leaps of Faith

Sometimes a little step just isn't enough to get the job done. Baby steps work great for self-discipline and developing new holy habits. But when it is our trust that needs attention, sometimes it takes something big and scary to make the progress we need. Several years ago, my wife Robin spent the summer teaching Bible School to children in Kerch, Ukraine. The trip was organized and led by a team from New Jersey and in the fall the team leader called Robin with the bad news that no one in New Jersey was able to return the following summer, so the school was going to be cancelled. Without thinking, Robin blurted out that she would lead the trip. The woman on the other end of the line was thrilled, promised to send Robin everything she would need, then hung up. Within seconds of ending the call, Robin turned green and instantly regretted it. "Why had she said she would lead? She had never led a mission trip before! She didn't even speak the language!" She spent the next year way in over her head. Sometimes that is the single best way to grow. She knew darn well what she couldn't do, so if this trip was going to happen God would need to show up. When we only attempt things for God that we know we can do, then we don't really need God. But when we are in over our heads, when we are out of our league, when we are out of our depth, we have to learn to trust God because there simply is no other way. In God's eyes, the dreams we have for ourselves are far too small. It takes saying "yes" to a God-sized dream to really experience the full power of God in our life. God pours out power in direct proportion to how much it is actually needed. The greater the risk, the more of God's power will be needed to see it through.

We call it a "leap of faith" because it is like jumping off a cliff trusting that God will catch us. It is taking a real risk which is why it can be terrifying. And yet, it can also be exhilarating! The next summer's Bible School in Ukraine went beautifully and Robin later confessed that she had never in her life experienced such an intense period of growth as a disciple of Jesus. Our next steps closer to God may be small, steady, and certain. But sometimes, the next step is massive and terrifying. Either way, it is normal. Keep moving forward on the Path with God.

V. Staying Connected

We keep living the Jesus Way of Life together and we keep stepping closer to God. We cannot emphasize strongly enough how important it is to stay connected to other Jesus followers you can trust to encourage you and hold you accountable to keep moving ahead. God has designed it this way. It is how things work. We need each other. Discipleship rarely works out well when we are all alone.

WHAT NEXT?

We have finished our introduction to the 'holy knowledge" and "holy know how' needed to follow Jesus on the "Way That Leads to Life." These are the Disciplines of Jesus that help us accept life as it is and help God change it for the better. It is now time to learn it, practice it, and live it. As a part of a 5x5 Discipleship Group, you are going to take part in a weekly holy adventure to explore the Kingdom of God in your own life and in the lives of your fellow participants. Trust and support these new found friends as they shall be trusting and supporting you.

Here is an important last reminder about 5x5 and how it got its name. Not only does it refer to the two lists of Five Undeniable Truths and The Five Disciplines of Jesus, it also refers to a greater goal of the process. When soldiers enter combat, they must be in constant communication with their commanding officers. When the military tests their radios, they test two qualities: signal strength and signal clarity. They rate the signals on a scale from one to five, one being the worst and five being the best. A rating of 5x5 is given to the best possible signal that is "loud and clear." That is exactly how we want to hear and experience God. Like soldiers in combat, we are deployed in a life or death mission led by our Savior and Lord. God makes these plans. God develops the strategies. God hands out the assignments. God equips us to serve. God sends in reinforcements when needed. A strong clear connection to God is essential. We cannot follow a God that we don't know, don't understand, and can't hear. This is what we desire in our relationship with God: excellent strength and perfect clarity -- the most understandable signal possible. By helping each other experience God with more clarity, we help each other surrender more of ourselves to God's control and mature as Christian disciples until there is no other motive in us than love of God and love of neighbor. Let's begin.

10
5X5 SMALL GROUP PROCESS

What you have read so far is an overview of the things a disciple should know and know how to do in order to serve God's plan for our world. I hope you find the material helpful in your walk with Jesus Christ, but we still haven't answered the most important question: "How do we use this material to disciple each other?" We turn now to small group process. If you do an internet search for "small group processes" you will find far more than is contained here. For that reason, we are going to limit this discussion to how 5x5 Discipleship Groups work rather than teach all the finer points of group dynamics. It will be helpful to continue indulging in that kind of research to prepare yourself for the traps and pitfalls that can derail even the best groups. We will begin with the thought process that led to the formation of groups and then describe a typical session.

Most small group experts teach that there is an optimal group size. Most recommend a group that consists of eight to twelve people. It is seen as important to have enough people to share the conversation yet not so many that it is impossible for all to participate.

Small Group, High Commitment, High Involvement

5x5 groups are about intentional life transformation. It is not a class through which we acquire information but a process through which lives are changed. There is plenty to learn and plenty to learn how to do, but the learning does not stop with our brains. It is not a place to learn by listening quietly from the corners of the room. We learn to live our lives as followers of Jesus by living them, which requires a strong desire to change and the commitment to put in the work that transformation requires. Like most things in life, we get out of the group as much as we are willing to put in. Everything costs something. A typical 5x5 group consists of five participants and a facilitator who meet for a minimum of sixty minutes and a maximum of ninety minutes each week. Groups are limited in size to allow every person sufficient time to discuss their walk with Jesus in the past week and make decisions about next steps that will be taken in the week ahead. It is focused on intentional improvement. As participants discuss daily life, teachable moments emerge, and the group then explores the material contained in this manual as it applies to the situation at hand. This practical approach contrasts with that of classes that necessarily teach material according to an arbitrary class schedule, whether we are ready to apply it to our lives or not. In 5x5 we have collected enough material for dozens of courses and keep it ready at hand in order to offer what is needed when it's needed. Group sessions go wherever they need to go and cover whatever they need to cover to meet the immediate needs of the participants. Unlike the groups mentioned above, attendance is not optional. Regular attendance and participation are part of the group covenant. We must stay engaged over time in order to grow in Christ. Not only that, our fellow participants are relying on us and need our encouragement and accountability for their growth and wellbeing. Everyone gets sick now and then and most people go on vacation, so it is expected that people may miss a weekly session now and then. These are expected but are seen as rare exceptions.

Gathering a Group

It is helpful to gather people who have enough in common to learn together. While we have successfully led groups with wildly different ages, gender, and spiritual maturity, we have also seen groups fizzle prematurely because the chemistry wasn't right. Personal chemistry, or the ability of a group to accept, like, and support each other, seems like something we wouldn't need to worry about in the Kingdom of God. We should all be able to accept each other and learn together, but in reality, some thought should be given to putting the right five people together. I have no hard and fast rules to offer here other than that you should select group members prayerfully and after conversation with each member allowing them to articulate their hopes and goals for the process. 5x5 is not right for everyone because it requires a deep desire and commitment to grow.

Without that inner desire, the process is less likely to change lives. I look for people who are hungry for Jesus. As I'm building a group, I will often ask members if they have any friends who would also be ready for a journey like this. That way, relationships already exist to help hold the group together. We have formed groups several different ways from personal invitation by the pastor, to volunteer sign-ups, to people who hear the positive testimonies of group members and ask to join. All have worked. Once a group is formed, it is important to model the mutual love, mutual acceptance, mutual encouragement, and mutual accountability of mature disciples. If handled well, even a group of misfits can learn to love and protect each other.

Group Covenant

Clear agreements on the front end avoid disagreements on the back end. Discipleship is about making promises to God and keeping commitments. Keeping commitments builds self-discipline and self-control. Clear agreements also keep a group united and aligned to a common purpose. We write these agreements out in a Group Covenant that is signed and kept handy by each participant throughout the process. While each group should be free to personalize these agreements for their particular group, there are some minimum recommended components that every Group Covenant should include.

Day, Time, and Meeting Place

Names and Contact Information of Facilitator and Participants

Group Expectations:

1. Sessions start on time.
2. Attendance and preparation are expected of all.
3. Every participant will share every week.
4. Every participant will keep a personal journal
5. Confidentiality is ruthlessly protected.
6. All are encouraged to be completely honest about what is happening inside and around them.
7. Covenant will be reviewed, renewed, or discontinued every three months.

5x5 Group Process

The 5x5 Framework gives us something concrete to measure ourselves against that is more reliable than how we "feel" we are doing. Everyone must be completely honest about what is going on inside and around them because there is way too much pretending and assuming in the Body of Christ. We assume that everyone is doing fine with Jesus and pretend that we are, too. When we pretend or assume, we give each other permission to live a lie and to frustrate the Kingdom of God. Life is too short and the Kingdom is too important to be anything other than an authentic disciple that helps God change lives and make the world better. Be honest with yourself. Be honest with God. Be honest with your group.

- Are you satisfied with your relationship with God?
- Is God satisfied?
- What areas give you the most concern?
- Where do you begin to improve?

These are always the first questions we ask in a brand new group. We zero in and begin where we actually are. After all, isn't that how salvation came to us in the first place? The Word became flesh and dwelt among us. God joined us right where we are but loved us too much to allow us to remain stuck there. The entire goal of each session is to take our next step closer to God. Therefore, a pattern emerges that is useful at every stage of our journey. We must first determine where we are at any given moment in our love relationship with God. We call this "zeroing in."

Step 1: Zeroing In

This is an important conversation in which we diagnose what is right and what is wrong in our relationship with God. We drill down deep into our lives to determine exactly where we are in our faith walk and compare that to where we would prefer to be. Sometimes the obstacle is something going on around us, like a busy schedule, loud traffic when we are trying to pray, or a person who is angry with us. Sometimes the obstacle is something going on inside of us, like a fear of being rejected, procrastination, or competing desires. Zeroing in often includes asking the word "why?" over and over until there are no more answers to give. It digs past excuses, blaming others, or our own unwillingness to reveal our true condition.

The 5 WHYs

We employ a relatively simple process called "The 5 WHYs and the 5 HOWs" which was developed by Sakichi Toyoda of the Japanese auto maker Toyota. He developed the technique in the 1930s as a process for identifying the root causes of problems that lead us to the best solutions and is still used by Toyota today. The process is simple. We begin with a problem and ask why it is a problem. We keep asking "why?" until we get to the root cause. For example, imagine your child failed to mow the lawn after school like you asked her to do. The conversation might go like this:

Father: Why hasn't the lawn been mowed?

Daughter: I didn't have time before it got dark.

Father: Why didn't you have time?

Daughter: I was late coming home.

Father: Why were you late coming home?

Daughter: Because I missed the bus.

Father: Why did you miss the bus?

Daughter: Because I had detention.

Father: Why did you have detention?

Daughter: Because I got caught cheating on a test.

Father: Why were you cheating on the test?

Daughter: Because I didn't study.

Father: Why didn't you study?

Daughter: Because I forgot we had a test today.

Father: Why did you forget?

Daughter: Because I didn't write it down when the teacher told us to,

Father: Why didn't you write it down?

Daughter: Because I wasn't paying attention.

Father: Why weren't you paying attention?

Daughter: Because my eyes hurt.

Father: Why do your eyes hurt?

Daughter: I don't know, but I get headaches looking at the board.

Finally, we have found the root cause of this problem, and it has nothing to do with the lawn. The root cause is the first domino to fall that caused the rest of the dominoes to fall. You can think of the lawn, the bus, the detention, the test, the cheating, the lack of studying, the failure to pay attention as symptoms, rather than the disease. If the father simply grounded his daughter for not mowing the lawn, it would do nothing to prevent missing the bus or detention or the lack of attention in class. The real problem that set all the others in motion is a problem with her vision. The "5 Why" process is that simple. State a problem and ask "why?" five times. You will eventually run out of explanations for the "why?" and that is where begin to develop effective solutions. You will not always need to ask five times. Sometimes it will take less than five and sometimes, like the example above, a few more. The key is to keep asking until you get to the real problem. Solving that problem will cause the most positive change.

Step 2: Determining our Next Steps

The only step we can ever take is the next one. Once we zero in on what is holding us back, we determine the next natural step to make it better. Sometimes we are disappointed in ourselves when we zero in and discover we are much farther away from God than we thought. That does not matter in the least. What matters is whether or not we will take one step in the right direction, which will be followed by another and another. As David Allen, author of "Getting Things Done" explains:

"The "next action" is the next physical, visible activity that needs to be engaged in, in order to move the current reality toward completion." ("Getting Things Done, Penguin Books, 2001)

We constantly ask each other this question: "What is your next step?" We may not know, which is where the teaching of the facilitator and the discernment of the group come in, but we do have a process for developing strategies and solutions. It is called the "5 HOWs".

The 5 HOWs

If the "5 WHYs" help us diagnose and identify problems, the "5 HOWs" help us solve them. The root cause needs to be addressed and we keep asking the question "how do we do that?" until we get to the concrete next step described by David Allen above. If we were to solve the problem above between the father and daughter, it might sound like this:

Father: So we need to deal with these headaches. How do we do that?

Daughter: Maybe I need glasses.

Father: Maybe you do. How do we make that happen?

Daughter: I probably need an eye exam.

Father: I agree. How do we make that happen?

Daughter: We need to call the eye doctor and make an appointment.

Our group will both equip us with strategies and solutions and encourage us to follow through. We identify what we need to know and what we need to know how to do in order to take our next step and move forward. The facilitator will guide the group into the relevant portion of the manual and teach as needed on the material and practices in question. Members of the group will help each other discuss and apply these ideas in a way that works for each.

Step 3: Committing to Action
Once the next logical step is determined, we commit to action. We actually do something differently. We dedicate ourselves for the next week to mastering this crucial baby step until we've formed a new habit and a new holy instinct. We will need that group encouragement to follow through. We take responsibility before God for our own wellbeing and seek God's grace to stay strong.

Step 4: Encouragement and Accountability
When the group gathers again after a week apart, it is time to report on our progress. We remind each other of the next steps we are taking and share openly about how it went. Here is where discipleship too often dies. If we have failed to take our next step with no compelling reason for that failure we cannot let the moment pass without pressing for more details. It may be uncomfortable which is why we may be tempted to let the moment pass. But if we accept weak excuses, and fail to challenge the lack of effort, we are giving each other permission to fail. We speak the truth in love and begin zeroing in on the real reason for the failure. Why do we go easy on each other? Perhaps we don't want to hurt anyone's feelings. Perhaps we don't want anyone to come down too hard on us when we've had a challenging week. It may seem kind, but it does far more harm to the Kingdom than good. If you are in a group that refuses to hold each other accountable for our actions, you need to find another group.

Step 5: Celebration

When one succeeds, we all rejoice. Each victory, no matter how small, is a Kingdom Victory. The Kingdom grows a little more powerful when someone who struggles to take time out for God has just completed seven days in a row spending twenty minutes of quiet time with God per day.

Through this process we are helping people take their next step closer to God by teaching holy knowledge and holy know-how. In the beginning, the facilitator will drive the process by helping people diagnose their current development, identify needs, assign next steps, and encourage progress. Leading people to spiritual maturity is as much an art as it is a science. If the facilitator drives too much of the process it can stunt the growth of group participants who never learn to think for themselves. If the facilitator takes a "hands off" approach, participants can wander around lost and lose hope in the process. The science comes in knowing what to provide for a growing disciple and what to encourage them to do on their own. The art comes in knowing the right moment for each approach. It is my firm belief that discipleship is 100% teachable. This art and science of discipling others is also 100% teachable. Let's break this down into smaller parts to understand better how to do the right thing at the right time.

How People Learn

When I was very young, I wanted to ride a bicycle. My parents bought me my very first two-wheeler with training wheels. I was so excited to ride, I hopped on and began to peddle around the driveway. I didn't have to know anything about speed or balance because the training wheels did all the work. I felt like I could ride across the country. Then came the big day. My father took the training wheels off, and everything changed. I wobbled, stumbled and fell. I was afraid to keep riding. I thought I would never get the hang of it. My Dad knew I needed some help, so he grabbed the back of my bike seat and jogged alongside while I pedaled. The whole time he told me I was doing great and that I should just keep going. I didn't realize that he started letting go until I pedaled away from him. I was so startled to be actually riding a bicycle I forgot how to stop and ran into a tree. My Dad put me right back on and encouraged me to ride. I was still a little scared and wasn't sure I could do this. Dad encouraged me, telling I could do it on my own, that I had in fact already done it on my own. I gave it a try, and slowly got better. Before long, I didn't need any help at all and could hop on my bike any time I wanted to ride anywhere in town.

By paying attention to both what I needed and what my Dad provided, this story reveals most of what we need in order to disciple someone else.

We will take a closer look at what learners need and what teachers and leaders provide. It does not matter what we are trying to learn, whether it be riding a bike, speaking a new language or following Jesus, we all progress through four common stages in our learning process. What I'm about to share with you is from "Situational Leadership" developed by Dr. Paul Hersey and Ken Blanchard. It is designed to teach managers how to lead their employees toward better performance in their jobs, but the wisdom applies to everyone trying to learn how to do something on their own. (Leadership and the One Minute Manager. HarperCollins, 1985)

Before we can help someone take their next step, we need to know exactly where they are standing. Otherwise, we can give someone advice they aren't ready to take. Diagnosing someone's developmental level is a combination of *Competence* and *Commitment.*

Competence is a function of demonstrated knowledge and skills that can be gained through learning and experience. There are things we need to know and things we need to know how to do. In order to ride a bike we need to know how to pedal, how to steer, how to balance, and how to stop. We can read a book or take a class about bicycles before we ride and we will gain much. We will gain far more by putting that information to use by actually riding, making mistakes, and getting better over time. Competence is different from potential. Potential is what we are capable of doing in the future as we learn. Competence is about what we've already learned and have done.

Commitment is a combination of our confidence and our motivation. Confidence relates to how self-assured we feel about our ability to pray, serve, or ride a bike. Our motivation is determined by how much interest and enthusiasm we have for what we are learning to do. Depending on the combination of our competence and commitment, we will need more than a one size fits all approach from our leaders. Using the story of my first bicycle, let's take a look at the four common stages of development as we learn anything as named by Blanchard and Hersey:

Four Developmental Stages: Competence and Commitment

Stage One: The Energetic Beginner
Low Competence, High Commitment

When my parents gave me that first bike, I didn't know how to ride it, but I didn't care. I just wanted to ride. You could say that my competence was low. I had never ridden before and didn't know much about it, but my commitment was high. My interest and enthusiasm were through the roof.

Stage Two: The Disillusioned Learner
Low Competence, Low Commitment

Once the training wheels came off, I realized that this was going to be much harder than I thought. Once I fell, I was afraid of falling again. Learning to ride free like the older kids in the neighborhood seemed impossible. I was ready to quit.

Stage Three: Capable but Cautious
High Competence, Low Commitment

After I crashed into the tree, my father put me right back on the bike. I was focused on the tree, but he was focused on the fact that I had ridden all the way across the yard all by myself. I knew what to do because I had done it. The only thing holding me back was my fear and uncertainty.

Stage Four: The Self-Reliant Achiever
High Competence, High Commitment

Not only was I able to eventually ride around town on my own, I began to love riding and wanted more. I would eventually spend an entire day riding 65 miles through the mountains where I grew up. I would eventually leave the blacktop for the backwoods trails, taking up mountain biking where I would ride over roots, rocks, creeks, and puddles. My bicycling knowledge now grew to include basic bike maintenance and how to safely take a spill over the handlebars. I even entered and finished a mountain bike race. I did not need my Dad to help me increase my mileage and skills over the years because I became a self-learner. I did my own research, read the right books, visited the right shops, and benefited from trial and error.

As I said earlier, we all go through these basic stages regardless of what we are learning, and it definitely applies to growing disciples of Jesus. As facilitators, we learn to recognize which stage a person is in as it relates to a specific goal. If we are learning to pray, we ask questions to uncover the competence and commitment level of the person we are helping. Have they ever prayed before? Has prayer been a positive experience or a negative one? Are they comfortable spending more time in prayer or is it something they are trying to avoid? We then determine their competence level (how much learning and experience they already have) and their commitment level (how much interest and enthusiasm they express). Is it high, low, or somewhere in between? You then the refer to the four stages explained above and get an idea of where they are in their development of the goal at hand. This then tells us what they need from a leader to help them make progress. Here are the four leadership approaches we use to address the specific needs of learners in different stages of development toward mastery.

Four Leadership Styles: Direction and Support

Learners need direction and support to do their best. When our competence is low, direction must be high. We provide learners with what they do not already have: knowledge and experience. We tell, teach, and instruct. When commitment is low, support must be high. We provide praise and encouragement and include them in the thinking and decision making process. Direction is always thorough, specific and clear. Support is always personal, including an interest in the physical, emotional, and spiritual wellbeing of the whole person. Each of the four developmental stages matches a corresponding leadership style that provides the best results.

Style One: Directing
High Directive Behavior, Low Support

When I first tried riding a bike, the training wheels did most of the work. Training wheels are not the most helpful image for directing, though. Think of an officer giving orders to a soldier. The orders are always clear and complete so that the soldier is not required to think and problem solve but to simply obey. If the problem that needs to be solved is a lack of physical fitness, directing is saying "drop and give me twenty push-ups!" This works best early in our discipleship process when we do not know what we do not know, and so are unable to come up with our own solutions.

Style Two: Coaching
High Directive Behavior, High Support

After the training wheels came off, more was required of me and I was scared and overwhelmed. My Dad continued to direct and teach, but now ran alongside holding the seat. He literally supported me, keeping me from falling but also encouraged me. He gave me the confidence to keep trying, praising me on making good progress even though I couldn't yet ride on my own. When coaching, both the teacher and learner are working hard together. The teacher will direct, offering solutions to try but will ask the student for their thoughts and questions as well. It is no longer enough to just do as we are told. We begin learning how to think for ourselves by exploring problems and solutions together.

Style Three: Supporting
Low Directive Behavior, High Support

After I crashed into the tree, I was hesitant to keep riding even though I had demonstrated that I could ride on my own. I needed to trust myself and my skills more than I did. Additional instruction was not what I needed. What I needed was encouragement to take more risks and prove to myself that I knew what I was doing.

Style Four: Delegating
Low Directive Behavior, Low Support

The leader delegates the job to the student by giving the student the freedom to direct and support themselves. This does not mean that we can now ignore the student and their progress, it just means they need less direction and support. We can now check in periodically and keep them headed in the right direction. To make it easier to see the natural relationship between the four developmental stages and their corresponding leadership styles, I have grouped them together below:

Stage One: The Energetic Beginner
Low Competence, High Commitment
Style One: Directing
High Directive Behavior, Low Support

Stage Two: The Disillusioned Learner
Low Competence, Low Commitment
Style Two: Coaching
High Directive Behavior, High Support

Stage Three: Capable but Cautious
High Competence, Low Commitment
Style Three: Supporting
Low Directive Behavior, High Support

Stage Four: The Self-Reliant Achiever
High Competence, High Commitment
Style Four: Delegating
Low Directive Behavior, Low Support

So the process is now very clear:

First, we choose a goal to pursue.

Second, we diagnose the learner's level of development related to that goal.

Third, we match the right leadership style to the developmental level of the student.

We learned a moment ago that giving direction is like giving orders. We tell, teach, and instruct. Supporting involves the person in the process through questions, conversation, and encouragement. Directing is one-way traffic while supporting is two way traffic. When we support, we encourage people to think, decide, and choose for themselves. The root cause analysis of the "5 WHYs" is always supportive in nature, allowing the learner to answer for themselves. The problem-solving work of the "5 HOWs" is directive early in the group process because learners may not yet know enough to choose the right solutions on their own. As you will see in the example below, once we have identified the root cause, we have stumbled upon a teachable moment. We offer instruction on the area of focus and offer some possible actions to try. As the learner gains knowledge and experience over time, choosing solutions becomes more supportive because he or she can now take more responsibility for themselves.

What Does a Group Session Sound Like?

We disciple each other by talking with each other about real life. That is what sets this kind of group apart from a traditional Bible Study or class. There is no other agenda besides what is actually happening with God in our everyday lives. Given our discussion of learning development levels and the leadership styles needed to become more capable and confident in our walk with Jesus, I want to let you listen in on a typical conversation from a group session. For purposes of example, we will observe the initial session that begins the 5x5 process.

Leader: Everything begins with our love relationship with God, so that is where we will begin today. I'm going to ask you a very direct question: Are you satisfied with your love relationship with God?

Student: I'm not sure how to answer that.

Leader: Why not?

Student: Well, I feel like if I say "yes, I am satisfied" that it's probably the wrong answer.

Leader: There are no wrong answers. Our only rule here is that we agree to be completely honest about what is going on inside of us and around us. How do you feel about God?

Student: I believe in God. I grew up in the church, but I don't know that I know what it's like to have a personal friendship with God.

Leader: What does that mean to you?

Student: I don't know.

Leader: What do you think it means to other people?

Student: I don't know. Some people talk about God like He's sitting in the room with them like we are. I've never heard God out loud. I'm not sure I've ever gotten any answers to my prayers that I know about. I'm just not sure how it can seem so real to some people.

Leader: Do you pray?

Student: Yeah. Some.

Leader: What is prayer like for you?

Student: Honestly?

Leader: Of course.

Student: I don't get much out of it.

Leader: O.K. What does your prayer life look like?

Student: What do you mean?

Leader: How do you go about it? What works for you? What doesn't work for you?

Student: I don't know. I guess I just don't pray enough.

Leader: Do you pray every day?

Student: I mean to, but…no. Not every day.

Leader: Why do you think that is?

Student: Well, it can be hard to fit in sometimes.

Leader: What gets in the way?

Student: Life.

Leader: Can you be more specific?

Student: Well, if I don't get it in before I go to work, it's probably not going to happen, because by the time things finally slow down in the evening, I'm tired. I feel bad if I fall asleep during prayer.

Leader: So mornings would be better?

Student: Probably.

Leader: How early do you need to be at work.

Student: Not until 9:00.

Leader: What time do you wake up?

Student: Usually between 6:30 and 7:00.

Leader: So from the time you wake up, you have two hours to get ready and get to work. Is there enough time in there to pray a little?

Student: I guess…if I get up on time.

Leader: How important is this love relationship with God to you? Is it worth getting up for?

Student: Sure it is. (Long pause) But I don't.

Leader: (Letting that sink in) Why don't you?

Student: I don't know.

Leader: You will find in the coming weeks that I will ask that question a lot. Once we land on something you want to do but don't, I'm going ask you what is keeping it from happening. There are only two kinds of obstacles: the ones around us and the ones inside of us. We don't have much control over the things happening around us, but we have complete control of what's going on inside of us. So, we started with your frustration that God doesn't seem real and moved from there into your struggles with prayer. Now we find that one of the struggles is finding the time to be in prayer, so that's actually where we need to start. You feel the morning would be best, but you don't always take the time. What's keeping that from happening?

Student: Me, I guess. I just need to make it happen.

Leader: What could you do to carve out, say, twenty minutes of prayer every morning before work? Is that possible?

Student: I think so.

Leader: What could you do to make that happen every day?

Student: I could set an alarm, but I hit the snooze button a lot.

Leader: Why?

Student: Because I'm tired!!

Leader: Why are you so tired?

Student: Probably because I stay up too late.

Leader: Why are you up so late?

Student: I like to stay up for the opening monologue after the news, but then I get sucked in and watch until after midnight.

Leader: Are you willing to trade that monologue for a love relationship with God?

Student: When you put it that way, Yeah. That makes sense. That's an easy fix, besides, I can probably see the monologue the next day online anyway.

Leader: So other than go to bed earlier, what else could you do?

Student: Well that's a big one. I could put a post it note on my nightstand near the alarm reminding me to pray. I could put my Bible on the kitchen table the night before as a reminder to pray when I sit down to breakfast.

Leader: It sounds like there are a lot of things you could do.

Student: Yeah, but I think the biggest one is deciding to do it. Once it's important enough, I will make sure to work it in.

Leader: Amen! You just discovered a cardinal truth! We always make time for the things that are important to us. We can watch three hours of TV a night, but just can't get around to fifteen minutes of prayer. What you've just done is decide to make God more important to you. Good for you. So what is your next step?

Student: Well, I should pray every day.

Leader: Good. But let's get really clear. Before you can pray, you have to carve out the time. That is actually your next step. Let me challenge you to do whatever it takes to carve out, how much time every day?

Student: How about twenty minutes?

Leader: Then that's your win for next week. I want you to set aside twenty minutes with God every morning for the next seven days. I don't even care right now what you do with it. Pray, read your Bible, sit in silence with God. It doesn't matter how good the twenty minutes is right now. What matters is that you learn to take it every day. Once you have that down, then we can talk about what you do with it. How does that sound?

Student: That sounds fine! I can do that.

Leader: Good. That is your Next Step for next week. Go ahead and write that down in your journal and we will all write it down in ours. You are going to want to remember exactly what you've committed to and we need to remember to ask you about it next week. We are also going to pray for you every step of the way. Now, there is a section in your manual you will want to read. Under the Discipline of Worship there is a section on "Sabbath Keeping" and it is all about the spiritual discipline of reserving time for God. Originally, the sabbath was a particular day that was set aside but it is broader than that. You will find some helpful stuff in there about how to carve out and protect your time with God. Are you clear on what you are doing?

Student: Yes.

Leader: Good! O.K. Who wants to go next?...,

Again, what you've just observed is what we call "zeroing in." It is peeling away the layers of an onion until you get to something you can't peel any more. The student started with the wish that God would seem more real. The leader questioned why God didn't seem real. Hopefully, you can now see how crucial a word "Why" is in this process. Notice how much of the process is driven by the student and not the leader. With no agenda whatsoever other than to get to the real problem to be solved, the leader encourages the student to talk about how they feel about things, describe how things actually are, identify what they wish were different, and explore all the things keeping that wish from coming true. This is highly supportive behavior, encouraging the person to talk, making it safe to be honest, and involving them in the discovery. It may be tempting to just hand the person a prescription to follow, but we take ownership of things we discover for ourselves. We are also teaching students to analyze their own situations and think for themselves.

Once we get to the real problem and the true next step, we become more directive, offering things to read and try at home. Over time, the leader will direct less and support and encourage more. Over time as the group becomes quite familiar with the process, the members can take turns leading as facilitator. As a facilitator, there is no arbitrary limit on the amount of time you should stay with a group as long as you allow the members to assume as much responsibility for their group as possible. You can become a "circle of equals" with each able to both disciple others and be discipled. There is however a definite minimum amount of time that a facilitator must stay with a new group before trusting it to run on its own. If you are committed to the ongoing life and health of a group, you must be willing to stay with a group until at least one member has grown to be a Stage Four "Self-Reliant Achiever" whose competence and commitment are high enough to disciple others. I have made the mistake as facilitator several times of leaving a 5x5 group already in progress simply because the semester ended and I planned on starting a new group. Our small group semesters are three months, which work great for short term Bible studies, but are rarely long enough to disciple a new group to the maturity needed to care for their own growth. We have had better success with groups that I facilitated for six to nine months. Groups can continue to meet together forever if they wish. However, as maturity increases it will be time for group members to pass on what they have learned to others by starting and facilitating groups of their own.

Discipleship is a team sport. Gather your team and walk the Path of Jesus together. Get ready to see lives change. The Kingdom of God is growing in you and through you. You are helping God change the world. That is an awesome privilege. Enjoy the adventure!

WORKS CITED

Allen, David. *Getting Things Done.* New York. Penguin, 2003.

Aurelius, Marcus. *Meditations.* Tran. Hays. New York. Modern Library, 2002.

Blackaby, Henry T., Richard Blackaby, and Claude V. King. *Experiencing God: Knowing and Doing the Will of God.* Nashville, TN: Broadman & Holman, 2008. Print.

Blanchard, Ken. *Leadership and The One Minute Manager.* HarperCollins, 1985. Print.

Bonhoeffer, Dietrich, Geffrey B. Kelly, and F. Burton. Nelson. *A Testament to Freedom: The Essential Writings of Dietrich Bonhoeffer.* San Francisco, CA: HarperSanFrancisco, 1995. Print.

Brinkman, Rick and Kirschner, Rick. *Dealing With People You Can't Stand: How to Bring the Best Out of People at Their Worst.* McGraw Hill, 1994.

Chappell, Paul K. *The Art of Waging Peace: A Strategic Approach to Improving Our Lives and the World.* Easton Studio Press, LLC. 2 July 2013

Cloud, Henry, and John Sims Townsend. *Boundaries. When to Say Yes, When to Say No to Take Control of Your Life.* Grand Rapids, MI: Zondervan Pub. House, 1995. Print.0

Covey, Stephen M. R. *The Speed of Trust: The One Thing That Changes Everything.* Free Press, 2006. Print.

Epictetus. *The Manual: A Philosopher's Guide to Life.* Trans. Torode. Ancient Renewal, 2017.

Fletcher, Colin, C. L. Rawlins, and Colin Fletcher. *The Complete Walker IV.* New York: Knopf, 2003. Print.

Forni, P. M. *Choosing Civility: The Twenty-five Rules of Considerate Conduct.* New York, NY: St. Martin's Griffin, 2003. Print.

Foster, Richard J. *Celebration of Discipline*. New York, NY.: Harper Collins, 1998.

Frankl, Viktor E. *Man's Search for Meaning*. Beacon Press 2006.

Grieg, Peter. *The Prayer Course*. Web. 15 Oct. 2017.

Hallesby, Ole. *Prayer*. Minneapolis: Augsburg, 1994.

Hawkins, Greg L., and Cally Parkinson. *Move: What 1,000 Churches Reveal about Spiritual Growth*. Grand Rapids, Mich: Zondervan, 2011.

Head, Tom. *Absolute Beginner's Guide to the Bible*. Indianapolis, IN: Que, 2006.

Hull, Bill. *The Complete Book of Discipleship: On Being and Making Followers of Christ*. Colorado Springs, CO: NavPress, 2006.

Irvine, William B. *A Guide to the Good Life: The Ancient Art of Stoic Joy*. Oxford University Press, 2009

Job, Rueben P. *Three Simple Rules*. Abingdon Press 2008.

Keating, Thomas. *Foundations for Centering Prayer: Open Mind, Open Heart; Invitation to Love; The Mystery of Christ*. New York: Continuum, 2002.

Krueger, James FR. *"This Restless Sea: Contemplative Practice and Prophetic Witness Amidst Violence."* (www.onbeing.com) December 26, 2015

Leas, Speed B. *Discover Your Conflict Management Style*. Bethesda, MD: Alban Institute, 1997.

Pennington, M. Basil. *Lectio Divina: Renewing the Ancient Practice of Praying the Scriptures*. New York: Crossroad Pub., 1998.

Rees, Erik. *S.H.A.P.E.: Finding & Fulfilling Your Unique Purpose for Life*. Grand Rapids, MI: Zondervan, 2006.

Reese, Martha Grace. *Unbinding the Gospel: Real Life Evangelism*. St. Louis, MO: Chalice, 2008.

Rosenberg, Marshall. *Nonviolent Communication: A Language of Life*. PuddleDancer Press, 2003.

Stockdale, James B. *Stockdale on Stoicism I: The Stoic Warrior's Triad.* Annapolis, MD: U.S. Naval Academy, Center for the Study of Professional Military Ethics, 2001.

Urban, Tim. *Taming the Mammoth: Why You Should Stop Caring What Other People Think.* www.Waitbutwhy.com, June13, 2014.

Warren, Rick. *The Purpose Driven Church: Growth Without Compromising Your Message & Mission.* Grand Rapids, MI: Zondervan Pub., 2011.

INDEX

ABOUT THE AUTHOR

Gregory Rapp was baptized into the Church of Jesus Christ on July 20, 1969, the same day Neil Armstrong walked on the moon. He was raised in the mountains of Northern Pennsylvania and has a great love of the outdoors. As a graduate of Indiana University of Pennsylvania with a degree in Theater, Gregory worked for several years as an actor, director and playwright before hearing a call to ministry from God in 1996. He graduated from Wesley Theological Seminary in Washington D.C. and has served as an ordained elder in the Susquehanna Conference on the United Methodist Church in Central Pennsylvania. He currently serves as the senior pastor of First United Methodist Church in Hanover, PA. where he is married to his wife Robin and is the proud father of two grown children, Autumn and Alex. He continues to write and teach about discipleship through live events and online at www.5x5discipleship.com.

Made in the USA
Columbia, SC
30 October 2018